RHS GROW YOUR OWN
FLOWERS

RHS GROW YOUR OWN
FLOWERS

Helen Yemm

MITCHELL BEAZLEY

Dedication This book is for Henry

GROW YOUR OWN FLOWERS
Helen Yemm

First published in Great Britain in 2010 by Mitchell Beazley,
an imprint of Octopus Publishing Group Ltd, Endeavour
House, 189 Shaftesbury Avenue, London WC2H 8JY
www.octopusbooks.co.uk

An Hachette UK Company
www.hachette.co.uk

Published in association with the Royal Horticultural Society

Design and layout copyright © Octopus Publishing Group Ltd 2010
Text copyright © Helen Yemm 2010
Text copyright © The Royal Horticultural Society 2010

ISBN 978 1 84533 536 6

A CIP record of this book is available from the British Library.

Commissioning Editor Helen Griffin
Art Director Pene Parker
Deputy Art Director Yasia Williams-Leedham
Designer Mark Kan, Miranda Harvey
Senior Editor Leanne Bryan
Copyeditor Joanna Chisholm
RHS Consultant Helen Bostock
Contributor Leigh Hunt
Picture Research Manager Giulia Hetherington
Production Controller Susan Meldrum
Proofreader Lynn Bresler
Indexer Isobel McLean

RHS Publisher Susannah Charlton
RHS Commissioning Editor Rae Spencer-Jones

Set in Frutiger, Glypha, and Interstate
Printed and bound in China

The Royal Horticultural Society is the UK's leading gardening
charity dedicated to advancing horticulture and promoting
good gardening. Its charitable work includes providing expert
advice and information, training the next generation of
gardeners, creating hands-on opportunities for children to
grow plants, and conducting research into plants, pests,
and environmental issues affecting gardeners. For more
information, visit: www.rhs.org.uk or call 0845 130 4646.

Note The Royal Horticultural Society's Award
of Garden Merit (AGM) helps gardeners to make
informed choices about plants. This award indicates
that the plant is recommended by the RHS. Awards
are usually given after a period of trial at an RHS
garden, often Wisley. Plants are judged by one of the
RHS plant committees.

Of the "tried and tested RHS varieties" featured in this
book, those that have been awarded the Award of
Garden Merit are followed by the trophy symbol (♔).

A full list of AGM plants may be found on the RHS
website at: www.rhs.org.uk/plants/award_plants.asp.

Contents

Introduction

Making a beautiful garden full of flowers takes careful planning, an honest appraisal of the realities of your plot, intelligent observation of how plants work, and, of course, not a little hard work. Even if there were such a thing, instant gardening this is not. But the rewards for effort are infinite. Gardening with flowers gives you endless opportunities for self-expression and, when it all goes right (as it increasingly will), a real sense of achievement.

Whether you realize it or not – your gardening aspirations may well be shaped and coloured by nostalgic fantasies of how you think you remember gardens of your childhood, or by romantic images in picture books. In that fantasy world of effortlessly planted flower gardens filled with glorious sights, sounds, and scents, lofty verbascums and phalanxes of perfect hollyhocks and delphiniums all stood to attention above unblemished hummocks of fabulous daisies. The air was always heavy with the scent of old-fashioned pinks; immaculate lavender hedges swayed and sagged under the weight of countless bees;

SOFT LIGHT ENHANCES the colour connections here between dusky-stemmed echinacea and its border companion, purple-flowered *Verbena rigida.*

every day was sunny, and the summers were endless.

You may, therefore, well feel that a garden without an abundance of flowers just isn't the real deal. Perhaps in a tiny urban patch or in a hemmed-in front garden that has to double as a car park – one that is largely devoid of the things flowers require to grow successfully – it may be appropriate to have a smart, wood, stone, gravel, and potted spiky-things set-piece garden. It is certainly better than having no outside space at all. However, since the very specific title of this book – *RHS Grow Your Own Flowers* – attracted you, probably such a modern minimalist garden just doesn't, quite literally, give you the right buzz. What you really hanker after is something altogether more complicated, more personal, and more beautiful, even though this is harder to achieve. For so

many people the very essence of a garden is the annually burgeoning and daily changing abundance of colour and scent that flowers provide.

A pretty garden in which to grow plants that you want to eat can, of course, be made with a little care and a modicum of artistic flair. Indeed, combining flowers and vegetables in one place is a style of gardening that has an increasing number of devotees. But a love of flowers, pure and simple, and a love of nurturing, growing, and picking them for no other reason than simply to embellish yourself, your environment, and generally cheer up your daily life, seems to be fundamental. After all, gardeners have been doing just this since time immemorial. Flowers have been used to decorate all the important social events and ceremonies of human life from birth to death.

While few people show an interest in growing things of any kind in childhood, this is clearly when their love affair with flowers begins. A child will instinctively pick a flower to give to his or her mother, both their faces wreathed in smiles, or later, loll around chatting with friends, idly making daisy chains.

But when and how does all the growing start? In all likelihood the flame is kindled when you acquire a less-than-perfect patch of sour soil or barely disguised builders' rubble outside your first real home. You may promptly arm yourself with a budget-range trowel and a watering can from a DIY store and pick up a packet of nasturtium seeds or a bundle of wallflowers from a bucket outside a local store. Your first steps into gardening may well just go on from there as you try things out, whispering your way hesitantly around local garden centres at weekends. There are glorious and surprising successes, heartbreaking catastrophes (often involving snails), and some dreadful and costly mistakes, but as you progress you slowly learn what to do and what definitely doesn't work. You may be seduced by plants plucked out of a steamy polytunnel in full flower, and then plonk them optimistically in the cold and inhospitable ground in quite the wrong place; it is dispiriting to watch them quietly fade away. Or you may have been taken in hand by generous but overbearing friends and relations, fluent Latin-speakers intent on passing on big-garden know-how acquired over decades and also, into the bargain, lumbering you with armfuls of their cast-offs that inevitably run amok in your own garden.

DRIFTS OF PALE tulips add to the illuminations in the golden spring borders at Parham House, in Sussex, UK.

GENTLY LEANING SPIRES and plants spilling over paths are, for some gardeners, the essence of a flower garden in high summer.

GROWING ORNAMENTAL VEGETABLES among the flowers can look good. Here, rigid black kale 'Cavolo Nero' contrasts with wafting stems of *Verbena bonariensis* and *Pennisetum villosum*.

FOXGLOVES ARE THE ultimate dingly dell plants that no woodland garden can be without.

There comes a point when you have to take control, make your garden your own, decide what you want the garden to look like, and just go for it. One way forward is to visit other gardens, not just grand and famous ones but those of more modest proportions, perhaps more akin to your own. Ask questions, take photographs.

It is also helpful if your plot has a well-placed tree or two, or a couple of agreeable shrubs or roses that can be pruned into shape and on which you can hang your floral ambitions. But management of the bones of the garden, the woody plants, is not what this book is about. Instead, *RHS Grow Your Own Flowers* shows you how to make the most of the spaces in between the trees and shrubs, how to carpet a woodland floor, or how to prepare the soil thoroughly before creating a border where once there was parking for three cars or simply far too much lawn. This book concentrates on suggesting flowers that are appropriate for the job – kiss-me-quick annuals, dark-horse biennials, and most importantly crescendos of perennials.

As you get more ambitious you will realize that there are more, and different, varieties of herbaceous plants to be found if you look beyond your local garden centre towards the small growers who specialize in herbaceous plants. A vast number of these can be found by trawling through the *RHS Plant Finder*. Many supply plants via mail order, and some have show gardens that are a great source of information and inspiration. Not to be forgotten either are the flower shows and privately run summer plant fairs, where specialist growers sell their wares and are happy to advise and share their extensive plant knowledge.

Of course, much of gardening simply has to be learnt by experience. And experienced gardeners will all stress that, even when you have got to grips with all the essential everyday horticultural nuts and bolts, the learning process never, ever stops.

When faced with a burning ambition to grow flowers that are intensely satisfying to you because they are where they want to be, where you want them to be, and, furthermore, growing well, you have to go right back to some fundamentals. What kind of flower garden are you after? Are the flowers for you to smell, touch, pick, or wander among, or just to sit and enjoy. Are you at heart a gardener who prefers formal, straight lines and neat edges or one who opts for blowsy schemes with the plants falling all over the paths? Do you crave the peace of a softly coloured dingly dell or the shouty drama of primary-coloured exotica? How much time have you got, and do you enjoy fiddling around with seedlings and taking cuttings? And, finally, the all-important gardening question is how do you successfully achieve what you want, that is growing the flowers you love in the space you have, given its various limitations - light levels, soil type, and soil quality - and all the other things that plants are fussy about? The aim of this book is to help you find some answers.

LATE SUMMER POKERS flourish in a hot spot among similarly coloured flowers at West Dean Gardens, in Sussex, UK.

The flower garden

Planting styles

For your garden you can choose from styles that range from the very formal through varying types and degrees of informality and cottage gardening to woodland planting and gardens that are no more than stylized versions of ideas normally kept firmly outside the garden gate. For most people, however, gardens end up somewhere in the middle of every style, with an individual atmosphere that is an inevitable compromise.

Before making any decisions it is helpful to understand the influences that have resulted in your current garden style. And it is worth remembering that the style you might now visualize for your plot may be dramatically at odds with what you can realistically achieve. You may well have to adapt your ambitions to cope with the site and its quite specific conditions (see "Know your plot", page 26).

FORMAL

Flower gardens in the ultra-formal style have beds set out in a decorative and often symmetrical way divided and intersected by grass - or more often stone or gravel – pathways wide enough for two people to move about comfortably and, just as importantly, to allow access for wheelbarrows. Formally arranged beds and borders are

SISSINGHURST CASTLE'S FORMALLY laid out White Garden is actually a harmonious mix of greys and greens, against which white flowers come and glow.

often planted with brightly coloured bedding plants (although the fashion for these has waned in recent years). They were generally open at the sides so that the flowers could be better appreciated, although more frequently nowadays they are edged with box (*Buxus*) or dwarf flowering hedges (lavender or teucrium, for example), the clean lines of which serve to enhance – to frame - the taller flowers grown within, as well as to hide their frequently less attractive undercarriages.

One of the best-known examples of a formal-styled garden is the White Garden at Sissinghurst Castle, in Kent, UK, where the monochrome of the flowers is enhanced by the greens and greys of the foliage and their contrasting texture. At all times of the year, the success of gardens such as this hinges on the rigidly formal layout of the box-edged beds and the paths, while the flowers and all the other vegetation come and go, ebb and flow.

Skilfully planted and managed formal gardens have layer on layer of planting, with flowering plants following in quick succession through the season: daffodils are superseded by tulips then annuals, perennials, and foliage foils, and often with something taller - roses, perhaps - as a permanent centrepiece to each bed. At the flower season's end, when everything is pulled out and cut down for winter, the essential formal framework remains – still neat, simple, and pleasing to the eye, the neatness accentuated when dusted with hoar frost.

There are, however, other ways of creating a formal style in your garden. The beds will take on an entirely new demeanour, for example, if the bedfellows within are massive and/or dramatically simple. Immaculate, starkly straight-edged beds look extraordinarily lovely when filled first with tall tulips in simple colour combinations, followed in late summer by a heady mixture of cannas, dahlias, and wildly exotic-looking leaves of bananas (*Musa*) or melianthus.

INFORMAL

Purely herbaceous borders – those that contain only perennial plants – were popular until the early 20th century but they are now few and far between because their creation and maintenance are highly labour intensive. Furthermore, unless you take pleasure from the sight of neat, naked soil, this kind of border provides little in the way of visual treats in winter. However, there are still some impressive herbaceous borders around to admire – one of the most magnificent being at Arley Hall in Cheshire, UK.

A mixed border contains shrubby plants that can create interest even when there is precious little in the way of flowers to look at. It is therefore a more user-friendly adaptation of the basic informal style and much more suitable for a smaller garden. In addition to a few flowering shrubs or climbers to add permanent body, a mixed border ideally contains a long-season mixture of bulbs for spring and perennial plants that flower throughout summer and well into autumn. Everything is planted in small groups or, where space allows, in huge drifts, to create maximum impact. There may also be pockets

AN INFORMALLY STYLED border is perhaps more organized than it looks. Designer Tom Stuart-Smith is a master of such carefully managed informality.

of lower-growing annuals, or taller gap fillers, as well as lilies, dahlias, and crocosmia.

Generally, small plants are placed at the front of the border, serving to hide the lower stems of the taller ones at the back. Seemingly artless drama can be created by using veil plants with more diaphanous growth habit (for example, *Verbena bonariensis* or similarly lofty, pale yellow-flowered *Patrinia scabiosifolia*) and by inserting groups or singletons of dramatic verticals such as verbascums into the planting scheme.

Getting the components and the balance of a mixed border right can take even a relatively experienced gardener several years to achieve. Even after that, the planting scheme may well be subject to changes year by year. This is part of the enjoyment that justifies the considerable mental and physical effort involved.

COTTAGE GARDEN

A house with roses, hollyhocks (*Alcea*), and honeysuckle (*Lonicera*) around the door is today's rose-tinted and very much stylized version of the cottage garden – the perceived rural idyll of pre-industrial revolution Britain, when hard-pressed agricultural workers supplemented their basic diet by growing fruit and a few vegetables along with enough flowers to attract pollinating insects in the tiny plots beside their homes. The cottage-garden style was adopted in the early 20th century as a reaction to the Victorian fashion for garish. hot-housed bedding schemes. Where early exponents such as William Robinson and Gertrude Jekyll led, other garden designers – most recently and notably Penelope Hobhouse – have followed, expanding the theme.

In this very English gardening style, the use of generous, informal masses of harmoniously coloured flowering perennials is *de rigueur*. It is all managed within an often almost deliberately lax, semi-formal layout (generally also using a substantial number of blowsy, old roses with French names, and adorned with clematis).

For the past century or so, such a cottage-garden style has graced the outside of small and not-so-small manor houses in the UK. It is, therefore, somewhat ironic that in the 21st century many gardeners try hard to emulate the same look in their tiny patches outside modest houses that are much more akin to the size of the lowly, original workers' cottages.

WILDFLOWER MEADOW

A natural summer meadow consists of a profusion of wild grasses and native wild flowers, locally different according to the soil type, moisture levels, and the cutting or grazing regime of its custodian. If you want this sort of meadow in a garden setting (an extension of a lawn or in an old orchard, say) you first need to impoverish the soil and get rid of coarse grasses by regularly close mowing for a season or two. After that you can gradually introduce patches of wildflower seed, removing small areas of turf first, or plant small plug plants of wild flowers, chosen from those appropriate to the local soil and climatic conditions.

A simple spring meadow, which will consist mainly of grass, cowslips or primroses, and early-flowering bulbs, is slightly easier to establish than a summer-flowering one (see "Wild flowers on a smaller scale", page 38).

NATURALISTIC

This style started to engulf gardeners and designers in the last years of the 20th century. Taking inspiration

THE RICH COLOURS and textures of nature have been allowed the upper hand in this attractive wildflower meadow.

from the textures, colours, movement, and effects of changing light in nature, designers used plants – mainly herbaceous perennials and grasses with strong shapes and colours – *en masse* in great interlocking swathes. Such a naturalistic style really works well in a rural setting, under big skies and on a big scale.

An intriguing example, however, of naturalistic planting within a formal layout (the garden even has vast hedges of immaculately but eccentrically shaped box hedges) is Le Jardin Plume in Normandy. It is interesting that Patrick and Sylvie Quibel, the designers and keepers of this highly regarded, 21st-century garden, acknowledge the influences of all that had gone before, specifically the informality-within-formality of Christopher Lloyd's garden at Great Dixter, in the UK, with its essentially traditional bones, as well as the great ebullience of the naturalistic planting trail-blazer Piet Oudolf from the Netherlands.

WOODLAND

There is something deeply peaceful and satisfying about gardening in shade as opposed to concentrating all your efforts on the floral hurly-burly of a sunnier garden. Indeed, having taken inspiration from the writing and from the garden of Beth Chatto's lovely woodland garden at Colchester in Essex, UK, a whole generation of gardeners has become inspired to plant up and enjoy parts of their gardens they might previously have considered inhospitable. It can, moreover, be quite a challenge to get plants growing happily in dappled shade under and between trees.

This style of gardening is restricted by lack of moisture in the soil and the lack of light in summer, and, worse, a woodland's fundamentally root-filled soil, which makes digging and getting new plants established difficult.

You can, however, create a truly magic woodland garden by carefully identifying patches of ground that receive more rain and more sunlight than others and by carpeting them with large swathes of appropriately chosen plants. You will need to nurture the plants painstakingly while they get established, and mulch extensively with natural leaf mould. In time you can enjoy your own leafy, flowering glades – a woodland garden that looks and feels totally natural.

Inevitably, early spring-performing plants fare best in a deciduous woodland garden, and as the trees leaf up and the dappled gloom intensifies, so white and pale coloured flowers and variegated leaves can make the area glow with life.

EXOTIC

For some gardeners, style is all about shock and awe. The shock is at the sight of plants with alien foliage shapes and textures and with dazzling flower colours sitting cheek-by-jowl with bright, bold but familiar border staples in a cool-temperate landscape. The awe is that anyone painstakingly manages to manipulate many of these alien plants into coping with an unsuitable climate. Indeed, many of these exotic plants are extremely high maintenance, needing overwintering under cover between midautumn and early summer. Even once they are moved into the garden they require the shelter of warm walls and careful summer feeding.

This is a style that has in recent years subtly embedded itself ever more deeply into the mindset of many gardeners who otherwise regard themselves as traditionalists. In the 1980s, on being presented with a flower colour combination of magenta, orange, and scarlet you might have winced. Now you might gasp, nod sagely, and acknowledge the great and innovative colour wisdom championed by the late Christopher Lloyd at Great Dixter.

A NATURALISTIC STYLE of planting using perennial plants and grasses works well here on a smaller scale.

PLANTS WITH WHITE flowers glow wonderfully in a woodland setting.

EXOTIC PLANTING AT its best. Cannas, dahlias, and verbena fight for attention at Great Dixter Gardens, East Sussex, UK.

The cutting garden

Until now, you may have felt that flowers belonged strictly in the garden: you grew them because you wanted to appreciate them as part of an ever-changing outdoor tableau. As your taste for flowers develops and your familiarity with how plants behave increases, the ultimate aim – the challenge – may become the creation not only of a harmonious flow of colour in the garden for as long a season as possible but also a floral bonanza that can be enjoyed in the house as well.

Slightly irrationally, perhaps, you may find it really hard to bring yourself to cut into the garden to any great extent, in case, as you see it, you somehow wreck the richness of the visual feast. However, by choosing to grow a few generously floriferous annuals among and between reliably repeat-flowering perennials in even the smallest beds and borders, you will be able to pick and tweak almost invisibly during summer and often either side of that season. By picking on such a relatively small scale you will encourage most plants to go on producing more flowers rather than going to seed. But you do need to be aware that some perennials cannot be persuaded to put in a repeat performance.

From experience you will learn which are the best cut-and-come-again garden flowers. When you have a little more time and space in which to experiment, you may also discover your dormant inner flower arranger, and want to create a larger cutting garden. You may also find that there is no space in a small garden for magnificent but space-greedy, spectacular, solo-performance artists such as peonies or oriental poppies (*Papaver orientale*).

CUTTING IDEAS

Sweet peas and their companions

However small your garden and however reluctant you may be to cut flowers from your beds and borders, you will probably be seduced by the ultimate cut flower, the universally loved sweet pea (*Lathyrus odoratus*). It is well worth finding 1sq m (9sq ft) of rich soil in a sunny (but not blisteringly hot) spot on which to grow a small wigwam of them. You can even grow sweet peas successfully in a large, heavy, and stable container such as an oak half-barrel. Or, more informally, you could just let a few plants clamber in among shrubs or even mingle

GLORIOUS SWEET PEAS always need a leg-up – in this case with a beautifully constructed bamboo framework.

1 DAHLIAS MAKE GREAT cut flowers, carefully snipped with secateurs and...

2 ...THEIR STEMS PLUNGED at once into plenty of water in a handy deep bucket.

3 A TRADITIONAL WOODEN trug is helpful for carrying cut flowers without damaging them.

with a few scarlet-flowered runner beans. 'Cupani' – a very old mahogany/maroon/violet sweet pea variety from which all modern varieties were bred – would look marvellous grown in this way. Otherwise, depending on your garden style, you may favour a dizzy mixture of sweet pea colours, or smart, single shades.

When grown *en masse*, it is important that you pick sweet peas almost daily (or at least deadhead those you missed) for several weeks, or they will start forming seed and gradually stop flowering. They are also thirsty plants and may develop unattractively mildewed leaves if they are allowed to dry out at the base on a regular basis. But even if you grow only a few plants on a single wigwam, you can make the most of less by combining sweet peas in a vase with lady's mantle (*Alchemilla mollis*) – an easy cottage-garden perennial with which sweet peas associate well and with whose flowering period they coincide perfectly.

To provide a succession of flowers, grow sweet peas in two batches: germinate one batch under glass in midautumn, pinch out their tips when they have made 8–10cm (3–4in) of growth and plant them out in spring; sow the other batch directly in the ground once the soil warms up. The lady's

mantle, meanwhile, will flower along with the sweet peas, but cut it to the ground before it goes to seed (otherwise it can become a somewhat overwhelming presence in the garden). It may even produce a few more flowers along with its subsequent, fresh crop of foliage.

Other simple-to-grow annuals that work well together and make great cut-flower companions for the tail end of the sweet-pea season are the annual culinary herb dill (*Anethum graveolens*), which carries lovely, lime-yellow, cow parsley-type flowers well above its aromatic froth of foliage, and the tall varieties of cosmos (*C. bipinnatus* 'Purity' – white; *C.* 'Sensation Mixed' – shades of pink and cerise). The cosmos will flower on and on, and even a single plant, both statuesque and airy in the border with its fine feathery foliage, will provide you with endless pleated-petalled daisies until the first frosts.

Other cut-flower options

Good cut-and-come-again performers to make a semi-permanent feature in your border also include the excellent, purple, woody-stemmed perennial wallflower *Erysimum* 'Bowles's Mauve' and various other slightly more tender, shrubby daisies such as the highly prized, pale yellow *Argyranthemum* 'Jamaica Primrose'. (Both these plants are easy to propagate from softwood cuttings; see page 46.) As they flower more or less non-stop for the whole summer (given ideal conditions, the wallflower will keep going for most of the year) they are favourites for cut flowers, along with prolific border perennials such as *Knautia macedonica* and *Astrantia major*. Many annuals, notably tobacco plants (*Nicotiana*), vivid red-orange Mexican sunflower (*Tithonia*), and pot marigolds (*Calendula*), are popular too.

Seedheads

Not to be forgotten, when considering plants for the cutting garden, are dramatic seedheads. Many of the spring-flowering ornamental onions (*Allium aflatunense*,

MANY SUMMER FLOWERS can be left to develop into seedheads, which can later be extremely decorative.

A. cristophii, and *A. schubertii* are the best), various poppies (particularly those of opium poppy, *Papaver somniferum*), and love-in-a-mist (*Nigella*) are all stunning in their husky beige-ness when left alone to dry *in situ* in beds and borders. At the end of the summer continue to enjoy their splendour by bringing the seedheads into the house before they deteriorate in the autumn damp.

Shrubs

While flowers are the main focus of this book, it is the woody backbone of any garden – the shrubs, and in particular those with evergreen or colourful leaves – that will be invaluable for providing a regular and ample supply of material with which to augment and enhance cut flowers.

Evergreen foliage shrubs conveniently need to be cut back and groomed in high summer, so that this marriage of flowers and foliage is one of great convenience to gardeners and flower arrangers alike.

RECOMMENDED SHRUBS FOR FOLIAGE
Evergreens
Brachyglottis monroi (crimped-edged, leathery, grey leaves)

Bupleurum fruticosum (leaden-green leaves, dusky-rose stems, olive-green "cow parsley" flowers)

Choisya ternata (shiny, pungent, evergreen leaves, with white flowers in early summer)

Elaeagnus x *ebbingei* (bronze/gold new leaves)

Eucalyptus gunnii (keep this tree stooled – shrub-like – for continuous, rounded, blue-green leaves)

Olearea ilicifolia (spiky, matt, grey-green foliage)

Pittosporum tenuifolium 'Irene Paterson' (marbled green/white foliage)

Pittosporum tenuifolium 'Purpureum' (chocolate/purple foliage)

Rhamnus alaternus 'Argenteovariegata' (small cream-variegated leaves, reddish stems)

Deciduous
Cornus alba 'Elegantissima' (soft cream-variegated leaves, also deep maroon mature stems)

Corokia cotoneaster (dark, wiry stems; also called "wire-netting bush")

Cotinus coggygria Purpureus Group (plum-purple, translucent leaves)

THE DEDICATED ANNUAL CUTTING PATCH

While a carefully planted cutting patch can be a visual riot of colour in the height of summer, essentially the growing of annuals purely for cutting is a practical exercise in which you need to concentrate on making the area as easy to manage as possible.

Selecting a site
For your cutting patch choose a plot that is open and sunny (not under the canopy of trees, for example), because if grown in the shade annuals will become leggy and flower less well. The site should also be as sheltered as possible from strong wind, but avoid areas that are subject to invasive roots from a nearby hedge. When the annual cutting patch becomes

vacant each autumn, improve the soil with masses of organic matter. This is needed because you are expecting a high yield year after year from a tiny patch of ground. If the site has beds edged with box (*Buxus*) or other evergreen dwarf edging plants, such enriched soil will generate rapid growth in these plants as well, so careful management and maintenance are needed.

Arranging your plot
Certain beds can perform a double function during a single season: one devoted to growing tulips for cutting can, once their bulbs are lifted and stored, then be used for growing dahlias that have been started off in pots.

When annuals are treated as a crop, grow them in rows. You can then hoe with ease, affording each plant a little more space than you might do in a crowded mixed bed.

If aesthetics are an issue, and your summer cutting patch is very visible during its off season, you might prefer to lay it out in a formal style, in square or rectangular beds. Ensure that you can easily reach across the beds for general maintenance and picking, and that there are wide paths between them. Even in formal beds, annuals can be sown in rows (their edges fudged at the thinning-out stage), or they can be started under glass and planted out in late spring, creating great blocks of colour.

THE CATASTROPHE CAN
During summer, there are bound to be casualties in a bed or border: foxgloves and delphiniums that topple; and stems snapped by pets, footballs, or careless mowers. There may be also an excess of foliage and flowers – the result of overenthusiastic planting or self-seeding that benefits from selective culling. None of this random vegetation may be suitable for cut-flower displays in the house. However, when such plants are put in a container (an old galvanized watering can looks particularly fetching) and placed outside a garden door or on an outside windowsill, they together form an often exotic, artless display of garden glories that once were or that might have been. You will need to refresh and top up the water regularly as well as groom the plants from time to time by removing spent flower stems.

How to grow flowers

The different types of flowering plants

While the backbone of most gardens will inevitably consist of flowering shrubs or roses of some sort, you are also likely to want to grow herbaceous - that is, soft-stemmed - plants in your flower garden. Some plants may be here-today-gone-by-frost-time plants, and you can experiment with different combinations that take your fancy. Others will almost become part of the fabric of the garden by seeding themselves around, while a third group of plants, carefully chosen to suit your site and its unique conditions and then treated with care, will go from strength to strength year after year.

ANNUALS

An annual is a plant that germinates, produces leaves, flowers, and seeds, and dies all within a single growing season. Most are brightly coloured flowering plants (some have interesting foliage as well), and most of them are suitable for growing in containers. Annuals can be bought as small plants in late spring, or else they can be grown at home from seed, in which case they are started off indoors in pots or seed trays filled with appropriate potting compost in or around early spring.

If you buy annuals ready-grown in strips or trays early in the growing season, it is important to remember that they will have been grown in commercial polytunnels and may not be sturdy enough to cope with strong light or cold night temperatures. They will need to be acclimatized gently to outdoor conditions (hardened off) before planting (see page 34). Because annuals live short and intense lives, and have less extensive root systems, they can succeed in soil that is less deeply cultivated than soil for more permanent plants. Indeed if annuals are grown in overrich soil they have a tendency to produce too much leaf at the expense of flowers.

Traditionally annuals were used in formal displays, but more often now they are grown as colourful additions

THE OPEN FACES of fast-growing annuals such as sunflowers are big players in a summer flower garden.

BY SEEDING THEMSELVES around, biennials such as foxgloves will in time form colonies that ebb and flow.

PERENNIAL BORDER PLANTS - here stout-stemmed *Echinacea purpurea* 'Kim's Knee High' - improve year after year.

and gap fillers in a mixed flower border, where their reliable performance can go on well into autumn.

Whole borders can be designed just with annuals, which are sown *in situ* or first raised as small plants under glass before being planted out. Plant them to best effect in large swathes and use their exotic colours, different heights, and leaf shapes for contrast.

Annuals are also often used to create short-term carpets of colour between young perennials and shrubs in a new mixed border. Huge statements can be made, too, with taller annuals – swathes of tobacco plants (*Nicotiana*), wafting clouds of delicate-leaved cosmos, spidery cleome, sunflowers (*Helianthus*), and their vivid orange-and-red relations, Mexican sunflower (*Tithonia*).

THE OVERPLANTING TRAP

When planting annuals in a young mixed border it is easy to get carried away and include too many plants. Therefore, take care to prevent the whole planting scheme from becoming overwhelmed by late summer.

Hardy annuals

A hardy annual is naturally able to withstand frosts and can be sown direct into the soil in spring. Some will also tolerate autumn sowing or can be allowed to self-seed *in situ*. Even when they are very young, hardy annual seedlings, as the name suggests, will survive winter cold and the plants are all the better for it. They will grow away quickly in spring as soon as light levels increase and the soil warms up, and they will flower in early summer. Love-in-a-mist (*Nigella*) is a great example of a hardy annual that is much more prominent in a garden if it is allowed to sow itself around, or is manually sown, during late summer.

Seedlings of many hardy annuals resent root disturbance, however, and naturally sown colonies are better thinned out so that each plant has room to grow and expand, rather than be transplanted around the garden. Hardy annual seeds sown outside in the ground in spring may form smaller plants and flower a little later than those from an autumn sowing.

F₁ hybrid annuals

In theory, F_1 hybrid annuals are superior plants. They will have been painstakingly bred by seed producers to enhance various qualities such as sturdiness, longer flowering season, and greater resistance to disease.

EXTENDING THE LIFE OF AN ANNUAL

Some of the plants sold as annuals, given certain treatment and conditions, may become short-lived perennials. For example: ordinary bedding wallflowers (*Erysimum*) will cheerfully carry on for another year or so if cut back almost to the ground after flowering. Annual snapdragons (*Antirrhinum*) will trundle on for a year or two in mild gardens, while even some of the older varieties of tobacco plant (*Nicotiana*) will withstand a certain amount of winter chill in sheltered gardens and will flower away merrily during the first warm days of the following summer.

BIENNIALS

This group of plants includes many of the much-loved, old-fashioned cottage-garden favourites such as honesty (*Lunaria annua*) and foxgloves (*Digitalis*). These plants germinate in early summer, and grow into small leafy and completely frost-hardy plantlets in their first year. They expand and eventually produce flowers in the following spring and summer, after which they seed prolifically and die. Foxgloves, often sold as one-year-old plantlets with a perennial label on them, may indeed go on for an extra year, but they are seldom as impressive and are not guaranteed to persist after their first year of flowering.

Biennials are wonderfully useful, particularly in an informal flower garden. They do not resent being moved around in the autumn of their first season's growth, and a floating population of them can, therefore, be used as admirable gap fillers.

PERENNIALS

If it is flowering and evergreen shrubs that provide the backbone to a garden, then it is perennials (herbaceous and evergreen ones) that flesh the whole thing out. Perennial plants are those that, given the right treatment and adequate conditions, will go on for year after year, forming thickening clumps or even spreading out sideways (sometimes a little too far) each year.

Their flowering times vary: some perennials flower as early as late spring, others don't start till early autumn, but most often the length of time they flower can be extended by deadheading (thus preventing them from making seed, and spurring them on to flower more) or by cutting down some or all of the stems in late spring (see The "Chelsea chop", page 42). Some of the earlier flowering perennials can also be cut down completely – leaves and all – after their first flush and will flower again during autumn.

Part of the skill in growing perennials lies in the original choice of variety and their placement in the garden – giving them enough room to expand and make a real statement. As you gain experience you will discover cultural tricks for individual perennials so that you get the most out of them.

Growing perennial plants well can be fairly labour intensive. Some of the most-loved perennials - delphiniums, for example - are particularly attractive to slugs and snails as their juicy new shoots emerge in spring. If they are to withstand freak summer storms, many perennials - particularly the taller ones - need to be supported as they become top-heavy with flower. All perennials need to be cut down at the end of the season (or at least before the beginning of the next one). Every few years they need to be lifted, split up (see page 44), and the soil around their roots revitalized.

Perennials can be grown under glass from seed sown in spring, but they will take two or three years to become substantial garden plants. Some tough-minded gardeners will remove any flowers spikes or flower buds during the first year of growth, in order to encourage the plants to put all their energy into making bigger and stronger roots.

In response presumably to gardeners' legendary impatience and a modern desire for instant results, the seed producers have developed ranges of perennials that will reliably produce stout plants that will flower in their first year of growth.

WHAT IS A BEDDING PLANT?

Use of the term "bedding plant" has become somewhat confused over time. Not all bedding plants are classed as annuals, and not all annuals are bedding plants. This term is generally applied to plants used in seasonal beds, and it may refer to tender perennials such as geraniums (*Pelargonium*) and argyranthemums as well as annuals such as busy Lizzies (*Impatiens*) and marigolds (*Tagetes*).

Plug plants

Buying ready-grown perennials as plug plants (generally to be found in squashy, little, black plastic pots at garden centres) is another option to sowing perennials from seed or as more mature and therefore expensive plants. Plug plants can be extremely vulnerable, and on arrival at your home they will fare best if they are potted on into larger containers (see "Potting on plug plants", page 33). Do not plant them in the ground at this time. Put them out in the garden only when they have developed a more extensive root system and are growing vigorously.

Bulbs

Some perennial plants - often loosely known as bulbs - produce growth each year from underground storage systems. They are a motley group. As well as true bulbs (such as snowdrops, tulips, lilies, and daffodils), there are tubers (such as dahlias and cannas), rhizomes (such as bearded irises), and corms (such as crocus and crocosmia). All need specific growing conditions. Although some are perfectly hardy, other bulbs are not reliably so. When carefully chosen and positioned, bulbs add a lot of charm and drama to a flower garden.

THE UNIQUE COMBINATION of shapes, textures, flowers, and foliage - sometime planned, sometimes somewhat random - will give your garden its own special character.

Know your plot

Giving your plants the conditions they need, observing how they behave, and if necessary gently manipulating them are all part of the challenge of growing glorious flowers – and you get better at it as you go along. But first and foremost, before deciding on the plants you want, you have to get to know your plot, understand the particular soil type you are dealing with, and how the light and the prevailing winds affect different areas of your garden.

SOIL

Plants need good topsoil, which can vary in depth from a few centimetres to a good, healthy 40cm (16in) or more. Topsoil comprises a mixture of ground-up rock particles that contain a variety of vital minerals plus water, air, and – vitally – natural nutrients formed from decayed and decomposing animal and vegetable matter (humus) as well as bacteria and microorganisms.

Beneath the topsoil, and between it and the solid rock that governs the soil's basic character, is subsoil. This is usually rough and stony and lacks most of the things that plants need to enable them to grow.

While colour will tell you quite a bit about your soil (a dark colour often indicates the presence of plenty of organic matter in the soil), it should be noted that the soil behind older terraced houses, for example, particularly where the only access to the garden is through the house, is often darkly sour and sooty-looking – that is, unfertile and unproductive simply because it may have been over- or poorly cultivated for years.

Some areas of your garden may be damper than others. The presence of greedy, thirsty tree roots, which extend at least as far as the tree canopy, can cause major problems but are nothing that you can do anything about as far as growing conditions are concerned. However, if the roots interfere with drainage systems you must get this dealt with professionally. Without extensive drainage work, you may not be able to alleviate areas that are excessively boggy. The simple answer in both these situations is to choose plants that can naturally cope with the prevailing conditions, rather than striving to work against nature.

A SIMPLE SOIL test will help you determine the acidity or alkalinity (pH) of the soil in your garden.

DIFFICULT SOIL

In new housing estates or gardens that have been severely tinkered with, the topsoil may be a real hotchpotch of churned-up soil. Frequently, it may contain areas where the potentially barren subsoil – generally identifiable by its pale colour – has been brought to the surface and merely covered with a thin, cosmetic layer of imported topsoil, which may or may not be a good match for the original. Even worse, builders' rubble contaminated with who-knows-what may be buried beneath the soil.

Soil pH

This is a measurement of acidity or alkalinity in soil on a scale that ranges from pH1 (acid) to pH14 (alkaline). The pH of any soil is usually dependent on the type of terrain and the nature of the underlying rocks. Soil that is pH7 is classed as neutral.

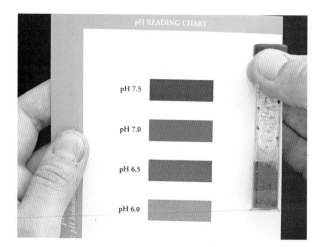

Plants have natural pH preferences, and some are so fussy that, given soil with an unsuitable pH, they may be unable to absorb nutrients in the soil and will, effectively, start to starve. The pH of your local soil can often be guessed at fairly accurately by looking at the local geological features, plants, and trees. For example, soil over chalk is alkaline, while soil in areas that were once ancient woodlands or marshland is often acid. A noticeable population of oaks (*Quercus*) and birches (*Betula*) in your area may indicate that the soil is neutral to acidic. But if old man's beard (wild *Clematis*) or sycamore (*Acer pseudoplatanus*) trees predominate, the soil is more likely to be alkaline. It also helps to look at the kind of plants your neighbours grow successfully. Azaleas, camellias, and ornamental acers (non-native woodland plants) will indicate acid soil conditions. Forsythia in every front garden and lots of happy-looking lavender means the soil is likely to be free-draining and slightly alkaline.

Of course, this is no more than a helpful generalization. A simple soil test kit will tell you more precisely what the soil pH of your own garden is, but be sure to test several samples of soil from different parts of the garden – the more the better – to get a more or less accurate overall picture of your plot.

Texture

To complicate matters further, basic soil texture – which affects its ability to retain water and drain well – is governed by the size of the rock particles from which the soil is formed. Very fine particles create a smooth, sticky, clay-ey soil (that feels almost soapy when you squeeze it between your fingers); it has a tendency to waterlog in winter and bake rock-hard in summer, which is tough on delicate plant roots. Clay soil does, however, retain nutrients well.

At the opposite end of the texture scale, soil that looks and feels gritty or sandy drains well and never becomes waterlogged – but nutrients, too, wash through too quickly. You can have acid or alkaline clay soil, just as you can have acid or alkaline sandy soil.

Very few gardens have perfect soil – called loam. This has a neutral pH and a perfect balance of everything, so more or less any plant will grow well. It has high levels of organic matter and, therefore, the fertility of clay, but without becoming cold and sodden in winter and baking

SOIL CAN BECOME weedy, nutrient-poor, and compacted during the season and so needs digging well to clear, nourish, and aerate it before planting can start.

dry in summer; loam also has the lightness (and ease to dig) of sandy soil, but without its thinness.

Drainage

Garden plants need moisture in order to thrive, but they also require air around their roots. Most will falter and eventually die if they are planted in ground that has a tendency to become waterlogged, especially in winter. Few gardeners go to the considerable expense of putting in land drains. However, you can improve the drainage of soggy soil by digging in coarse-textured organic matter to open up its texture (dig a wide area so as not to create local sumps around individual plants). Choose plants that are more tolerant of, or enjoy, damp soil. If a part of your garden is seriously wet, even in summer, you might consider creating a bog garden.

FERTILIZERS

Of the three main nutrients that benefit plants, nitrogen (N) supports rich, green foliage. However, too much nitrogen in the soil will encourage the production of lush leaf growth at the expense of flowers. Phosphates (P) stimulate the formation of healthy root systems, and potash (K) will promote better flowering.

Fertilizers come in many forms, with a different balance of the above essentials for varying purposes. The NPK content (expressed as a ratio) can always be found in small print on fertilizer packaging.

High-nitrogen fertilizers are used most extensively to keep lawns healthy and green. Fertilizers labelled "high potash" will help plants to flower and keep on flowering – and are particularly useful for short-life, high-energy annuals. More or less balanced fertilizers – those with roughly equal proportions of N, P, and K (blood, fish, and bone, or growmore, for example) can be applied as a top-dressing around flowering plants in spring to get them started, and again in midsummer to keep them going. Slow-acting fertilizers such as bone meal are high in phosphates and must be dug quite deeply into the soil before planting perennials and other plants that are to be left to grow undisturbed for a long time. The benefits of such fertilizers will last for several years.

Popular with some gardeners are controlled-release fertilizers – small pellets containing fertilizer. Their shells start to break down only when soil moisture and temperature levels are perfect for plant growth, and the effects last for the entire growing season. Fertilizer pellets are also available for clearly labelled specific purposes – to be added to potting mixes for container plants or as a boost for bulbs, for example, or they can be incorporated into the soil around plants.

There are, too, water-soluble and liquid feeds, both organic and inorganic, which will boost plant growth or promote flowering according to the balance of nutrients. Such quick-fix feeds are useful when plants are under stress after a pest attack or drought, and many can be applied as foliar feeds, since plants can absorb nutrients through their leaves as well as through their roots.

LIGHT

Light has an enormous part to play in plant growth. While there are plenty of plants that will grow in dappled shade, few – if any – will thrive and flower well in deep all-day shade. The vast majority of colourful flowering plants do best in gardens that get plenty of sun during the growing and flowering months. If they are positioned in too little sun, plants will flower poorly and grow lean and lanky in

MOST SMALL GARDENS are shadier than their owners would like to believe and may receive sunlight for only a few hours.

their efforts to reach the light. They will consistently under-perform and then gently fade away.

There are very different kinds and degrees of shade, so a really hard-nosed appraisal of the light conditions in every part of your garden is important before you plan where to have your beds and borders and what to put in them. (Most gardeners like to convince themselves that their gardens are more sunny than they actually are.) Bear in mind that even a so-called sunny part of the garden may receive little if any sun until the summer months because of the presence of house walls, other buildings, fences around it, and trees in the vicinity.

Deep shade

The shade cast by overhanging evergreen trees and shrubs is perhaps the worst kind. The problem is compounded by the inevitably impoverished and dry soil, due to the presence of so many tree roots in the ground – many of them extremely close to the soil surface. This is, quite simply, no place for a flower

garden, even if the sun does slant seductively in under the canopy for much of the day in summer.

Partial shade

Dappled shade cast by deciduous trees is hard but not impossible to deal with, so here you can concentrate on flowers that perform in spring, before the canopy of the trees thickens. You can also prune out the lower branches or the overall canopy of the trees, where possible, to introduce more light and vital rain. This is an ideal place to plan a garden using woodland plants (see page 14).

Light from one side

The proximity of lofty fences and house walls will ensure that even what seems like a sunny spot will in fact have direct light that is completely one-sided, and may last, realistically, for a few hours of the day. This can prove unsatisfactory for a flower garden. Rainfall will also be uneven, and this causes problems too.

WIND

Identifying the direction of the prevailing wind in your plot is important, since summer zephyrs can turn to destructive icy blasts in winter. Many of the most desirable, tall flowering plants detest endless buffeting, and need physical protection. Therefore, introduce hedges, or trellises or open-slatted fences well clothed in plants, to soften the effects of harsh winds and draughts. The construction and establishment of some sort of harmonious-looking windbreak of this kind should be a priority if you are planning a grand scheme from scratch. But such living protection doesn't happen overnight, and it may be necessary to install semi-permanent mesh screening while the hedging or other protective plants become established.

Wind funnels

While tall walls, buildings, and solid fences may appear to make smaller gardens seem sheltered, they can in fact cause damaging - and infuriating - wind eddies and strong back draughts (in the opposite direction to prevailing winds) that can seriously affect plants. It helps if you can identify these vulnerable spots before you plan the layout of your borders and beds.

PROTECTIVE WINDBREAKS AND screens can be used to great effect, such as this wattle one included in the re-creation of a medieval apothecary's garden at Chelsea Flower Show 2001.

MAKING THE MOST OF YOUR GARDEN

Finally, before drawing up a new planting scheme take a long, hard look at what is in the garden already. Are the existing climbers or trees stealing too much light or water from the area in which you want to grow flowers? Should they be cut back, or removed altogether? Is the best and sunniest part of the garden currently under concrete or paving, while what passes for a border languishes in the shade - and should the layout and the emphasis of the garden therefore be radically changed? This is your best chance to achieve that clean slate, and you may - will - live to regret it if you are indecisive at this point.

Even if the layout is basically pleasing and practical, are the existing borders deep/wide enough? Think, too, of access paths. With a little manipulation of the space you could even put a useful service path down the back of a border, or stepping-stones through the middle of it. What you need to do is think ahead, imagining the garden full of flowers that may need to be accessed.

Preparing and planting

The vast majority of gardeners grow flowers in more or less traditional flower borders, either as they were laid out by previous owners – sometimes which they renovate and replant – or which they make from scratch, most often by digging up grass. Thorough preparation is the name of the game, and it pays not to be in too much of a rush to start planting. Plants and seeds really do very much better if they start off in soil that is pretty much weed free, well dug over, and enriched with masses of organic matter. The benefits of really good site and soil preparation will last for years.

An existing border that is basically in good condition will undoubtedly contain a few sitting tenants that you may want to keep. Learn something about these before giving them a permanent place in your new scheme. Also, identify any shrubs in the border and familiarize yourself with their growth habits. Some of these may have to go if they are high-maintenance space invaders that don't earn their keep in a flower border.

Before doing any planting, take the opportunity to improve every available centimetre of soil in the bed or border, incorporating plenty of well-rotted organic matter such as manure or garden compost (see page 37).

CREATING YOUR PLANTING SCHEME

Making a sketch – back-of-an-envelope style – is helpful, as is making a wish list of plants suitable for the conditions in your border, along with their flowering times and heights. But try not to be overambitious or see this as gardening-by-numbers. At least half the pleasure of flower gardening is about learning as you go, discovering plant combinations that work for you and intrigue you – which may just as likely happen quite by chance instead of after days or sleepless nights spent mulling over colour combinations, leaf textures, relative heights, and planning everything out with a tape measure.

Realistically, you are really unlikely to get a border right first time. The first year should be about growing things well and observing what they do, and filling in gaps (with annuals, perhaps). Fine tuning happens in year two – and for ever after.

Marking out a bed or border

To help visualize a border, some gardeners mark out areas for planting, using fine sand to make the subdivisions into which the plants or groups of plants are to go. This is useful not only when creating blocks of colour with annuals and other bedding plants but also in a planting scheme using perennials and bulbs.

1 DRY SILVER SAND is helpful for marking out seed-sowing areas.

2 IF YOU SOW seeds in rows within the marked areas it will be easier still to spot the weeds from the germinating plants.

3 COVER SEEDS WITH a light sprinkling of soil. Tamp the soil down lightly and water it with a rose attachment on the watering can.

WHEN BUYING CONTAINER-GROWN PLANTS, always make sure that the rootball is in good shape, with plenty of pale young roots visible, barely filling the pot.

PURCHASING PLANTS

If you buy plants at a garden centre or nursery, seek out ones that possess plenty of vigorous shoots rather than those that have only one or two, or that are flowering prematurely. Check the rootball of any potential purchase to ensure that the plant has not become rootbound. Gently turn the plant upside down and remove it from the pot. Its roots should be fine, pale, and fresh looking – not matted and dark; they must not stick out of the base of the pot. Leaves should be a good green, and the surface of the compost moist and weed free (beware of tired, previous-season plants that have been topped up with a few centimetres of fresh compost).

If you buy small plants, pot them on and grow them for a few weeks before transferring them to the garden. You should be able to split really vigorous, newly purchased plants into two plants (see page 44).

PLANTING PERENNIALS IN A BED OR BORDER

Let the soil rest for at least two or three weeks after thoroughly digging and enriching the site. Before planting, water your plants well by soaking them in a bucket of water until they start to sink. This is particularly important if plants have been grown in a loam-free compost that may have dried out completely. If you are planting several plants, prepare a planting mixture: mix two fistfuls of bone meal into a bucket of well-rotted garden compost.

For each plant, dig a hole at least twice the size of its pot. Sprinkle two or three generous fistfuls of planting mix into the planting hole and fork it into the base. Also add about the same quantity to the backfill soil. Tip the plant out of the pot and nestle it gently into the planting hole. Backfill with the surrounding soil/compost mix and firm it gently by hand. Water in the plant to settle the soil around the roots. Mulch with garden compost.

SIZE OF PLANT GROUPS

Most flowering plants look more impressive if planted in groups – which does not mean adhering rigidly to the rather grand "plant in threes, fives, or sevens" dictum. Five delphiniums in a small border? Massive *Crambe cordifolia* planted in threes? Common sense should prevail at all times.

PLANTING PERENNIALS IN A CONTAINER

Gardeners with little space to play with generally feel the need plant up a few seasonal containers – bulbs in spring, annuals in summer, and maybe some winter-flowering pansies or marginally tender cyclamen. To create huge impact, plant perennials – both hardy and slightly tender – singly in big pots (as with dahlias or cannas) or even more dramatically group them with other plants in large containers so that they dry out less. Magnificent changing displays can be created this way, taking as an inspiration the spectacular groups of potted flowers and foliage around the doorway of Great Dixter, in Sussex, UK.

1 WITH YOUR FINGERS either side of the main stem, carefully remove the plant from its old pot.

2 TEASE OUT THE PLANT roots extremely gently to help them spread into their new potting soil.

3 PUT IN THE PLANT. Top up the compost and firm it well, ensuring there are no air pockets around the roots. Water well.

Use soil-based potting compost (John Innes No 3, lightened with a little garden compost or leaf mould). For a long-term arrangement, choose a container large enough to accommodate the expanding plants.

PLANTING BULBS, CORMS, RHIZOMES, AND TUBERS

Plant true bulbs, such as daffodils and lilies, in free-draining soil improved with a little bone meal, burying them under twice their height of soil. However, each member of this disparate group has special needs, and it pays to do some research to make sure that you plant them at the correct depth – on which success or failure frequently depends.

Plant all bulbs, corms, rhizomes. and tubers as soon as they are acquired, and if this is not possible store them somewhere cool, airy, and dry. Set them in groups or seemingly natural drifts, remembering to mark their positions with short canes. Leave those that are truly hardy – the bulbs mentioned above, and corms such as crocosmia and crocus, and tubers such as irises – in the ground from year to year. Dig up slightly tender plants (see "Autumn tasks", page 43).

GROWING FLOWERS FROM SEED

It is quite possible to start an entire flower garden from seed sown directly into the ground or by growing your own

1 HOLD FINE SEED in the crease of your hand. Gently tap your hand to distribute the seed evenly over the compost.

2 TREAT SEEDLINGS GENTLY when you prick them out, lifting them by their leaves and not by their delicate stems.

3 USE A PENCIL or thin stick as a dibber to make a hole for each seedling into its newer, more spacious accommodation.

POTTING ON PLUG PLANTS

Plug plants are too small to survive in the garden straight away and will need to be potted on and gradually acclimatized to outdoor conditions. As soon as you bring them home, transfer them to individual small pots or larger-celled trays, using a stronger, loam-based compost (John Innes No 2). This will prepare them for planting later on in garden soil or into larger containers.

1 GETTING TINY PLUG plants out of their cells can be a bit of a challenge. Use a pencil to poke each one out from below.

2 POT THEM ON, handling them with care when they are small. They will soon expand and become viable, little plants.

annuals under glass. This is particularly fun to try in a new garden or if you want to grow annuals simply for cutting.

Some seeds – mainly of annuals or biennials – can be sown directly in the ground where they are to flower, while others need a little more nurturing in order to make it to flowering stage. These, therefore, have to be started off in pots or trays in the comparative warmth of a greenhouse or on a light windowsill; plant them out when the weather warms up in late spring or early summer.

SEED CAUTION

When seed packets contain thousands of tiny seeds, think carefully how many plants you actually want. You may need only sufficient seed to sow in a small pot, and you can then swap the rest of the seed packet with other gardeners.

GROWING FROM SEED INDOORS

In many ways, growing seeds under glass or on a windowsill is easier than cultivating them outdoors in garden soil. Germination and early growth are not dependent on weather conditions (although light levels play an important part), and young, healthy plants, once gradually acclimatized to outside temperatures, grow on quickly. Annuals will flower earlier than those that are dependent on outside soil and air temperatures. However, do not be in too much of a hurry with starting your seeds

indoors – the most common problem is one of timing. Sowing too soon in spring will mean seedlings grow spindly and weaken before you can plant them outside. Seeds sown later tend to do better in the long run.

Large seeds, particularly those of space-greedy climbing plants such as sweet peas (*Lathyrus*), benefit from deep containers from the start to accommodate their rapidly growing root system. A lot of other seeds can be started off in any container – even recycled food packaging – that has one or two drainage holes in the base and can hold about 10cm (4in) of potting compost. Simple propagators to maintain initial humidity can be made using clear plastic bags or clingfilm, or you can buy one. There is a dazzling array of seed-growing equipment on the market.

Preparation

Multipurpose composts can be used for seed growing but sift out any large lumps and add a little sand, for good drainage. Otherwise, choose a proprietary seed or cutting compost, both of which are low in nutrient and generally comprise a 50/50 mixture of sand and peat-substitute such as coir fibre. Fill a pot or other container with the potting compost and tamp it down lightly.

Germination needs humidity, and tiny seedlings are particularly vulnerable to fungal disease. Therefore, water pots and containers of compost with a fungicidal solution (Cheshunt compound or liquid copper) immediately before you sow. Having dampened the compost evenly, drain it well – the compost must not be waterlogged.

To soften their tough seedcoat, soak seeds such as morning glory (*Ipomoea*) in water overnight before sowing. Nick (chip) others such as sweet peas with a sharp blade opposite the just-visible eye.

Sowing the seed

Before sowing, always read the instructions on seed packets as they are very important.

Sow larger seeds individually, pushing them gently into the compost to the required depth with the end of a pencil or your finger. Then cover them carefully with compost.

Mix very fine seed with dry silver sand. Using a V-shaped piece of card, sprinkle the seed mix evenly on the compost surface. Then cover the fine seed mix with a layer of vermiculite, to help germination.

Some seeds need darkness and warmth in order to germinate; others simply need light and humidity. Refer to the seed packet for relevant information.

Once seedlings have germinated, place them in humid conditions and good light. Avoid strong sunlight, which can harm delicate seedlings.

Thinning seedlings

Thin or prick out seedlings as soon as they can be easily handled by their first true leaves. Never hold seedlings by their delicate stems. Keep the strongest-looking seedlings unless you have sown a mixed pack, in which case prick out a selection of seedlings, otherwise you may be in danger of getting all white ones, for example.

Depending on their size and vigour, plant the seedlings either in pots or seed trays in twos and threes or in small clusters, or pot them on individually in 8cm (3in) pots. At this stage they need a more nutrient-rich potting compost such as John Innes No 2 or a multipurpose compost.

Position the plants in good light and give them regular water so they grow on well. Seedlings of larger plants may need potting on again before they are ready to be planted in the garden.

Hardening off seedlings

Before being planted out, it is really important to acclimatize seedlings to the weather conditions outdoors for a week or 10 days. Otherwise the shock, particularly of low night temperatures or cold draughts, will stop young plants in their tracks, and leaves of tender annuals will scorch or become yellow and unhealthy looking.

To harden off young plants, put them outside in a sheltered, shady position, during the daytime only at first. Eventually leave them out at night as well, in their pots, unless very cold temperatures are forecast. They should then be ready for planting in the open ground.

Planting seedlings in the garden

Once thoroughly hardened off, plant seedlings in their permanent positions, suitably spaced to take account of their eventual size. Water them - and the patch of ground where they are to go - the night before. Once planted, protect them if necessary with, for example, a dome of bent chicken wire or a small forest of wooden kebab sticks (particularly unappealing to cats). Check on their progress daily while they become established. Water them only if really necessary, and in the evening, using a rose on the end of the watering can.

YOUNG TENDER PLANTS should be hardened off - that is, gradually acclimatized to outside temperatures and weather conditions. Plant out once there is little risk of frost.

Planting up in a hanging basket or other container

Use a loam-based compost (John Innes No 2) mixed 50/50 with peat substitute-based compost, which will hold water well. Add water-retaining granules in the mixture as summer flowers grown in a hanging basket or other container will otherwise dry out readily. Take care not to overplant hanging baskets and containers, which will make the problem worse.

GAP FILLING

Often gaps just appear in a planting scheme because of unforeseen casualties, so it always pays to have a few healthy, potted young annuals on standby for emergencies. Many a gardener has resorted to standing magnificent pots of lilies in a border simply for impact or to distract the eye from local difficulties.

GROWING FROM SEED IN THE OPEN GROUND

Many annuals can be sown directly into the ground where they are to flower, following the guidelines on the packets of commercially bought seeds. Direct sowing may sound like a lot less trouble, but in fact the process can be fraught as you may not be able to recognize your seedlings from potential weeds.

It is, therefore, important to sow in relatively weed-free ground, unless you are familiar with your own particular population of weedlings. Also, if you sow seeds in rows, these can then be fudged by selective thinning out.

Preparing a seedbed

In the autumn prior to sowing, cultivate the site well by digging it over and incorporating well-rotted organic matter, to improve the soil.

In spring, rake over the soil to create a tilth. If you think your soil is still fundamentally heavy and lumpy, rake fine sand into the top few centimetres of the soil at this point, or even cheat by adding bags of seed and cutting compost to make it easier for your seeds to get established. Never sow seeds too thickly as thinning out young plants seems wasteful, and any little transplants

TENDER PERENNIALS SUCH as *Argyranthemum foeniculaceum* are useful border gap fillers and can be planted out in early summer.

often resent the disturbance and don't take well. The best way to ensure the fine seed is distributed evenly is to mix it with fine, dry silver sand (or play sand) – but not with builders' sand.

Sowing seed in drills

Mark out a shallow drill or drills with the corner of a hoe and moisten the soil via a fine-rosed watering can before you sow. After sowing in the drills, shake dry soil through a fine-meshed riddle to cover the seed to the right depth: barely hide fine seed, but add 1–2cm (½–¾in) of soil over large seeds.

Caring for the seedbed

Place chicken wire or twigs over the seedbed to deter cats, birds, and the like. Freak weather conditions can also play havoc. If the soil dries out, seeds may germinate poorly. Water, if necessary, with the finest rose on a watering can: heavy-handed watering, like heavy spring rain, can knock tiny seedlings sideways.

Borders old and new

The prospect of creating a floral masterpiece on a completely blank canvas is probably for most of us less appealing than adapting an existing garden, however dishevelled. But there may be lots to do. Much clearing, weeding, digging, pruning, even moving shrubs and marking out new beds with sticks, string, and whatever props are to hand - all with one aim: to create an environment in which flowering plants will thrive.

RENOVATING AN OLD FLOWER BORDER

Dig up any herbaceous plants that you want to keep and pot them up temporarily, each with a label, or store them on plastic sheets in deep shade, their roots covered in damp newspaper.

Remove as many weeds and their roots as you can. Then pile on a thick layer of well-rotted organic matter all over the border. Fork it in deeply, taking care not to damage any shrub roots. Before replanting, wait two or more weeks for stray weeds to resprout, and for air pockets in the soil to settle.

Clearing the weeds

Is the soil covered in little seedlings? If so, they are highly likely to be annual weeds, and a carpet of them indicates that they have been allowed to seed themselves unchecked. Are there tell-tale, dried-up, brown, twining wisps of last year's bindweed clinging to the fence, or thick, white roots just under the soil surface (indicating the presence of ground elder or couch grass)? All plants such as these should be dealt with before you invest time and money in creating your flower garden.

Annual weeds such as chickweed and hairy bittercress should be hoed out, preferably when the soil is dry, as soon as they appear. If they have been allowed to flower there will be a potential weed problem from their dormant seed for several years to come.

Perennial weeds will need to be dug out or treated with a root-busting weedkiller such as glyphosate, when they are in full leaf, and a second application may be necessary before it is safe to plant. Dig up any desirable plants that have become infested with perennial weeds and remove every scrap of invasive root. Gently wash the soil off the desirable plant's roots in order to ensure this.

Spreading, rampant border plants - lovely but thuggish Japanese anemones (*Anemone* x *hybrida*), *Lysimachia punctata*, and Cypress spurge (*Euphorbia cyparissias*) for example - should be viewed unsentimentally as perennial weeds and dealt with accordingly. It is tempting to leave scraps of them *in situ* to ensure that the border has instant body - but remember, if they ran amok once, they will do so again, so be tough.

SERIOUSLY WEEDY PLOTS

The realistic way to cope with totally neglected sites is to grow some tall, dramatic annuals from seed for the first year; do not plant perennials at all. The annuals will hide or disguise any residual weed problem (you could hoe between them to stop weeds from flowering) and you can have another go at cleaning the site when the annuals have finished flowering and been cleared away during autumn.

ONE OF THE most irritating of annual weeds is chickweed, which can flower and set seed for 11 months of the year in the UK.

Improving the soil

Ideally dig in autumn, so the soil can settle over winter, although this job can be done in spring. The easy way to improve both the texture and fertility of the soil in an old bed or border is to spread at least a 10cm (4in) deep layer of rich organic matter over the surface of the soil and systematically dig it in. Make sure that you turn the soil to at least the depth of your spade, and preferably half as much again. Digging can be very tiring, and it may be better to tackle the plot in more than one session.

The organic matter could be home-made garden compost if you are lucky enough to have enough of it; otherwise use well-rotted farmyard manure, commercial bagged and blended manure, recycled council green waste (which tends to be quite high in nitrogen), or mushroom compost. Look in your local directory or on the internet for a company that supplies and delivers ton bags (builders' bags) of composts, which is much more economical than buying small bags. A ton of compost is not nearly as overwhelming as it sounds.

If your soil is light and sandy or heavy clay, choose organic matter that is coarse-textured and increase the quantity you dig in. For some generations it has been the accepted practice to add grit to clay soils, but nowadays there is a move away from this towards the addition of organic matter, which does a much better job of improving poorly drained soil.

WITH DISTINCTIVE, WHITE, invasive roots and twining stems, perennial bindweed is one of the worst weeds. It may need to be treated with a glyphosate weedkiller.

ALTERNATIVES TO MANURE

Well-rotted, straw-based animal manure is increasingly hard to source and a suitable alternative for the garden are wood chips (even though they add little to the fertility of the soil and take a long time to break down). Manure that has been left uncovered in the open to rot down may contain unwanted weed seeds, so watch out for these vigilantly.

CONVERTING PART OF A LAWN INTO A FLOWER BED

The soil in a lawn is likely to be quite compacted so digging will be tough. However, there are several ways to convert a lawn into workable soil for your flower garden.

Using black plastic

A rather lengthy method is to kill the grass area by covering it in a sheet of black plastic (in spring) and leaving it for an entire growing season. This is the length of time it will take to kill the grass off completely, as well as any perennial weeds (such as dandelions) that may be growing in it. When you uncover the plot, you will have to dig it over, turning the soil to break it up, then incorporate organic matter (see "Improving the soil", left), and dig the soil a second time before planting.

Using weedkiller

A quicker way to clear an old lawn is to water the area with a glyphosate-based weedkiller. Once the grass has turned a rather lurid yellow/orange colour (after 2–3 weeks), skim it off the top surface of the soil (the roots will have started to disintegrate). Then start digging the soil and preparing it for planting, as above.

By double digging

A third, laborious, but intensely satisfying way to prepare a bed is by double digging, but do not do this if perennial weeds such as couch grass are present. To double dig an old lawn, remove 5cm (2in) layers of turf in spade-width strips and stack them nearby, then thoroughly dig the whole area in a series of trenches. As you dig the first trench (about a spade's depth or slightly more), put the soil to one side (so it can be used to fill the final trench). Break up the trench base with your fork and add well-rotted garden compost if the soil is heavy. Line the trench base with strips of saved turf, green side down, and add a fistful of bone meal per metre (yard). (These turf pieces will rot down and feed your plants for several years.)

As you dig your second trench, tip what is on your spade into the first trench – thereby burying the turf a spade's depth down – and chop the turned-over, compacted soil repeatedly with your spade to break it up.

Continue to dig and fill a series of trenches, gradually working your way across the plot. By the time you have dug the entire area, you should have got rid of your stack of turf completely. It will all be out of sight more than 30cm (12in) down under ground, and you can retire – to rest your back – knowing that your new bed is well and truly prepared for planting.

WILDFLOWER MEADOWS

As many gardeners have learnt to their considerable cost and frustration, a wildflower meadow is not achieved by buying a few seductive-looking packets of wildflower seeds and broadcasting them into the lawn. Wild flowers find it hard to compete with vigorous domestic lawn turf and do far better in grass that is rather poor and has been naturally grazed by animals. Success with wild flowers in a garden, therefore, requires a considerable degree of stage management.

The most successful way to establish a natural-looking, summer-flowering meadow in your garden is to remove the existing grass together with the fertile layer of topsoil. Then use weedkiller to clear the remaining soil or remove any residual perennial weeds (such as dandelions) manually, the roots of which may have escaped or been severed in the topsoil removal procedure.

Once the site is prepared, the easiest way forward – and one that will give the most natural-looking results – is to sow a suitable wildflower seed mix that also includes seeds of nonvigorous grasses. These are readily available from specialist suppliers, who will advise you on an appropriate mixture, bearing in mind the soil type, pH, moisture and light levels, and so on, and will also provide guidelines about sowing rates.

FLOWERS OF WILD knapweed and hardy geranium hold their heads up in among the ripening grasses of a summer meadow.

WILD FLOWERS ON A SMALLER SCALE

With a bit of time, work, and ingenuity you can establish a natural-looking, mini wildflower area on the margins of the lawn, perhaps, or under a hedge, or around and between fruit trees.

To establish wild flowers artificially in a piece of former lawn, you have effectively to imitate old farming grazing regimes, as you can't really combine a spring-flowering patch with a summer-flowering one. Therefore, you have to decide to have one or the other.

For a spring wildflower garden

A spring-flowering bed is possibly simpler to maintain than a summer one, and it fits slightly more neatly into a domestic mowing routine. In it you can grow snowdrops (*Galanthus*), aconites (*Aconitum*), crocuses, fritillaries (*Fritillaria*), daffodils (*Narcissus*), and camassias in grass, as well as early-flowering wild perennials such as primroses (*Primula vulgaris*) and cowslips (*P. veris*).

You can mow the grass for much of the year, but leave it well alone from very early spring (when the first bulbs emerge) and for the next three or four months (while the spring bulbs and other flowers come and go, their leaves die down, and they drop their seed). Start to mow again in early to midsummer and carry on for the rest of the growing season.

For a summer wildflower garden

Robust perennials such as campion (*Lychnis*), ox-eye daisy (*Leucanthemum vulgare*), hawkweed (*Hieracium*), and knapweed (*Centaurea*) are among the easiest to establish, by planting specially grown plug plants or by raking seed thinly into bare soil, having first removed patches of turf. By sowing patches of yellow rattle (*Rhinanthus minor*) – a semi-parasitic wild flower that feeds off grass – you will gradually weaken the grass growth even further, which will in turn make life easier for the flowers to colonize and spread.

To maintain a summer wildflower garden, mow the grass until late spring, then leave it well alone for the next three months while the summer flowers come and go. When flowering is over, mow the area short, leaving the mowings to lie on the ground (as in making hay) until the wildflower seeds have shed themselves into the ground. Then mow again, very short this time, picking up all the clippings (which gradually reduces the soil's fertility). Continue to mow as necessary until the following late spring, when the cycle starts again.

WOODLAND BEDS

It is worth noting exactly where the smothering weeds are growing in a woodland setting – for this, somewhat irritatingly, is the best growing space, where most light and rain falls, and where you will, therefore, find it easiest to establish your own plants.

Before starting to plant, you should clear your plot of weeds, although this needs a bit of ingenuity in a woodland.

The weeds may include rafts of nettles and hard-to-eradicate bracken and brambles. Fork out the spreading, yellow roots of nettles, and treat bracken with glyphosate (in late summer) – but it may take several seasons to control bracken in this way. Rip out young bramble runners, and dig out or at least fatally wound the older plants. As long as you sever bramble stems with a spade or loppers below the lowest pink growth buds, they will not return.

The challenge in planting a woodland plot lies in the fact that you are doing something more than a little artificial – trying to establish new plants in already root-filled soil, under a summer-heavy leaf canopy, which allows in little rain. If trees are really large, it may be helpful to thin out the upper branches and remove one or two lower ones.

As well as clearing the site and choosing plants that are completely suitable for the site, the other real key to success is in providing your plants with a comfortable mulch of leaf mould or failing that the nearest commercially available substitute – composted bark, which is similarly neutral and moisture retentive. And however careful you are when you plant, you may have to do a considerable amount of nurturing during the first year by scraping back and replacing the mulch after deeply watering once or twice during the driest months.

THE DAPPLED SHADE of a woodland margin provides a perfect home for ferns, hostas, and ground-hugging polygonums.

Growing healthy plants

All plants need light for their leaves to photosynthesize, grow, and flower. They must have air and water around their roots to enable these to develop strongly, and they require nutrients and minerals in order to sustain growth and keep healthy. But different plants have varying and sometimes very specific needs. Some herbaceous plants, for example, require staking or some protection from the wind, while others will grow happily without such assistance.

Some plants tolerate cold winters, while others thrive in dry or waterlogged soil. Rich and water-retentive soil is important for some plants even in summer, yet others will do better in poor soil or in a very well-drained one. And some plants will need more, or less, of a particular mineral (such as iron or magnesium) to enable them to stay healthy. Putting together and maintaining a successful flower garden depends to a large extent on getting to grips with these basics, for there is no sadder sight in the garden than a plant struggling against the odds and in the wrong place.

FEEDING

In the artificially tweaked and tidied environment that is a garden, plants benefit from a little help to make them perform well and for a long season. So not only is careful improvement of the soil important before planting begins, but also the application of an annual mulch of well-rotted organic matter to the soil is beneficial. Many gardeners take a belt-and-braces approach and as a matter of routine apply a fistful per square metre (yard) of a balanced fertilizer (such as blood, fish, and bone) to beds and borders in spring.

Annuals

When you plant annuals out in the garden, add a sprinkle of a slow-release balanced fertilizer to the planting hole. When the temperature and moisture content of the soil reach a certain level, the slow-release element becomes active and will last for two or three months. Slow-release fertilizer mixed into the compost of containers filled with flowering annuals will last the whole season.

As annuals reach maturity and burst into flower give them a boost of flower-inducing potash such as tomato food. Easiest to apply is a solution, which can be watered into the soil around their roots every two weeks.

Perennials and bulbs

If they have been planted in deeply dug and enriched soil, with a slow-acting fertilizer and plenty of organic matter around their roots, perennials and other long-term plants need little in the way of extra food during their first year. Thereafter, they will benefit from a fistful of balanced fertilizer sprinkled evenly around (but not on) their crowns. Gently fork it in, together with a little well-rotted garden compost or manure.

Perennials and bulbs in containers, planted in soil-based compost such as John Innes No 3, will need repotting in fresh compost every other year. In between times replace the top few centimetres of potting soil, and add some slow-release fertilizer.

WATERING

By giving plants appropriate growing conditions you should dramatically reduce the need to water them, but sometimes after a few weeks without significant rain it is necessary to water artificially. You may also need to water in the first year after planting perennials while plants get their roots properly established. How and when you water plants is important.

Water in the cool of the evening and water deeply, once a week, rather than just a little bit each day (which simply encourages a plant to make shallow surface roots that are vulnerable to drought).

If you use a hose, get a lance attachment with a soft-spray rose on the end. Aiming the spray low down, below plant foliage, water in a circle a few centimetres away from the stem, which is where the roots of the plant will be; don't direct the nozzle (or a watering can rose) straight at the base of the stems of the plant (which is almost instinctive). If the soil seems really dry, make a shallow gully by scraping back the mulch

SWEET PEAS NEED support even when they are tiny; here they have minature wire cages to cling to.

WIRE SUPPORT GRIDS put in place over the new growth of perennials in late spring will be undetectable a month later.

ONCE THEY GET going, sweet peas will scramble anywhere – here over a simple wigwam made of canes and twine.

around each plant and direct the water into that, drawing the mulch back afterwards.

A container closely packed with thirsty flowering plants may need daily watering. Again, try to do it in the evening, and water the plants deeply. Stand each container in a saucer of gravel rather than drenching the plants from the top and causing the water (and nutrients) to cascade out of the base.

Don't waste water by regularly wetting all the leaves of your plants with a hose or watering can with a rose. This, too, is another instinct that is hard to fight.

CARING FOR CONTAINER-GROWN PLANTS

Flowering plants grown in these somewhat restrictive conditions require daily watering in hot weather. Once they start to flower, give them a high-potash soluble feed (such as tomato food), at the rate recommended by the manufacturer. Flowers also need regular deadheading.

SUPPORTING PLANTS

Many, but not all, tall summer-flowering plants will need to be supported as they grow, particularly in less than full sunlight or in exposed sites. Knowing just how tall each plant, or group of plants, is going to grow and giving each an appropriate method of support is part of the skill of putting together a traditional flower border. The secret

is to get all necessary supports in place by the end of spring, so that they vanish in the following weeks.

The simplest method of support is often the most effective and appropriate for a large number of plants. You need a single cane the same height as the eventual height of the plant to be supported and a length of jute twine. Secure one end of the twine around the cane using a sheepshank knot, then loop the twine around each stem in turn, eventually tying the end of the twine to the cane. Result: the stems are held in a loose circlet, each one able to move independently in the wind with very little restriction, while being supported firmly – and the plant looks entirely natural.

Frameworks for annuals

Create a series of enclosures of wide-meshed, galvanized chicken wire of various dimensions and in appropriate configurations, in which the sheer mass of stems and foliage of tall plants will be held upright. Alternatively, support entire blocks of plants using even wider-meshed, nylon pea/bean support, which is virtually undetectable once the plants have grown up through the mesh. Stretch the mesh horizontally over beds or sections of beds and attach it firmly to canes.

Fast-growing annual climbers can be grown up trellises, through other plants, or over a simple wigwam – the choice of support depending on how the plant actually climbs. While morning glory (*Ipomoea*) will twine happily up bamboo canes, if you use bamboo to make a wigwam for sweet peas (*Lathyrus*), which climb via little, hooked tendrils, you will need to clad the base of it - at the very least - with some kind of netting on which the tendrils can get a grip. Tall annual sunflowers (*Helianthus*) will need stout individual canes, while other annuals (such as annual rudbeckia and cosmos) can be given twiggy sticks or grids - in the same way as you would support perennials (see below).

Staking perennials

Tall, many-stemmed perennials (such as sanguisorbas) are also best supported by a forest of twiggy sticks that becomes virtually undetectable as the plants grow up through them. The spires of delphiniums can be held up

THE SPIRES OF the tallest delphiniums become top-heavy as their flowers open, and they should be supported with individual canes.

in this way too, or, somewhat more laboriously, they can be gently tied individually at 15cm (6in) intervals to tall canes, as can stems of heavy-headed plants such as lilies.

A mass of short, twiggy sticks is also useful to hold aloft the flowerheads of shorter-flowering plants that are matt-forming but which tend to flatten down after rain (such as *Geranium* 'Johnson's Blue'). Otherwise grow them through wire-mesh supports.

Place metal hoops or grids on legs around clump-forming perennials (such as phlox), or for *Helleborus argutifolius*, for example, place the stems together in an intricate but wind-tolerant cat's cradle that supports stems both individually and as a group.

Whatever method of support you use for your perennials, you must check regularly all your grids, hoops, canes, and twine as the plants fill out and mature during the season. Loosen off ties where these might constrict stem growth. It is indeed rare to get through an entire growing season without having a disaster in this particular department - but you will improve at providing the right support for each plant type you grow as you gain experience and start to know your plants better.

THE "CHELSEA CHOP"

This is a fashionable manipulation trick. During late spring (at around the time of the Chelsea Flower Show, hence the name), cut down tall perennials by about half, to induce later flowering, bushier growth, or smaller, less heavy flowerheads - or a combination of all three. If you chop just half of the stems on a plant, you will promote a longer flowering season. The Chelsea chop is particularly successful for the large, stately, succulent sedums, whose stems frequently, in rich soil, flop open in the middle and do not lend themselves to being supported. It is also useful on some of the daisy family - heleniums, asters - as well as on phlox and campanulas.

DEADHEADING

Once flowering plants, particularly annuals, produce seed - thus performing their ultimate natural aim - they eventually stop flowering. Gardeners can put off the time when they cease flowering by regularly removing blooms as they fade.

SNIPPING OFF SPENT flowers (along with a short length of stem) will prolong the flowering season of numerous garden flowers.

In truth, the term "deadheading" is a misnomer. For if you were to go around merely removing dead flowerheads, you would soon end up with a sorry sight – a forest of browning stems among the next pristine generation of developing flower buds. Deadheading, therefore, should involve the removal of stems as well as heads – down to a point where you can see clearly that new flowering growth emerging. Do not deadhead, however, if you want to keep seed in order to propagate your own plants, or if you want self-seeding to occur naturally.

Deadheading can become an almost pleasurable daily chore – a chance also to soak up the pleasures of just being out among the flowers, as well as to spot any little local difficulties that might be developing (pest attacks, snapped shoots, and so on). It is vital to deal with these as soon as any damage or symptoms are spotted.

MIDSEASON CUTBACK

Crowded beds and borders that have been flowering away for weeks can be given an effective face lift around midsummer by having some of the excesses of effervescent foliage cut away. By this time, fresh leaves and a little space around them are quite welcome.

Certain plants do not respond to deadheading. Early-summer flowering *Geranium magnificum* and pulmonaria, for example, will not repeat flower whatever you do to them. For plants such as these, cut away the flower stems and foliage after flowering, after which each plant will produce a new, smaller crop of attractive, fresh foliage. The extra space thus created can be filled with later-flowering annuals.

Having cut off the flower stems on early summer-flowering delphiniums, feed the plants with a soluble fertilizer, then cut off the lower foliage once new leaves appear from the base. Treated in this way, delphiniums may be persuaded to flower a second time in early autumn.

Midsummer flowerers such as *Astrantia major*, after their admirably long flowering session, can be similarly cut back and will produce new leaves as well as a prolific second crop of flowers.

AUTUMN TASKS

As the growing season draws to an end, there are important tasks for the gardener to do such as pulling up annuals, cutting down perennials, planting bulbs, and improving the soil (see page 213). Other jobs include lifting plants that are slightly tender (such as cannas and dahlias) before the ground becomes frosted. Store and dry them or plant them in pots of dry compost, in a frost-free shed or garage.

As clump-forming perennials grow and thicken up, the centre of each clump becomes visibly weaker and less productive. To retain the vigour of these plants, dig them up every three or four years, throw away the exhausted central portion, splitting the vigorous outer section into two or three plants, and replant them – or donate them to friends (see page 44).

Propagating plants

Without doubt the most economical way to fill out a flower garden is to propagate your own plants. You may have started growing seeds of some sort in childhood, so the whole idea is not exactly new to you. However, you may perhaps be less familiar with other ways to increase your plant population, such as by dividing them or to taking cuttings – short lengths of young shoots – which when inserted into potting compost will root spontaneously during the appropriate season, given the correct encouragement.

DIVIDING PLANTS

You can divide tubers and rhizomes, take offsets from bulbs, and, simplest of all, split the roots of many young, vigorous perennial plants in order to increase your plant stock.

Perennials

Dividing mature perennials is perhaps the simplest form of plant propagation. Most perennials do better if divided in autumn, but on others – certainly those with woody roots such as hostas – this job is better done in spring, when their new shoots can be easily seen.

Dig up the naturally expanding clump of fibrous-rooted plants such as primulas and tease the small, very obvious plantlets apart or insert two forks back to back into their centre, to prise each plant apart. Divide tough, woody-rooted perennials such as astilbe with a spade or a sharp knife, ensuring that each potential new plant has visible growing points and some undamaged roots – you may need to wash the soil off the plants to check this.

After dividing any of these perennials, replant the new divisions in soil that has been reinvigorated with well-rotted garden compost or manure mixed with a little bone meal. Alternatively, you can offer your new plants to friends or neighbours.

Bulbs

Mature bulbs of tulips and allium propagate themselves by producing smaller, attached, little bulbs called offsets. If you lift these bulbs for storage after the leaves have died down, detach their offsets and replant them in autumn; they will eventually grow on and flower. Lily bulbs are slightly different, being made up of scales, which can be carefully detached and grown on separately for a year in pots of sandy compost.

1 CONGESTED ROOTS can cause a plant to flower poorly. Here an agapanthus is gently cut through the centre with a knife.

2 COMPLETE THE JOB of dividing the plant by using your hands to wrench the roots apart, creating two new plants.

3 REPOT THE NEW DIVISIONS in John Innes No 3 compost – loam-based compost being suitable for long-term containerized plants.

1 TO DIVIDE A clump-forming perennial – here a healthy but overlarge primula – dig the entire plant out of the ground.

2 PUT TWO FORKS back to back through the middle of the clump and tease the roots apart.

3 REPLANT THE DIVISIONS in soil that has been reinvigorated with plenty of organic matter. Firm them well in.

A MIXED BLESSING

Many a new gardener has started out as the grateful recipient of gifts of plants. These are too often divisions of overexuberant perennials that are deemed by the generous giver as essential in every garden. Some of these – such as *Alchemilla mollis*, *Geranium* 'Claridge Druce', and *Euphorbia cyparissias*, can become seriously invasive until and unless you get the measure of them. Also if you decide to reciprocate, take care not to trowel out little pieces from the edge of your most admired perennial to give to your friends. By taking such pieces you will be donating the best bits of your plant, and what may eventually remain will be the tired core.

Corms

Crocosmia and gladiolus produce new corms annually, either on top of or around the base of the old corms. Detach these and grow them on the following year.

Rhizomes

To increase irises, remove the outermost parts of the rhizome, with a knife, every few years in mid- to late summer. Replant the new pieces horizontally in the soil, with leaves neatly trimmed back. Divide and replant cannas in spring, when they already have visible growing points. These perennials expand rapidly and if planted in pots quickly outgrow them.

Tubers

The tuberous roots of dahlias have fingers, which can be separated with a knife in spring and then replanted at once. As with cannas, it is important that each section has a visible growing bud.

TAKING CUTTINGS

Raising plants from cuttings is a relatively quick and easy way to increase your plant stock. A cutting is any part of a plant which, when taken from the parent plant and treated appropriately, becomes an individual plant in its own right. Most cuttings are taken from stems, but in some cases plants can be propagated from little pieces of stem with a small amount of root attached.

Basal cuttings

Some herbaceous perennials such as short-lived, slightly tender penstemon and those that have particularly loose crowns such as Michaelmas daisies (*Aster novi-belgii*) are best propagated by taking a small piece from the crown of the plant to which a few roots are attached. Once these Irishman's cuttings, as they are sometimes called, are potted up they grow away quickly and need less attention than softwood cuttings (*see page 46*).

Softwood cuttings

Although cuttings can be taken from soft, bright green, young shoots at any time throughout the growing season, they root extremely quickly if taken in midspring just when plant growth is accelerating.

Cut off fast-growing stem tips, 4–8cm (1½–3in) long, just below a node (leaf joint) with a razor blade or very sharp knife. Remove the lower leaves and dip the stem base in a fungicidal solution. Then insert two or three cuttings around the edge of a pot filled with a proprietary sandy compost or a home-made, 50/50 mixture of horticultural sand and fine leaf mould. Because softwood cuttings are green and sappy they dry out easily, so seal the whole pot of cuttings in a polythene bag, to keep them moist. Position the pot somewhere warm (16–18°C/61–64°F), in a light but not sunny place.

When there are signs of new growth, make an air vent in the polythene bag, and eventually remove it. Pot on the individual cuttings into a more nutritious, soil-based compost (such as John Innes No 2) and water well. They will develop into young plants within weeks.

Semi-ripe cuttings

One or two essential players in the flower garden (sage and lavender, for example) are in fact soft-stemmed shrubs that are best propagated from semi-ripe cuttings. These are cuttings taken from non-flowering shoot tips of the current season's growth. Take cuttings 5–10cm (2–4in) long, trim them just below a node, and remove the lower leaves. Slot them into a pot filled with John Innes No 1 or a sand/peat mixture to about a quarter of their length. Water with a fungicide (Cheshunt compound) and place in a shaded cold frame. If necessary, cover the cuttings to keep them humid until they have rooted.

SAVING SEED

There is something fundamentally satisfying about growing flowering plants and collecting seed that you can then use to make further generations of plants or to give away to friends or neighbours. Always save seed from healthy, vigorous plants. It is worth bearing in mind, however, that you won't necessarily get what you expect from the next generation of seed-grown plants. For example, seed saved from plants grown from F_1 seed will not be true to the parent plant.

If you want to save seed, stop deadheading the plant well before the end of the flowering season so the seedheads have time to mature fully. You should – almost literally – catch the seed as the seed pods and cases are ripe, on a dry day, just before the plant drops them by itself. Put the seeds and seed pods into paper (not plastic) bags or envelopes; don't bother to sort everything out or remove all the husky bits until you are ready to sow. Then label and store the seeds in a dark, dry place below 4°C (39°F),

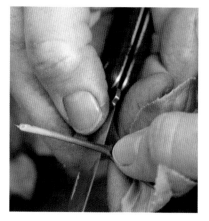

1 TO TAKE A SOFTWOOD cutting, cut cleanly below a node (leaf joint) on a non-flowering shoot of the current year's growth.

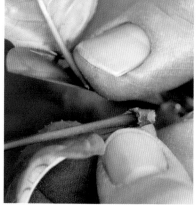

2 REMOVE THE LOWER leaves from each softwood cutting and dip the bottom of each stem in a fungicidal solution.

3 INSERT THE CUTTINGS into a pot filled with a sandy compost or a home-made mix (see above). Water them with a fungicide.

1 SAVE SEED (here of *Lunaria rediviva*) on a dry day when it is fully ripe but before it has been naturally distributed.

2 MAKE SURE YOU label the envelope with the type of seed and the date it was collected and saved.

3 SEAL THE WHOLE SEEDHEADS in the envelope and store them in a dry, cool, and dark place.

where they can completely dry out, unless they need to be sown straight away while the seed is still fresh. If you are unsure whether to sow seed immediately or in spring, sow a little of what you have saved immediately and save some to sow in spring. Bear in mind that seed stored for more than a year deteriorates slightly and therefore not all of it may germinate.

There are seeds, generally those of plants from high altitudes or cold climates, that need to go through a period of extreme cold before they will germinate. Some of these may need their hard seedcoats artificially broken in order to break the dormancy of their seeds. This can be done by soaking, chipping with a sharp knife, or, if the seed is too small for this, by rubbing the seeds with an abrasive substance to wear down the seedcoats.

ENCOURAGING SELF-SEEDING

As you increase your knowledge of plants and how they behave, it can be great fun to encourage the formation of more or less natural small colonies of favourite plants in your flower garden. This can be readily achieved with some of the more common, sun-loving hardy annuals such as love-in-a-mist (*Nigella*) and pretty cultivated forms of annual poppies such as *Papaver rhoeas* 'Fairy Wings'. If you allow a few of these plants to seed naturally, hoards of seedlings will germinate in early autumn, some of which will survive and start the following spring as

manageable-sized seedlings that can, with a bit of care, be moved to new locations.

Hellebores can also be encouraged to spread this way, although seedlings will take three or four years to mature and flower. Other perennials with recognizable seedlings include astrantias and short-life perennial verbascums.

Taking advantage of self-seeding is nowhere more effective than in a woodland or woodland-margin garden. There you will find prolific self-seeders such as perennial hellebores, the white campion *Silene fimbriata*, and such biennials as easy-to-grow foxgloves (*Digitalis*) and honesty (*Lunaria*). Allow plants to drop their seed (and in the case of biennials die, as they will after they have flowered). Then in their first leafy year, thin the new seedlings out and even move groups of them around.

SAVING GOOD COLOURS

If you are particular about colour, it pays to be wary when encouraging self-seeding. Unless you are quick off the mark and remove any rogue seedlings of the wrong colour, white honesty or white foxgloves or dark-flowered hellebore hybrids, for example, will gradually become dominated by the native colours (purple, pink, and dull pinkish white, respectively). Often you can tell future flower colour by examining the stem colour of seedlings closely.

A-Z of flowers

Achillea *Yarrow*

There are some 100 species of garden yarrow, although the one with which most people are first familiar is a rather scruffy roadside - or worse - mower-defying lawn weed. Yarrow was traditionally a useful medicinal plant used for staunching blood flow, as some of its old, traditional names - sanguinary, soldier's woundwort - would imply (although when used by Achilles it was clearly ultimately unsuccessful). This plant has strongly aromatic, very dissected, almost feathery foliage (often grey-ish), and flat corymbs of closely grouped, tiny flowers - spectacular when grown *en masse* and seen from a slightly elevated viewpoint.

Site and soil

First and foremost, yarrow is extremely fussy about drainage and is indeed relatively drought-tolerant. It, therefore, needs an open and sunny site. It is happiest in limy, even chalky soil, but can be grown in most garden soil except unimproved heavy, cold clay. If you do want to grow yarrow in heavy ground and clay soil, dig in plenty of coarse-textured organic matter, coarse sand, or grit before planting, to aid drainage.

When deciding where to plant yarrow, the fact that the flowers have a habit of fading and changing colour as they mature can be used to great effect where space permits by including several different-coloured plants together in a mass. The essential flatness of their flowers also looks good when set against strongly contrasting, statuesque, vertical border plants such as verbascums and sisyrinchiums.

Buying guide

Buy and plant out yarrow in early autumn, remembering that colours rarely stay vivid as the flowers fade. Because it is often sought out in rather subtle colour variations, yarrow is often - somewhat alarmingly - to be found for sale in high summer in its first year of flowering. It is hard to detect and select a good plant in a nursery in winter, because few yarrow are evergreen, and most die back completely at the end of the growing season.

Plant care

It would be easy to assume that these relations of pernicious lawn weeds were easy, low-maintenance plants, but this is not necessarily the case. Depending

THE FLATTENED FLOWERHEADS of yarrow are a perfect foil for softly wafting or vertical stems of grasses.

on conditions, plants can run out of steam quickly, and may need lifting and the soil revitalizing every other year. However, very rich soil combined with the lack of full light can induce floppy growth in yarrows.

Some species have a tendency to produce sprawling sideways growth, and therefore fall about if not carefully supported with simple metal grids, a forest of twiggy sticks, or a cat's cradle of sticks and twine (see "Supporting plants", page 41).

Deadheading

In smaller gardens where every leaf and flower are viewed at close quarters, removal of the first-flowering corymbs will enable the secondary ones a few centimetres lower down the stems to expand and take their place in the overall picture. Subsequent, more serious cutting back of spent flower stems will force the production of a second or even then a third flush of flowering stems.

Overwintering

If plants need to be lifted and revitalized or divided, this should be done in early autumn so that yarrow can re-establish in the still-warm soil. Otherwise cut down plants in late autumn, once their flat seedheads are no longer looking good. Leave some old flower stems a few centimetres high as markers.

In spring, apply a mulch of organic matter around each plant, taking care not to smother emerging foliage.

Propagation

Although yarrow can be increased by seed, it is more often propagated by division in early autumn, or otherwise in spring (see page 44). Take basal cuttings in late spring (see page 45).

Recommended varieties

A. 'Moonshine' ♛
Probably the most popular and one of the most spectacular varieties, it has neat, silvery, feathery foliage and pale lemon-yellow flowerheads, to 10cm (4in) across, between early summer and early autumn. H: 60cm (24in); S: 50cm (20in).

A. 'Walther Funcke'
The dusky red/orange, fading flowers, each with mustard-yellow eye and pale foliage, look good in a bright colour scheme. It tolerates slightly more shade than other achilleas and flowers early, from late spring onwards. H: 60cm (24in); S: 30cm (12in).

A. millefolium 'Red Velvet'
The deep red, pale-centred, tiny flowers of this variety dramatically darken, rather than fade, with age. H: 75cm (30in); S: 50cm (20in).

A. ptarmica 'Nana Compacta'
By contrast with the above, this is a smaller, mound-forming, grey/white-flowered achillea with dark green foliage. It is suitable for the front of the border. H&S: 30cm (12in).

Aconitum *Monkshood*

These clump-forming perennials are not grown often enough. Among the most wary gardeners there is possibly a slight prejudice against them, since all parts of monkshood are known to be poisonous, especially its black, tuberous roots and its sap. Indeed, perhaps it would be wise to wear gloves when handling these plants generally. However, they are tough, pest-resistant plants, with coarse leaves that resemble buttercups (to which they are related), and they bear curiously hooded flowers on stately stems in late summer. Their growth habit is superficially similar to, and therefore appreciated and beloved by, those gardeners who can't grow delphiniums (because of buffeting exposure or dire slug/snail infestation, for example).

Site and soil

Monkshood is not fussy about site and soil, although it performs best in moisture-retentive, rich soil in dappled shade. Flower colours may be paler when the plants are grown in acid soil.

The key to growing these plants successfully is to improve the soil massively with leafmould or other moisture-retentive organic matter and a little slow-acting, long-life phosphate fertilizer such as bone meal at the time of planting in autumn or spring.

The taller varieties make excellent back-of-the-border backbone perennials, and they associate well with shade- and moisture-loving *Persicaria amplexicaulis*.

Buying guide

Considering that monkshood is thought by many to be an easy alternative to delphiniums, it is surprising that it is not more commonly found in garden centres. You may, therefore, need to seek it out at specialist nurseries. Buy and plant it in spring or autumn.

Plant care

These plants somewhat resent disturbance and do not need frequent division (and because of their basic toxicity you don't want to handle them too much).

All but the tallest varieties of monkshood are wonderfully self-supporting, and therefore do not need staking.

THE CURIOUSLY HOODED flowers of monkshood stand tall in a late-summer border, somewhat resembling delphiniums with their eyes closed.

DEADLY ATTRACTION

While the toxicity of monkshood can make gardeners shy away from this good garden plant, the same deadly reputation has resulted in a rich cultural history. *A. napellus*, a species widely grown in gardens, was used in the Middle East for an arrow poison that proved effective in the hunting of ibex, the curl-horned, wild goat. Another common name, wolf's bane, will be familiar to Harry Potter fans as it was made into a potion that prevented one teacher from turning into a werewolf. Medicinally, extracts were used to help numb pain until far safer alternatives took over in the mid-20th century. In the garden, sensible advice about monkshoods comes from Victorian gardener William Robinson: "They should not be planted where the roots could be by any chance dug up by mistake for edible roots." It may sound like an unlikely blunder, but the roots look remarkably like horseradish once the foliage has died down in winter.

Deadheading

By deadheading monkshood you can encourage the lower, bud-bearing laterals to plump up and flower better. The latest-flowering varieties can then provide colour in the border well into autumn.

Overwintering

Monkshood is totally hardy and can be cut down in autumn. An organic mulch at either end of the winter is beneficial. When the new leaves appear early in spring, they are totally ignored by slugs and snails.

Propagation

Propagate monkshood by division in very early spring (see page 44).

Recommended varieties

A. x cammarum 'Bicolor' ♀
'Bicolor' is a tall variety with dark green leaves and pale blue, white-streaked flowers. The lower petals are an intense blue. H: 1.2m (4ft); S: 50cm (1½ft).

A. carmichaelii 'Arendsii' ♀
With its typical, deep blue flowers carried in late summer and early autumn, this variety definitely tolerates partial shade. H: 1.5m (5ft); S: 30cm (1ft).

A. 'Spark's Variety' ♀
This midseason flowering plant has very deep violet-blue flowers and more serrated leaves than other monkshood varieties. H: 1.2m (4ft); S: 50cm (1½ft).

A. carmichaelii (Wilsonii Group) 'Kelmscott' ♀
The flowers of this tall, late-flowering variety are light lavender. H: 1.5m (5ft); S: 30cm (1ft).

Actaea *Bugbane*

Formerly known as *Cimicifuga* (when the name *Actaea* belonged to a shrubbier relation), this is a useful group of shade-tolerant perennials with low-growing, sometimes darkly coloured and finely cut leaves. During late summer and early autumn, bugbane produces lofty, often arching wands of fluffy flowers, most of which are surprisingly and intoxicatingly fragrant.

Site and soil

These plants belong in a cool, moist border or in a light leafy-soiled woodland – preferably in soil that is neutral or slightly acid. The leaves of the most often-grown, dark-leaved cultivars tend to wilt, scorch, and curl if they are grown in full sun and without the benefit of extremely moisture-retentive soil.

Bugbane looks stunning growing in the dappled shade of woodland margins, among hostas, ferns, and with Japanese anemones. In a more traditional garden setting, it is interesting, despite its height, to grow bugbane somewhere near the front of a border where its low foliage is in itself attractive for most of the summer, and the nose-height perfumed wands of flowers can be appreciated at close quarters in the cool, autumn air.

When planted, the crowns should be set 2.5–5cm (1-2in) below soil level in ground that has been much improved with composted bark or leafmould and given a good surface mulch of the same.

Actaea can be grown from seed, but germination is unreliable, so division is a better method of propagation.

Buying guide

Buy and plant bugbane in spring or autumn. Fashionably dark-leaved *A. simplex* 'Brunette' is commonly found at garden centres, particularly in spring as the first showy leaves are emerging. Green-leaved varieties are harder to find, and you may need to visit a specialist herbaceous nursery.

Plant care

Water bugbane well during its first summer to make sure it gets used to its new site. Young plants take some time to settle down and to produce more than one or two

THE GLORIOUS EARLY autumn scent of the soft, white wands of bugbane are simply not in keeping with its distinctly unprepossessing common name.

flower stems each year, but once they have become established they seem to go on for year after year, improving as they age.

An annual leafmould mulch and application of a general fertilizer each spring are beneficial.

Deadheading

Deadheading is not necessary or productive: these late perfomers will only do so once.

Overwintering

Once their attractive seedheads have been thoroughly appreciated, cut down plants completely in winter. Bugbane is hardy and needs no winter protection.

Propagation

Increase bugbane by division in autumn (see page 44); do not do this in spring, as the plants start to emerge early and new shoots could be damaged. Bugbane can also be propagated from seed sown outdoors.

MEET THE FAMILY

Actaea may not be an instantly recognizable member of the buttercup family, Ranunculaceae, yet the similarity can be found when you take a closer look. The bottlebrush-like flower stems carry dozens of fluffy whorls, each one akin to the centre of a meadow buttercup bloom. This examination also makes you realize one of the main differences: there are no petals, the stigma and stamens are more than enough to draw the pollinating insects needed to set seed. The attraction might seem at odds with the plant's common name of bugbane, but the insect-deterring properties come from the aromatic leaves of species such as *A. cimicifuga*. Thankfully, most of those grown in gardens are sweeter smelling, although the foliage's musky overtones are unlikely to win them favour with every Parisian perfumer. Still, the elegant, willowy flowers and deeply cut leaves cut a dash when twinned with *Geranium phaeum* 'Album' and blue-grey *Hosta* (Tardiana Group) 'Halcyon'.

Recommended varieties

A. simplex 'Brunette' ♀
This tall, dark-leaved variety produces flower stems carrying pinkish white, highly fragrant blooms between early and midautumn. H: 1.8m (6ft); S: 60cm (2ft).

A. racemosa ♀
Despite its nickname of black snakeroot (as it was traditionally used as a tincture for snake bites), this variety actually has bright green foliage and white flowers. H: 30-150cm (1-5ft); S: 60cm (2ft).

A. simplex 'James Compton'
'James Compton' has slightly less dark leaves than *A.s.* 'Brunette', but produces stems of flowers that are of a purer white than it. H: 1.2m (4ft); S: 60cm (2ft).

A. matsumerae 'White Pearl'
Another smaller-stemmed variety, 'White Pearl' produces large, pearl-like buds that open to white, frothy flowers. H: 1.5m (5ft); S: 60cm (2ft).

Agapanthus *African lily*

This group of highly attractive plants belongs to the lily family. African lilies have strap-like leaves, 60cm (2ft) long, and stiff stems carrying large umbels of various shades of blue or white, funnel-shaped flowers. Hardier species tend to have narrower leaves that die back in winter. Some broad-leaved varieties are more or less evergreen but dislike cold winters; in cool-temperate climates they are often grown in pots and overwintered in a frost-free place.

Site and soil

African lilies need a site that is perfectly drained and preferably in full, year-round sun. They also appreciate light, slightly acid soil. Even hardy varieties are frequently grown in pots by gardeners who do not realize that African lilies will do perfectly well in a border as long as other plants are not allowed to crowd them.

Buying guide

It pays to buy African lily plants that are in flower, so you can see exactly what you are buying. There are nurseries that specialize in these plants, and they often appear at summer plant fairs with their latest offerings, all with enticing-sounding names. It is hard to keep track of all these new hybrids. Headbourne Hybrids, however, is a loose group of African lily hybrids raised in the 1940s, all of them known to be reliably hardy. Plant out or pot up African lilies as soon as you acquire them, disturbing their roots as little as possible.

Plant care

African lilies do well with the minimum of care, except for the addition of a fistful of general fertilizer roughly raked into the soil around each plant crown in spring. They might appreciate extra water during hot summers.

Deadheading

When plants are young, remove the flowerheads (and stems, for aesthetic reasons) to stop them making seed. This will help the plants to put their energy into root growth. Once mature, this is less important.

In fact, if left *in situ*, African lily seedheads are particularly attractive for several weeks in early winter, and good clumps therefore make excellent punctuation marks on border corners and beside wide paths and steps.

Overwintering

In colder areas, apply a protective mulch of dry, half-rotted leafmould or bracken in winter. African lilies can survive surprisingly cold temperatures as long as the soil around them drains perfectly.

Propagation

Divide plants in spring (see page 44). The new plants should establish themselves and flower the following year, given the right growing conditions. African lilies can also be raised from seed, although it takes three years for seedlings to reach flowering stage. Note that plants hybridize freely and therefore you will be nurturing an unknown quantity (and quality) for some time. Root cuttings can also be taken in spring.

Recommended varieties

A. 'Septemberhemel'
Pale blue flowers open from dark purple buds on this late flowerer. H: 70cm (28in); S: 40cm (16in).

A. 'Queen Elizabeth the Queen Mother'
This tall variety is an elegant, large-leaved, blue-and-white bicolour. H: 1.2m (4ft); S: 60cm (2ft).

Alcea *Hollyhock*

This short-lived, cottage-garden perennial of magnificent proportions has a reputation for bad behaviour and only made it into this book because of protestations by the author, who considered that its omission would constitute a crime against horticulture, since hollyhocks are almost universally loved by flower gardeners. Belonging to the large family that also includes herbaceous and shrubby mallows, hollyhocks are European and Asian natives, where they are to be found – miraculously rust-free – on rock, dry, and grassy wasteland.

Site and soil

Grow in full sun and moderately fertile soil. Treat hollyhocks as biennials if rust is an insurmountable problem (*see below*).

Hollyhocks are suitable for planting in the back of a mixed border or for growing in minimal soil along the base of a warm, sunny wall.

Sow seeds in containers in spring or *in situ* in mid- to late summer.

Buying guide

Buy and plant hollyhocks in spring or early autumn. A certain amount of pragmatism is required if young seedlings of named varieties and colours are bought. Such plants all too frequently fail to meet the characteristics promised on the label.

Plant care

Snails can be very damaging to the first leaves produced in spring, so be extra vigilant and take protective measures (see page 215).

If hollyhocks are grown on a windy site, tall flowering stems may need to be tied back gently to a wall or be supported by bamboo canes to which stems can be discreetly and individually tied. Cut down all stems at the end of the season.

The main enemy of hollyhocks is rust, which is ultimately terminally debilitating and makes plants ugly into the bargain. Rust is symptomatic of rainy spring weather, as overwintered spores splash up from the soil to infect lower leaves. One way to combat rust,

AN ESSENTIAL INGREDIENT of every cottage garden are the crepe-paper flowers of hollyhocks, which just keep on coming for weeks in summer.

Recommended varieties

A. rosea 'Nigra'
Slightly shorter-stemmed 'Nigra' bears flowers that are deepest chocolate-maroon (so-called "black"), with yellow throats. H: 2m (6½ft); S: 75cm (2½ft).

A. rosea Chater's Double Group
The very double, peony-form flowers come in very diverse colours, including apricot, pink, and lavender-blue. H: 1.8-2.5m (6-8ft); S: to 60cm (24in).

A. ficifolia
Fig-leaved hollyhock has finger-like leaves that resemble those of a fig tree. Its creamy yellow flowers are single or sometimes double. This hollyhock is far more rust resistant than others. H: 1.5m (5ft); S: 30cm (1ft).

A. rosea
Some gardeners prefer this old-fashioned single hollyhock in every shade of pink, red, and even white. H: 1.8-2.5m (6-8ft); S: 60cm (24in).

therefore, is to remove all the lower leaves from plants as their stems start to grow upwards. Any subsequent legginess will go completely unnoticed when plants are grown at the back of a border with lower-growing plants in front of them, as they so often are. Couple this essential grooming with a certain amount of vigilance – such as removal of any leaves with orange spots on their undersides and the application of a preventative systemic fungicide - and rust can be conquered and plants will live longer as a result.

Young plants will flower a little in their first summer, extremely well in their second, and possibly in their third year, but may go downhill after that. It pays, therefore, to allow plants to self-seed fairly freely, or to save seed and grow potential replacements every year.

Deadheading
Hollyhock flowers, like foxgloves (*Digitalis*), open in succession up each lofty stem. Once the main stem has finished flowering, it can be cut back so that the secondary flower stems (which will very probably still be flowering well) become more visually prominent. Whether you go to the trouble of doing this is all about aesthetics rather than about prolonging the flowering season.

Overwintering
Hollyhock stems are tough and woody and should be cut back with secateurs or loppers in late autumn. Small amounts of tatty foliage may appear during mild periods of the winter. Remove these in spring so that the plant gets away to a clean start.

Propagation
Hollyhocks are extremely short-lived perennials and where disease is a problem, it is perhaps best to replace them with young seedlings every two years or so.

Sow seed in spring or mid- to late summer (see above). Young self-seeded plants develop deep roots quickly, and resent being transplanted once they have started to grow upwards and make their flower stems. It is, therefore, safer to transplant hollyhocks to permanent sites, if needs be, when they have developed three or four true leaves, in early autumn.

Alchemilla *Lady's mantle*

Because they hold onto silvery droplets after rain, it is the leaves of lady's mantle that give these somewhat ubiquitous, pretty, clump-forming perennial plants their common name. The flowers, carried aloft for several weeks in early and midsummer, are lime-yellow and fluffy-looking, those of *A. mollis* being perfect bulking-out ingredients for informal posies of other garden plants. These plants are great, front-of-border, thoroughly drought-tolerant ground cover; moreover, they seem to be unattractive to slugs and snails. Lady's mantle is, therefore, treasured in equal measure as a real cottage-garden must-have, and it looks superb with blue or pink herbaceous geraniums.

Site and soil

Lady's mantle will grow almost anywhere, and will cope with (and the flowers will last longer in) a certain amount of shade. It is a good plant for the edges of beds and borders or used as a simple edging for a brick or paved path.

Lady's mantle seeds can be sown in a pot of seed compost in an open cold frame in early spring.

Recommended varieties

A. mollis ♀
Its froth of lime-green flowers and matt, pale green leaves decorate many a cottage garden, but this carpeting species may be invasive. H&S: 50cm (20in).

A. erythropoda ♀
With its small, delicate flowers carried between early and midsummer on raspberry-red stems (*erythropoda* = red-legged), this plant is pretty when edging flagstone paths. H: 25cm (10in); S: 35cm (14in).

Buying guide

There should be no need to buy this plant. Ask around among your friends – someone will sure to be trying to offload young plants of this prolific self-seeder. Tiny plants achieve a significant size within a single growing season. Clumps of *A. mollis*, for example, eventually spread to around 50cm (20in) wide and high (when in flower). Plant lady's mantle in spring or early autumn.

Plant care

Lady's mantle grows well with little intervention from the gardener. Feeding, mulching, and a soluble feed after the midseason cutback results in larger, rather bulkier plants.

Deadheading

Unless you are trying to establish a random colony, cut down the plants (flowers, leaves – everything) with shears in midsummer, before they have a chance to self-seed all over the garden. Plants will immediately produce a new crop of pristine leaves and a few more flowers.

Overwintering

Layd's mantle is totally hardy and dies right back in winter, at which point all the old foliage can be sheared off.

Propagation

Increase lady's mantle by division, in spring or autumn, although this job can be done at almost any time of year (see page 44). You can also allow the plants to spread by self-sown seed. Young seedlings transplant well.

Allium

These often stately bulbous perennials are just extraordinarily fancy and rather fussy members of the onion family. The relationship is clear to anyone who has let their leeks go to seed, or even has been tempted to grow them in the border specifically for their flowers. Many tall alliums make a great, early summer statement, their globular flowerheads towering over the burgeoning new growth of other plants that are yet to flower. Many have attractive, long-lasting seedheads.

Site and soil

The most important requirements for alliums are absolutely perfect drainage and full sun. They do best in free-draining soil into which coarse-textured organic matter, grit, or sand has been dug. You can even plant them in a raised bed filled with especially bought-in gritty soil. Remember that many garden alliums come from the rocky soil of the eastern Mediterranean, and you need to replicate those harsh, dry conditions as nearly as possible if these bulbs are to be reliably perennial.

Exact planting depths depend on the bulb size, but as a rough guide you should plant alliums so they have about twice their bulb height in soil on top of them. Set larger bulbs, perhaps, even more deeply than this, to give them greater stability when they are in flower. In soil that is basically heavy, make the planting holes slightly deeper and drizzle a handful of grit into them before putting the bulbs in place and earthing them up. No additional fertilizer is necessary.

WHEN PLANTED *EN MASSE*, the flowerheads of alliums will hover over the surrounding burgeoning foliage in a late spring border.

NOW ON SHOW...

The gardening world is far from immune from fashion. Just as silver, grey, and purple were the colours of the Millennium, these shades were quickly reflected in the plants chosen for RHS Chelsea Flower Show gardens. And no single plant appeared more conspicuously than purple drumstick alliums, their sculptural heads making chic additions to traditional and modern gardens alike. Since then, interest has remained high.

Buying guide

Buy bulbs in early autumn and plant them as soon as you can, meanwhile keeping them cool, dry, and in the dark. You can find alliums in bags off the peg in nurseries and garden centres, but check that the bulbs are firm, dry, and unblemished. All bulbs are cheaper if bought loose direct from specialist growers.

Plant care

When left *in situ*, and in growing conditions that suit them, alliums are trouble free and need no special care.

Deadheading

Most allium heads look wonderful as the flowers fade and the seeds are formed. They can be picked at this point (and hung upside down to dry) for use as decoration in the home.

Overwintering

Alliums are hardy as long as their growing conditions are perfect. They can, therefore, be left *in situ*. If they do start fading away (producing just leaves in subsequent years), the plants are telling you that conditions were not to their liking. In this case, improve the soil before replanting or choose a different and more appropriate site for them.

Propagation

Given the right conditions, alliums may multiply naturally. They will also self-seed (see page 47), or you can collect seed and sow it the following spring. If left undisturbed, their offspring will take at least three seasons to get to flowering size.

Recommended varieties

A. hollandicum 'Purple Sensation' ♔
This lovely allium, of deepest rich reddish purple, is the first to flower (in early summer). It bears flowerheads of 50 or more small starry flowers and long, strappy leaves. H: 1m (3ft); S: 10cm (4in).

A. cristophii ♔
A marvellous sight when grown in groups among low-growing shrubs, this allium has shorter leaves that will have virtually gone by the time the starry violet/mauve flowers – on umbels the size of a small football – come out. H: 15–40cm (6–16in); S: 15–20cm (6–8in).

A. 'Globemaster' ♔
As the name suggests this is a seriously imposing allium, with enormous leaves and flower stems, 80cm (32in) long, carrying umbels up to 20cm (8in) across. The colour of the flowers is deep purple. H: 90cm (36in); S: 20cm (8in).

Nectaroscordum siculum (formerly known as *Allium bulgaricum*). This prolific self-seeder has pointed buds that open to reveal umbels of enchanting, pendulous, creamy white bells flushed with green and chocolate pink. As the flowers fade the seed pods become erect. H: 1.2m (4ft); S: 30cm (1ft).

Alstroemeria

Also known commonly as Peruvian lilies, alstroemerias are not in fact lilies at all. They are hardy, clump-forming perennials with numerous fleshy, brittle tuberous roots. Banish from your mind memories of the bland orange, spreading weed in your grandmother's garden. New cultivars are altogether more colourful, more interesting, and to a large extent non-invasive. In spring, the plants produce a close forest of midgreen, brittle stems, which have alternate, lance-shaped leaves that are curiously twisted at the base. Most of the stems carry flowers with beautifully marked or striped petals, which last well in water.

Site and soil

Alstroemerias need a sunny site. If they experience less than full light, this encourages growth that is too tall and too floppy and generally untidy – and this is a difficult plant to support subtly or successfully.

Plant the tubers with due care (because of their brittleness) in late summer or early autumn in ground that has been prepared with the addition of organic matter, grit, and a little general fertilizer. Set the tubers at the same height in the ground as they were in the pot (that is, don't bury them too deeply), and mulch around, but not over the top of them.

Recommended varieties

A. 'Apollo' ♈
This eye-catching hybrid has white flowers with yellow, darkly freckled throats, from mid- and late summer. H: 1m (3ft); S: 75cm (2½ft).

A. 'Friendship' ♈
'Friendship' is a shorter variety with large, cream flowers. H: 60cm (24in); S: 75cm (30in).

Buying guide

Because there are so many colourful cultivars from which to choose, this is yet another perennial that is perhaps best bought when in flower, in summer, when you can see exactly what you are getting.

Plant care

Protect new growth from slugs and snails in spring (see page 215).

Water clumps in dry spells, to prevent the leaves from turning yellow and dying right back and the plant becoming temporarily dormant.

Clear away the old stems in autumn.

Deadheading

Remove stems as they fade. Some gardeners recommend pulling them sharply out of the ground (but do this only on established plants), or you can cut off the stems at ground level. This is more difficult to do without damaging other stems.

Overwintering

During the first and second winter after planting, apply a dryish mulch of half-rotted leafmould or bracken as frost protection. Once they become established, alstroemerias are totally hardy but may be slow to reappear in spring following a hard winter.

Propagation

Alstroemerias are best propagated by division in late summer or autumn (see page 44). Their brittle roots need to be handled with care.

Anemone

This is a variable genus, ranging from the small and delicate, native, perennial, spring-flowering wood anemone (*A. nemorosa*) to the towering 1.2m (4ft) plus stature of some of the so-called Japanese anemones (*A. x hybrida*). These tall border perennials are, perhaps, the best known and are indispensable for the beauty of their open, saucer-shaped flowers, for their height, and for their long, late flowering period.

Site and soil

Border anemones are undemanding, being content to grow in partial or dappled shade in soil that is humus-rich, moist but well drained. Being one of the few flowering perennials that will put up with such conditions, gardeners frequently feel inclined to plant them at the base of north-facing walls, away from which, it should be remembered, they will inevitably lean as they grow tall. Their prolifically produced and handsome leaves are a good foil for white tulips.

Wood anemones need dappled shade and a leafy

ANEMONES, TALL AND SHORT, all flower well in the shade. Here *Anemone x hybrida* 'Robustissima' shows off the delicate shading of its petals.

woodland-floor soil that is moist in spring. They will gradually form mildly spreading colonies.

Buying guide

Border anemones have large, woody roots and seldom appear happy or floriferous when growing of necessity in the confines of nursery pots.

Woodland anemones are often found for sale in flower, and the tubers of *A. blanda* are also either sold loose or in packets off the peg in garden centres in autumn.

Plant anemones in the open ground in autumn.

Plant care

Although border anemones have a reputation for becoming invasive - their roots eventually suckering

Recommended varieties

A. hupehensis 'Hadspen Abundance' ♀

Slightly shorter than *A. x h.* 'Honorine Jobert' , this is a pleasant, rich pink form. Intriguingly, some petals are more deeply coloured than others. H: 60-120cm (2-4ft); S: 50cm (1½ft).

A. nemorosa 'Robinsoniana' ♀

On this charming, midspring-flowering woodland anemone are slowly spreading rafts of foliage and pale blue flowers. H: 10-12cm (4-5in); S: 30cm (12in).

A. x hybrida 'Honorine Jobert' ♀

This is the best-known, best-loved, statuesque, single, white-flowered Japanese anemone – unsurpassed by all others. H: 1.5m (5ft); S: 60cm (2ft).

A. blanda blue-flowered

A few centimetres from the ground, from soil-coloured, knobbly tubers, come in late spring small, vivid sky-blue, fluttery-petalled flowers and dark green foliage. Leaves die away entirely in summer. H: 5-10cm (2-4in); S: 10-15cm (4-6in).

and spreading around – they sometimes take two or three years to really get going in the garden, so patience followed by vigilance should be the order of the day. Once they are safely established, border anemones are pretty trouble-free, needing little attention. Apply a mulch before the new growth appears in spring.

Pests are not a problem, although leaves can become black spotted with a fungal disease (see page 214).

Wood anemones become dormant in summer until the following spring, and their leaf growth will, therefore, have vanished from sight by midsummer. Until you have become familiar with your garden geography, it pays to mark the spot where you planted them.

Deadheading

Deadheading border anemones will prolong the flowering season slightly. Wood anemones do not seem to flower longer if they are deadheaded.

Overwintering

Anemones are totally hardy. Old stems can be cleared away in late autumn.

Propagation

You can propagate border anemones by digging up some of the already deeply rooted suckers, potting them up and growing them on for a year before planting them out. This is trickier to do than it sounds, and you should expect casualties. Root cuttings are more reliable and can be taken in autumn or winter.

Divide woodland anemones once they have become dormant in summer (see page 44).

HISTORY LESSONS

Wood anemones are a stalwart of the wild garden. If you find them growing in a woodland, they provide one of the best indicators that it is ancient (dating from at least 1600 in England and Wales, and pre-1750 in Scotland). This is because the native anemone spreads through creeping underground stems, rather than being widely dispersed by seed. As a result, it may take a century for a plant to grow to 1.8m (6ft) across, and a millennia to carpet a wood. In the garden, it still takes time, but the display can easily be supplemented with the readily available bulbs of *A. blanda*.

Anthemis

Anthemis belongs to a family of cheerful, useful, clump-forming, fairly short-lived perennial daisies that flower in midsummer. All have attractive, airy foliage that is aromatic when crushed (chamomile is another member of the same tribe). Flowers are in various shades from white through to deep orangey-yellow via soft cream. Anthemis has an extremely long, first flowering period and, if cut back, may repeat flower in early autumn.

Site and soil

Anthemis is fussy about drainage and dislikes baking sites with hot, dry soil as well as those that are excessively wet during winter. Therefore, plants grown in basically clay soil have shorter lives and generally falter more often than those cultivated in lighter soil.

Plant anthemis in spring in improved and lightened soil containing well-rotted organic matter and a little grit, together with a little bone meal.

Buying guide

Purchase plants in spring, when you can see growth already emerging in the pot. Be slightly wary, however, of the fact that these are vigorous plants that do extremely well in their first year. One plant may be sufficient in a smaller border, and when in flower will take up a considerable amount of space.

Plant care

Anthemis flowers are so prolific that they make a good posy-picker's border plant. However, clumps become top-heavy when in flower and may need supporting using sticks and string, or better still by being grown through a large grid (see "Supporting plants", page 41). If inadequately supported, the plant may sag and smother its neighbours.

Divide or at least replant every other year especially if plants are growing in soil or a site that is not ideal.

Deadheading

In midsummer, after the first flush of flowers has faded, shorten the by now slightly woody stems by two-thirds; then apply a liquid feed and a mulch. With luck the anthemis may flower again slightly, or at the very least produce strong, new growth that will toughen up the whole plant and prolong its life.

Overwintering

When grown in well-drained soil, anthemis will survive cold winters and needs no protection.

Propagation

It is easy to increase your plants by division in early spring (see page 44) and by softwood cuttings in the same season (see page 46). Even stray, midseason shearings left lying on the soil are likely to root and grow.

Recommended varieties

A. Susanna Mitchell
Slightly earlier flowering Susanna Mitchell has soft, large, lemon-yellow-centred flowers and silvery grey, filigree foliage. H: 60cm (24in); S: 90cm (36in).

A. tinctoria 'E C Buxton'
One of the most easy anthemis to find in nurseries, it has midyellow-centred flowers and midgreen leaves. H&S: 1m (3ft).

Antirrhinum *Snapdragon*

These colourful, cottage-garden annuals with curious, rabbit-lip flowers are familiar plants. They are not true annuals, however, but short-lived perennials – cultivars of *A. majus* – that flower well as very young plants. There are dwarf and tall forms, some with more open or upward-facing flowers, and myriad flower colours – from white through the whole colour spectrum (except blue) to deepest maroon and bronze, as well as many that are quite exotically bicoloured. Snapdragons are spectacular when grown *en masse*, but are more often used as single-colour fillers in a mixed border. They are useful for their exceptionally long flowering season.

Site and soil

Snapdragons like full sun and soil that has previously been enriched with well-rotted organic matter. Treat as you would high-performance annuals and remember that recently manured soil encourages plants to produce leaves at the expense of flowers.

When grown from seed, sow snapdragons on the surface of moist compost either in autumn (for earlier flowering the following summer) or in spring.

Buying guide

When bought as plantlets in spring choose the sturdiest plants you can find. Unless you like the surprise element of mixed colours, buy in single colours only and mix your own. Harden off the plantlets for a week before planting.

If growing from bought-in seed take note of the flowering height and other details, and don't just get dazzled by the colour picture.

Plant care

Water young plants well as they get established in early summer. Removal of the first flower stem will obviously encourage less vertical, more branched and slightly more compact growth, which may or may not be what you want. It will also encourage more and later flowers.

Rust can be a problem, particularly among closely packed plants grown in dry soil. There are rust-resistant varieties.

Deadheading

By deadheading regularly you will be rewarded with snapdragon flowers well into autumn.

Overwintering

If plants are allowed to grow on through mild winters and flower a second year, they often acquire a magnificent, almost shrubby stature. They will then probably deteriorate.

Propagation

Sow seed in autumn or spring (see above).

If allowed, snapdragons will seed themselves around mildly, but seedlings will not be the same colours as the parent plants and they have a tendency to turn up in unlikely places – crevices in walls, for example.

Recommended varieties

A. majus 'Night and Day'
Suitable for small spaces, this compact variety bears slightly upward-facing flowers that are deep crimson with white throats. H&S: 45cm (18in).

A. majus 'Diana'
Make a strong, vertical statement in a border with this superb, tall, white snapdragon, or use it for cut flowers. H&S: 25–50cm (10–20in).

Aquilegia *Granny's bonnet*

The *Aquilegia* genus is wonderfully varied and contains some refined species from the Americas – with elegant, long-spurred flowers – as well as the more familiar cottage-garden and woodland hybrids (the granny's bonnet types) with short spurs and altogether more dumpy, sometimes pleated and double flowers. Flower shades range from inky purple to pink, white, and even (almost) green, and every combination in between. Granny's bonnet will self-seed and naturalize in dappled shade, interbreeding randomly. All have very beautiful spring foliage that gets somewhat tatty as the season progresses.

Site and soil

Granny's bonnet grows well in a cool site and relishes dappled shade, preferring deep, rich soil. Before planting in spring or autumn, work garden compost or leafmould into heavy soil.

Sow Granny's bonnet *in situ* by broadcasting seed in suitable shady places in late summer.

Buying guide

Granny's bonnet has become rather modish and collectable over recent years, and aware of this many nurseries carry a wide choice of new varieties, sometimes selling them in flower. Some of these will be smaller, alpine varieties that are short lived and prefer well-drained, gritty soil.

Plant care

Unless you want your plants to set seed after they have finished flowering, cut plants down completely – even removing the old and tired foliage, which will be replaced by a few, much more attractive leaves within a week or so.

During spring, clear away all the vestiges of the previous year's leaves.

Greenfly can infest flowerheads (see page 216), and leaf miners sometimes create unsightly patterns on leaves, which can simply be pinched off.

Deadheading

A certain amount of deadheading very slightly lengthens the fairly short flowering season of granny's bonnet –

GRANNY'S BONNET CERTAINLY gets about a bit. In any cottage or woodland garden it will self-seed and colonize any area in dappled shade.

Recommended varieties

A. vulgaris 'William Guiness'

This distinctive, short-spurred hybrid has flowers that are (almost) black and white. They look intriguing in dappled shade. H: 100cm (39in); S: 50cm (20in).

A. vulgaris 'Nivea'

White granny's bonnet was beloved by Gertrude Jekyll. It comes true from seed and has the greyest foliage among granny's bonnets. 'Nivea' remains reasonably true if isolated. H: 100cm (39in); S: 50cm (20in).

A. chysantha 'Yellow Queen'

From America, this exceptionally long-spurred granny's bonnet has soft yellow flowers. H: 1.2m (4ft); S: 60cm (2ft).

A. vulgaris var. stellata 'Nora Barlow' ♀

You either love or hate the Barlows. This one is a curious, very double, spurless variety bearing flowers that are a subtly coloured, deep rose-red and pink. H: 100cm (39in); S: 50cm (20in).

from late spring to early summer. Flowers, however, become increasingly small and less significant.

Overwintering

Granny's bonnet is hardy, so will cope with just about all conditions during winter.

Propagation

Short-spurred granny's bonnet (generally *A. vulgaris* hybrids) will self-seed efficiently and hybridize freely (see page 47). Given the right conditions, colonies can become congested, with new plants almost growing on top of each other. For this reason it may be wise to collect seed and sow it around more widely yourself. New plants will start flowering in their second year.

If you prefer less of a hotchpotch and want to maintain a certain purity among your plants, you can propagate plants by division (see page 44).

SPURRED ON

The cosy name of granny's bonnet is thought to have gained greatly in popularity over the last 50 years. More traditionally, and widely, *Aquilegia* was referred to as columbine in the UK. This name comes from the Latin for dove, *columba*; and the short-spurred flowers do look like a circle of birds drinking from a bowl. *A. vulgaris* is a plant native to Europe and is known to have a long history in cultivation, which is shown by the flowery meads of many Renaissance paintings. By contrast, the long-spurred hybrids are relative newcomers, as at least some of the American parents were not described until the late 19th century. However, they offer a bolder range of flower colours, including rich reds and oranges. Yet, while vibrant shades have their place, gardening doyenne Gertrude Jekyll favoured the white *A. vulgaris* 'Nivea', which she teamed with white foxgloves and the tall stems of white, peach-leaved campanula in her own garden, at Munstead Wood in Surrey, UK.

Aster

There are numerous excellent species and hybrids in this tribe, some of them lofty, back-of-big-border plants, others more suitable for a smaller garden, while others are distinctly hummock-forming varieties that can be grown in containers. No garden deserving the name can surely be without at least one or two clumps of perennial daises such as these, as they provide such a colourful flourish at the end of the summer. Don't therefore be put off growing asters by the fact that the genus also includes the now much-shunned, distinctly wishy-washy, mildew-prone and invasive Michaelmas daisy (*A. novi-belgii*).

Site and soil

While all asters thrive in more or less sunny conditions, there is at least one – *A. divaricatus* (with small, white flowers carried on blackish stems) – that flourishes in distinctly shady conditions and looks extremely fetching alongside hostas and ferns on the edge of a woodland garden. Hybrids involving *novi-belgii* ancestry are mildew-prone, especially if grown in soil that dries out in high summer, while *A. amellus* and *A. novae-angliae* hybrids seem to be resistant to the disease.

The solution to the mildew problem is to prepare the soil carefully before planting and improve it with moisture-retentive organic matter and then to apply a moisture-retaining mulch in spring. It is also important not to crowd plants together too closely.

Buying guide

Buy and plant asters in spring, or more easily in autumn, when many plants can be bought in flower. For a really good choice you may need to approach a nursery that specializes in herbaceous plants. Those recommended on page 70 are available at most garden centres.

Plant care

Protect new growth from slugs and snails in spring (see page 215). In addition to mulching, plants known to be mildew-prone can be sprayed preventatively with a systemic fungicide in midspring and should be watered in hot, dry weather. Tall varieties suffering

AT THE VERY tail end of summer there is no more spectacular sight than a border bursting with colourful asters putting on the last show of the year.

Recommended varieties

A. x frikartii 'Mönch' ♀

Possibly the best aster of all, this wonderful plant has clear lavender-blue, yellow-centred flowers that go on and on well into autumn. If you have room for only a single clump of asters, this should be the one you choose. H: 75cm (30in); S: 45cm (18in).

A. ericoides 'Pink Cloud' ♀

The fine, pale pink flowers are carried over fine, heather-like foliage. H: 75-100cm (30-39in); S: 45cm (18in).

A. 'Little Carlow' ♀

Small, clear blue flowers shine out on this hybrid, which is tolerant of some shade but is slightly prone to mildew if it is grown in dry soil. H: 1m (39in); S: 45cm (18in).

A. novae-angliae 'Andenken an Alma Pötschke'

Bright salmon-magenta flowers make a strong splash of colour in late autumn towering over pale, bright green foliage. H: 1-1.2m (3-4ft); S: 60cm (2ft).

from lack of water develop unattractive, brown lower leaves. Tall varieties may also need staking, particularly in an exposed site.

INSPIRATION FROM THE MOUNTAINS

If you have already read my enthusiastic description for A. x frikartii 'Mönch' (see left), you may already be tempted to grow it. And, indeed, one notable plantsman, Graham Stuart Thomas, wrote: " 'Mönch' is not only the finest perennial aster, it is one of the six best plants, and should be in every garden. (Please do not ask for the names of the other five!)." Yet where did this plant come from? Its origins date back to the 1920s, and it is one of the first-known hybrids from crosses made between A. amellus and A. thomsonii. Raised by Frikart in Switzerland, three seedlings were named after a trio of famous mountains: Eiger, Jungfrau, and Mönch. It is the last one that has stood the test of time. Even the subsequent A. x frikartii 'Wunder von Stäfa' (this time named after a Swiss municipality) has less perfect, more washed-out blooms that need staking.

Deadheading

Little is achieved by deadheading asters as these plants flower late in the season. They cease their generous and colourful floral display at the start of the frosty weather.

Overwintering

Cut all plants down to the ground in late autumn and apply a protective organic mulch.

Propagation

Asters are best propagated by division every three years or so, at which point the less vigorous centre of each spreading mass can be thrown out and the outside runners retained (see page 44). A. amellus and A. frikatii can also be propagated successfully by taking basal cuttings in spring (see page 45).

Astilbe

Also known as false goat's beard, these useful perennials that originate mainly from China and Japan give a slightly exotic and other-worldly air to any garden. They have handsome, dissected foliage and soft, pointed plumes of tiny flowers that appear quite late in the season (midsummer onwards), and they brown attractively as they age. In all, astilbes have an exceptionally long season of interest.

Site and soil

Astilbes will grow in most quite rich and leafy garden soils but must be grown in ground that is never allowed to dry out completely as they require a degree of moisture at all times of the year.

They grow well in extremely shady places, and planted *en masse* astilbes associate well with waterside plants and with other moisture- and shade-lovers such as hostas and ferns.

Buying guide

Buy and plant in spring or autumn. Astilbes are easy to find in garden centres and are often sold in flower.

Plant care

These are trouble-free plants to grow. They are not attractive to slugs and snails, nor are they susceptible

THE FEATHERY SPIRES of shade and moisture-loving astilbes last for many weeks, first highly coloured and then as a bronzy autumn and winter feature.

Recommended varieties

A. 'Sprite' ♀
This small, white-flowered cultivar has dark, very divided leaves.
H: 50–60cm (20–24in);
S: 100cm (39in).

A. chinensis var. **taquetii 'Superba'** ♀
'Superba' carries bright pinkish purple flowers in late summer and early autumn. H: 100cm (39in); S: 35cm (14in).

A. 'Bronce Elegans' ♀
Reddish stems bear reddish pink flowers on this tiny hybrid.
H: 30–50cm (12–20in);
S: 50cm (20in).

A. x crispa 'Perkeo' ♀
Another small hybrid, 'Perkeo' has glossy, dark leaves that are tinged bronze when young. It carries narrow plumes of rich pink flowers.
H: 15–20cm (6–8in);
S: 10cm (4in).

to attack by other pests or fungal diseases. Astilbes require no staking.

Being shallow-rooted, they benefit from a mulch of composted bark or leafmould each spring.

Clumps become wide-spreading, and after three years they should be divided and split.

Deadheading

There is nothing to be gained by deadheading astilbes. In fact, faded flower plumes should be left untouched since they are considered by some to be part of the plant's basic attraction and should, therefore, be cut down only when they are no longer decorative.

Overwintering

Astilbes are hardy and need no winter protection.

Propagation

Although astilbes do set seed – and you may occasionally find seedlings popping up around established plants – propagation is most easily done by dividing plants in spring or early autumn (see page 44).

COME OUT OF THE SHADE
Considering that astilbes are long flowering, colourful, and a stalwart of the summer border, praise has not always been heaped on these plants. Even its name is lacklustre. Astilbe comes from the Greek for "without brightness", which alludes to the matt leaf surface of some species. Likewise, garden writer Christopher Lloyd waspishly commented: "These moisture-loving perennials are in the top flight of second-rate border plants." However, this was largely because he didn't like the stiffness of some of the cultivars – a habit that is very useful as a cut flower. So it seems time for gardeners to set the record straight and enjoy growing this shade-loving plant.

Astrantia

This, the ultimate non-flashy border perennial, carries flowers that have nevertheless a strange and intricate beauty. They consist of a convex head of tiny flowers surrounded by a ruff of attractive, pointed bracts, which may be white with pronounced, green tips, or pink or deep red, depending on the variety. The flowers, which first appear in late spring and last for several weeks, are held well above the leaves, which are strong, deep green, and nicely shaped.

Site and soil

Astrantias grow well in sun and, unlike many border perennials, will flower even better when planted in even quite deep shade. They also cope well with moderately fertile, heavy soil. Astrantias require a degree of moisture in high summer, however.

Buying guide

Buy and plant astrantias in spring or autumn. They are plants that hybridize freely, and too often you find that named varieties are not quite what they seem, having been grown from seed rather than propagated by division. If you are paying over the odds for hard-to-find *A. major* 'Shaggy', for example, buy it in flower. Plants labelled *A.* 'Hadspen Blood', meanwhile, too often turn out to have rather insignificant and murky-coloured flowers unlike the rich crimson of the true plant.

Plant care

Young plants benefit from being grown through a grid support. Thickened mature clumps hold themselves together better, but may need a restraining sticks-and-string girdle (see page 41).

Apply an organic mulch in spring and a fistful of a general fertilizer. In midsummer, cut back old leaves and flower stems quite hard so you reveal the second flush of leaves and flowers already growing from the base. The plant will then flower again in early autumn. Divide clumps of astrantia every four years.

Slugs, snails, and other garden pests are not a problem.

Deadheading

Deadheading as the flowers turn brown will ensure that the plant flowers for six weeks or more in its initial spell.

Overwintering

Astrantia dies right back in winter, is thoroughly hardy, and needs no protection against the cold.

Propagation

If not deadheaded, astrantia will self-seed prolifically, but the seedlings will not come true. Propagation is, therefore, more reliable if done by division, in either spring or autumn (see page 44).

Recommended varieties

A. 'Hadspen Blood'
Dark green foliage and stems are topped by rich crimson flowers and bracts on this slightly smaller, eye-catching plant, which is not as prolific as the pale varieties. H: 60cm (24in); S: 45cm (18in).

A. major 'Shaggy' ♀
Undoubtedly the best white astrantia that will subtly illuminate darker corners of the garden, it has large flowers that carry generous ruffs of distinctly pointed, green-tipped bracts. H: 75cm (30in); S: 45cm (18in).

Begonia

Many of these tropical and subtropical plants are familiar as foliage houseplants or (as in the case of Semperflorens begonias) are useful in a flowering-summer bedding scheme, particularly in shade. Among the tender tuberous begonias are many with fleshy leaves and top-heavy flowers in eye-watering shades of pink and orange. Such begonias are undeniably somewhat alien-looking, but they add a touch of exotica to a sheltered and shady, possibly urban garden.

Site and soil

Grow in moist but well-drained, fertile, slightly acid soil. Like many plants from tropical and subtropical regions, begonias will grow happily in the shade, and they dislike direct midday sun.

Buying guide

Plug plants of tender begonias featured here (Tuberhybrida and Semperflorens types) can be found easily at garden centres in spring or (in the case of B. 'Carmina') as dormant tubers for planting in containers under glass in early spring. B. 'Carmina' has a pleasantly trailing habit and makes an excellent plant for a hanging basket or other container (use loam-free compost or John Innes No 2). It is particularly impressive when grown on its own (or several of the same variety) unaccompanied by the usual bedding razzmatazz.

Plant care

Water sparingly, since begonias resent waterlogging and tubers may rot.

Apply a soluble feed every two weeks while in flower.

Deadheading

One of the chief attributes of begonias is their ability to flower prolifically all summer without the need for deadheading to encourage further blooms.

Overwintering

Tuberhybrida begonias need winter protection. In autumn, lift the plants from open ground or remove them from their containers, dust their tubers with fungicide, and overwinter them in a frost-free environment. Replant them the following year, with the hollow side of each tuber uppermost.

Semperflora begonias are not frost hardy, although container-grown plants may survive winter if kept barely moist at the roots in a cool but light environment indoors.

Propagation

As tubers and plug plants of these plants are readily available, propagation by seed (although possible) would seem a labour of love too far for most gardeners.

Recommended varieties

B. 'Super Olympia White'
One of the best bedding begonias, and one that will flower in shade, is this Semperflorens begonia which bears dark reddish, fleshy leaves and yellow-centred, white flowers. H&S: 15-30cm (6-12in).

B. 'Carmina'
With its attractive, gently trailing habit and vivid red flowers, this Tuberhybrida begonia impresses even the most hardened begonia sceptics. H&S: 30cm (12in).

Bergenia

Bergenias are also called elephant's ears and pig-squeak plants, from the sound made if you rub two leaves together. They originate from meadows and moist woodland in central and east Asia. Formerly known as *Magaseas*, there were beloved by Gertrude Jekyll, who used them extensively in her plantings. They have thick, coarse roots and large, glossy, evergreen leaves that, in the case of many varieties, colour reddish at various times of year. Flowers in varying shades of whitish pink to magenta are borne in spring.

Site and soil

Bergenias prefer moist and leafy soil, and are well suited to growing in light or dappled shade. Their leaves, for which this plant is most often cultivated, will be smaller but better coloured if plants are grown in thin, poor soil, while their flowers will be more prolific if the plants are put in a sunny position. They may not do well in a very exposed and windy site.

These perennials look best if allowed to form a substantial matt of foliage. As a rough guide, three plants placed with 30cm (12in) of clear soil between them will have covered an area about 1sq m (1sq yd) in a couple of years.

Bergenia leaves associate with those of ferns and the feathery foliage of astilbes, while the appearance of their blooms will coincide with, or slightly overlap, the flowering period of many spring bulbs. They look better with clean, white snowdrops in attendance rather than cheek-by-jowl with acid-yellow daffodils.

It has to be admitted, perhaps, that bergenias are not eye-catching plants when not well coloured in winter nor in flower. In a small garden, therefore, they should be used sparingly.

Buying guide

B. 'Ballawley' is easy to find in garden centres and nurseries, but you may need to hunt around for other varieties. These perennials can be planted with equal success in autumn or spring.

Plant care

Once established, bergenias spread sideways rapidly, their woody rhizomatous stems hugging the ground and creating a close forest of thick leaves. Therefore, during winter or early spring, it is a good idea to

STRIDENT EVERGREEN LEAVES of *Bergenia* 'Sunningdale' are lit up in spring by equally robust flowers. This is a welcome relief, at this time of year, from the usual surfeit of yellow.

groom the entire patch to smarten it up before the flowers appear. Remove old, brown leaves and any unproductive, woody growth and, inevitably it would seem, a fine crop of hibernating snails.

In time the whole area covered can become gappy, so every five years or so, once the patch has finished flowering, cut out some of the older growth and propagate

Recommended varieties

B. 'Ballawley' ♀

This is a bold bergenia with 30cm (12in) long leaves that turn bronze-purple in winter. On bright red flower stems it carries deep pink flowers in mid- and late spring. It prefers a sheltered site. H&S: 60cm (24in).

B. 'Overture'

Magenta flowers and deep green leaves – flushed red in summer and with darker purple hues in winter – adorn this neater variety. Unlike most varieties, it has a strong second flush of flowers in autumn. H: 30cm (12in); S: 45cm (18in).

B. 'Wintermärchen'

This attractive variety has green leaves that are purplish red on the undersides, and rose-red flowers. H: 30cm (12in); S: 50cm (20in).

B. purpurascens var. delavayi ♀

Smaller leaves and rose-red flowers typify this tall variety of bergenia. H: 50cm (20in); S: 40cm (16in).

new plants from young shoot tips (*see* below). At the same time, apply a general fertilizer around the whole patch, forking it in gently with a hand fork, and also mulching with leafmould.

Snails and slugs can cause some damage to foliage (see page 215), but by far the worst pest is the adult vine weevil, which feeds on the edges of the leaves. Seldom if ever seen, it leaves its evidence in the form of minutely notched leaf margins. This is unsightly – and more ominously – is a clear indicator that other plants in the area with soft and juicy roots are certain to be being devoured by vine weevil grubs in the soil. The best control is achieved by treating the grubs in the soil (among pansy and heuchera roots, for example, and in pots). Adult weevils can be caught in the act of feeding on the leaves on warm nights: place newspaper under the plants in the day. Then venture out in the dark and shake the leaves gently – you can hear the weevils dropping off the leaves, and they are very slow moving. Destroy the catch, and repeat the procedure the following night.

Deadheading

Some varieties will flower a little in autumn, but there is not much to be gained by removing the spent flowerheads and stems, except as part of a general tidy-up. This is a plant that does not rampantly self-seed.

Overwintering

Bergenias are thoroughly hardy, although leaves may wilt badly in the frost.

Propagation

To make new plants, sever shoot tips with 5-7.5cm (2-3in) of woody stem. Either insert them in pots of sandy compost or – if you are gap filling an existing colony – replant directly into improved soil. Keep an eye on them until it is clear the cuttings have rooted.

Brunnera

Brunnera belongs to a small group of woodland perennials, which are members of the same plant family as borage and forget-me-nots, and they originate from eastern Europe and north-west Asia. They are extremely useful mainly for their ground-covering foliage, which is slightly hairy without being coarse, but also for their refined and pretty, blue flowers, which appear in spring.

Site and soil

Brunneras grow best in leafy, woodland soil in a cool, shady site. Plant them where they can be appreciated as they first come into leaf and flower in spring. The green-leaved variety is not particularly attractive when not in flower, and the leaves of variegated brunnera varieties can scorch and generally lose their looks in summer if they receive too much sun or wind or during periods of drought and heat.

Sow brunnera seeds in pots of seed compost in a cold frame in March or April. Young plants will be ready to plant out in their permanent site the following autumn.

Recommended varieties

B. 'Jack Frost' ♛
Softly greenish white leaves with green edges and ribs enliven the deepening shade in a woodland garden. The blue flowers are almost a pretty irrelevance.
H: 40cm (16in);
S: 60cm (24in).

B. macrophylla ♛
Perhaps more suitable for a larger garden, this plant looks particularly good when its pretty bright blue flowers appear *en masse* above a significant-sized swathe of foliage. H: 45cm (18in); S: 60cm (24in).

Buying guide

Brunnera dies back completely in winter, and for this reason plants are generally to be found for sale in spring, when they are at their most attractive. Green-leaved *B. macrophylla* is quite a spreader – more than its variegated relations (as is generally the case) – so bear this in mind when deciding how many plants to buy.

Plant care

Newly planted specimens need a little care during summer, when woodland soil tends to dry out quickly.

All plants are extremely attractive to slugs and snails early in the season, when the first new and tender leaves may be eaten away completely. As protection, cover the entire crown of the plant and the soil around with coarse grit.

In a small garden, where every leaf matters, nip off scorched or damaged leaves from the plant in summer, to tidy things up. This will also encourage the production of bright and fresh foliage.

Deadheading

Remove old flowers, which will considerably tidy up the plants, particularly the variegated varieties when they become full-blown foliage plants.

Overwintering

Brunneras are all hardy and die right back in winter. Cover their crowns widely with grit (as a slug/snail defence) before the first leaves emerge.

Propagation

Plants will sometimes self-seed (see page 47), or they can be divided in late spring, after flowering (see page 44).

Calendula *Pot marigold*

Also known as pot marigolds, these easy-to-grow annuals are a real cottage-garden and informal-border staple. In its original form, wild calendula, which is native to southern Europe and northern Africa, has lax and untidy (albeit charming) growth and single, orange/yellow flowers. The numerous calendula varieties that have been produced have taller stems (up to 65cm/26in) and double and more subtle coloured flowers in shades of bronze, lemon-yellow, and a more pinkish orange, for example. All of them last well in water so are ideal for bringing into the house for informal cut-flower arrangements.

Site and soil

Pot marigolds grow best in a bed or border situated in a sunny position, although they will flower reasonably in partial shade. They flower most prolifically in soil that is not too rich.

Sow seeds in spring, where they are to flower and thin out the seedlings as they grow. In very sheltered sites, autumn-sown seedlings will survive and flower considerably earlier than spring-sown ones. Seeds can also be sown under glass in spring and small plants transferred outside when the weather warms up.

Buying guide

Small potted plants - generally of double varieties - are sometimes to be found in garden centres in spring. Acquiring one or two and letting them set seed might be a simple way to start off a more or less permanent self-seeding population in a cottage garden. Plant these calendula annuals in spring.

Plant care

Once they start flowering, water young plants with a high-potash feed. Blackfly (aphids) are sometimes to be found clustering along the flower stems, so remove these (see page 216). By the end of the season, exhausted plants that are dry at the roots may succumb to powdery mildew. There is nothing you can do about this.

Deadheading

Deadheading dramatically lengthens the flowering season of these plants, although some seedheads should be allowed to develop - either to save and sow later or to allow the seeds to cast themselves around.

Overwintering

Pot marigolds cannot tolerate winter temperatures in cool-temperate climates.

Propagation

Increase by seeds sown in spring *in situ* or in autumn.

Recommended varieties

C. officinalis 'Indian Prince'
Dark orange flowerheads, tinted reddish brown, are produced on this tall variety, which is suitable for cutting. H: 60cm (24in); S: 40cm (16in).

C. officinalis 'Bon Bon Orange'
This very early flowering, lower-growing variety is suitable for the front of an informal border. It has double, orange flowers. H&S: 30cm (12in).

Campanula *Bellflower*

The campanula family is a vast and varied one, all 300 members – annuals, biennials, and perennials – being native to the northern hemisphere, including Britain and the European mainland. There are tiny campanulas, and there are giants. Those mentioned here are all reliably hardy border perennials, with blue or pale lilac-coloured, bell-shaped flowers, although there are other species with white, dull pale pink, or deep purple flowers.

Site and soil

Bellflowers all appreciate sun and fertile, moisture-retentive, neutral to alkaline soil. However, delicate flower colours last better if plants are grown in a little shade. Stems of taller species are not particularly robust, and so they do better planted among other rather stouter border plants; otherwise they definitely need to be staked.

Campanula seed can be sown in spring on the surface of moist seed compost in pots sealed in plastic bags and placed in a cold frame. Germination may take 1-2 months.

Buying guide

Buy and plant bellflowers in spring or autumn. Potted specimens of *C. lactiflora* 'Prichard's Variety' are particularly easy to find at garden centres and nurseries. Also readily available is a useful shorter form, *C.l.* 'Pouffe', as is *C. latiloba* 'Hidcote Amethyst', which is a more robust plant with stronger stems, and less need of support.

Plant care

It is important to protect new growth from the attentions of slugs and snails (see page 215). Small slugs operate below soil level in early spring. By mulching around – not over – the crown of vulnerable plants, you reduce the likelihood of terminal damage to emerging shoots.

Put stakes and string, or a tall circular grid on legs, in place early for stems to grow through so that by flowering time supports are invisible.

Clumps expand slowly and are best left undisturbed.

GIVEN LITTLE DISTURBANCE and a sunny spot, bellflowers such as the beautiful china-blue *C. lactiflora* 'Prichard's Variety' just get better every year.

Recommended varieties

C. lactiflora 'Prichard's Variety' ♀
A single plant of majestic 'Prichard's Variety' makes a big statement in a small border, especially in midsummer with its pale lavender-blue flowers in loose, conical panicles. H: 1.2-1.5m (4-5ft); S: 60cm (2ft).

C. 'Burghaltii' ♀
This smaller bellflower that forms a slightly untidy mound above which appear long, tubular, pendant flowers of a greyish lavender-blue in midsummer. H: 60cm (24in); S: 30cm (12in).

C. 'Kent Belle' ♀
'Kent Belle' does best on slightly moist soil, with some shade. It carries large, deep violet flowers. H: 1-1.5m (3-5ft); S: 75cm (2½ft).

C. latiloba 'Hidcote Amethyst' ♀
Each stem on this robustly growing, erect bellflower carries massed, blue-violet bells that are slightly upward facing. H: 75-90cm (30-36in); S: 50cm (20in).

Deadheading
Cut back flowering stems of *C. lactiflora* by 2-3cm (¾-1in) below the flowers, to encourage a later useful but less generous flush of flowers. This species responds particularly well to the "Chelsea chop" (*see* page 42), resulting in delayed flowering on shorter stems, but it is worth experimenting with other species, by thinning out or shortening some of the stems in late spring. *C.* 'Kent Belle' may also flower again if cut back.

Overwintering
While a few bellflowers are evergreen, *C. lactiflora* dies right back in winter, so it is wise to put markers in the soil to indicate where plants are sited, particularly if you mulch haphazardly.

Propagation
Grow bellflowers from saved seed outside in an open cold frame in spring. Take basal cuttings from mature plants in spring (*see* page 45), or whole plants can be divided in either spring or autumn (*see* page 44). Propagate *C.* 'Kent Belle' by removing short runners and potting them up, replanting them when they form viable plants.

HURRAY FOR HIDCOTE
There are upwards of a dozen plants that are named after Hidcote Manor in Gloucestershire, UK, including *C. latiloba* 'Hidcote Amethyst'. All are generally noted as good plants, often recognized with an RHS Award of Garden Merit, and many set the standard, such as the low-growing, dark-purple lavender 'Hidcote'. These plants are the valuable legacy of one of England's most perspicacious plantsmen, Lawrence Johnson (1871-1958), who was actually a naturalized American. Although he was known as a gardener and garden designer, he certainly liked the finer things in life. On a plant-hunting expedition to Africa, he took his valet and cook and, whenever possible, travelled in his chauffeur-driven car. Back at home, Hidcote became noted as an influential garden, setting the 20th-century fashion for garden rooms filled with lush planting of a very high standard. The gardens continue to inspire as they are open to the public under the National Trust.

Canna *Indian shot*

Indian shot, also wrongly known as canna lily (it does not in fact belong to the lily family), is a showy-looking, slightly tender rhizomatous plant from forest margins and moist areas of Asia and North and South America. It is grown mainly for its huge, banana-like leaves, which can be green, burgundy, or even variegated. The scarlet or orange flowers – also less commonly salmon-pink or yellow – are produced late in summer on stems between 60cm (2ft) and 1.8m (6ft) high. When they appear in cool-temperate climates, the flowers are regarded as a bit of a bonus. In recent years, Indian shot has become an exotic-garden staple.

Site and soil

If grown in the ground, Indian shot needs a sheltered, sunny site, with fertile soil. It intensely dislikes heavy, winter-cold clay. Even if it survives in clay, it will perform late the following year and probably not flower until just before the frosts. It is, perhaps, more successfully grown in a large container in soilless compost.

Buying guide

Purchase Indian shot as a bare rhizome in spring and pot it up. Then when it has made substantial growth, plant it out carefully in soil improved with leafmould in early summer, if so desired. More often, Indian shot is bought in early summer as a leafy young plant that has been brought on prematurely under glass. By buying it in such an advanced state of growth, you can choose its leaf colour; it also ensures flowering in that year at least.

Plant care

Slugs and snails find Indian shots irresistible and can be a problem in mild springs (see page 215). Also inspect mature foliage daily for tell-tale signs and damage.

Deadheading

Carefully remove the withered petals of spent flowers, to improve the look of the plants.

Overwintering

Even in the most sheltered (and generally urban) gardens, Indian shot needs the protection of a dry mulch in winter. Use bracken or straw, pegged down under horticultural fleece. In cool-temperate climates, however, it is safer to lift plants from the ground in autumn, put them in pots of dry compost for the winter, and keep them somewhere frost free. In spring, gradually bring these pots into the warmth and light, to encourage them to start to leaf up in late spring. They can be replanted or potted on thereafter.

Propagation

Indian shot rhizomes expand rapidly and can be divided and potted up in spring, making sure that each division has a noticeable growing point (see page 44). Water young plants sparingly until growth starts.

Recommended varieties

C. 'Phasion' ♀
Green-, bronze-, and pink-variegated foliage and orange-red flowers make this medium-sized Indian shot a really eye-catching addition to an exotic planting scheme. H: 1.5m (5ft); S: 1m (3ft).

C. 'Stuttgart'
This tall variety produces orange flowers and cream-and-green, variegated leaves. H: 2m (6½ft); S: 1m (3ft).

Centaurea

Most of the numerous centaureas, also called knapweeds, are European natives. They are handsome in bud as well as when they produce their almost thistle-like – but softer – flowers in mid- to late summer. These are highly attractive to bees and butterflies. Their interesting seedheads last well into winter, and several species have greyish or distinctly silver foliage. Many centaurea are slightly weedy or invasive. The annual cornflower (*C. cyanus*), which is best known in its vivid blue form, makes an excellent cut flower and also makes a good gap filler in a perennial border.

Site and soil

Centaureas thrive in poor, very well-drained, limy soil, in full sun. The taller border centaureas are suitable for the middle or back of a sunny border, and also look at home in a grassy planting scheme. Plant them in spring or autumn.

Sow seeds of annual cornflower *in situ* during spring in a sunny site.

Buying guide

Border centaureas are usually represented at garden centres by the easy-to-grow perennial cornflower (*C. montana*), while silver-leaved *C. cinerarea* subsp. *cinerarea* is often sold as a bedding plant in spring. The more imposing centaureas, including the giant, yellow-flowered *C. macrocaphela* and *C. atropurpurea*, need to be sourced from specialist nurseries.

Plant care

Thin out seedlings of *C. cyanus* to 30cm (12in) apart as they develop.

Stake tall varieties with twiggy sticks as they grow.

In midspring, shear *C. cineraria* subsp. *cineraria*, to keep this front-of-border plant compact, and again after flowering in midsummer, to induce the production of fresh, silvery foliage.

Deadheading

Deadhead all centaureas – particularly *C. cyanus* – to prolong their flowering period.

Overwintering

While most centaureas are hardy, silver-leaved *C. cineraria* subsp. *cineraria* is not reliably so. If it does survive winter, it will need to be cut back when new growth is well under way the following spring.

Propagation

Increase hardy border centaureas by division in spring (see page 44). Take softwood cuttings of *C. cineraria* subsp. *cineraria* in late summer or autumn, when they should root easily (see page 46). Keep them under glass until the following spring, then plant out in the open ground.

Recommended varieties

C. cinerarea subsp. cinerarea ♀
With its silvery, intricately dissected leaves, this centauria is grown as much for its foliage as for its purple flowers. H&S: 75cm (30in).

C. atropurpurea
This species has feathery foliage and showy, ruby-red flowers from early summer to midautumn, followed by handsome seedheads. H: 1.2m (4ft); S: 75cm (2½ft).

Cerinthe

Cerinthe, which is also known as honeywort or wax flower, is a member of the borage family. It comes from southern Italy and Greece, where the green-leaved, yellow-flowered variety (*C. minor*) is regarded as an unremarkable weed. The plant that became much admired and sought after in recent years is *C. major* 'Purpurascens'. Amid its vaguely mottled, glaucous leaves are the blue-purple flowers almost hidden by nodding, grey-ish violet bracts, which darken as the season advances to give the plant a curious luminosity. Greek cerinthe (*C. retorta*) has more mottled leaves and purple-tipped, yellow flowers also produced under bluish bracts.

Site and soil

Cerinthe is not particularly fussy, but dislikes excessively moist soil. Rich soil will produce tall and sturdy plants that develop a lot of leaf at the expense of flowers. Although all cerinthes tolerate some shade, the bracts colour best in a sunny site.

Sow seed, one to a small pot, during late spring, soaking it for 24 hours first. Set the seed 1cm (½in) deep in loam-based seed compost and place the pot under glass. Make sure the seedlings get good light once they have germinated.

Recommended varieties

C. major 'Purpurascens'
Glaucous leaves and purple, bell flowers almost hidden beneath the greyish violet bracts make this an arresting, front-of-border annual. H&S: 60cm (24in).

C. major
With grey-green leaves, this cerinthe has distinctly yellow-tipped ruddy-purple flowers. H: 60cm (24in); S: 30cm (12in).

Buying guide

Buy cerinthe as small individually potted plants from nurseries in late spring.

Plant care

Harden off young plants properly before planting them out in early summer, as this is a plant that responds badly to shock or root disturbance. Pinch out shoot tips of young plants to encourage flowering, and water them during dry spells. Take precautions against slug damage (see page 215). Support floppy plants with short twiggy sticks (see page 41).

Deadheading

Cerinthe bracts remain colourful for a while even when the plant is going to seed. Therefore remove spent flower stems only when they lose their looks.

Overwintering

Large, black seeds will be produced throughout the season, some of which may germinate at considerable distance from the parent plants in early autumn. Thin these out and pinch out each growing tip. Depending on the prevailing weather, some seedlings may survive the winter. They may not make very robust plants but will start to flower in early summer, burning themselves out by midsummer.

Propagation

Allow cerinthe to self-seed (see page 47) or save seed and sow it under glass (see above). It would seem that some strains of *C. major* 'Purpurascens' are considerably more colourful than others.

Chrysanthemum

There are several distinct types of chrysanthemum – from annuals such as *C. segetum*, a cheerful-looking, yellow-flowered, Mediterranean weed, to the highly manipulated, generally slightly tender florist's chrysanthemums, some of which are grown for their dramatic sprays of flowers, while others have all but a single bud removed from each flowering stem, for exhibition purposes. All chrysanthemums have distinctively aromatic leaves and daisy-like flowers. Hardy perennial chrysanthemums are suitable for beds and borders. Later-flowerers, these overlap with asters, and a few chrysanthemums flower through to late autumn and even beyond. Their yellow, orange, and russet-coloured blooms look wonderful with the colouring leaves of autumn trees and shrubs.

Site and soil

Border chrysanthemums do best in moderately fertile soil and in sun. They are tolerant of alkaline soil. Many chrysanthemums flower extremely late in the year, and it makes sense, therefore, to site them somewhere that they can be appreciated from indoors, where they will be spot-lit by low, late afternoon sun, or where you will pass by them on a regular basis. This refinement is something often overlooked when planning a garden.

Buying guide

Most garden centres carry a fairly limited selection of popular border chrysanthemums in autumn when they are in flower. For unusual varieties you may have to purchase via mail order or online, or visit specialist nurseries.

CHRYSANTHEMUMS, MANY OF them with petals that are bronze, soft pink, and yellow, totally reflect their season, echoing the shades of autumn leaves perfectly lit by low, slanting sun.

Plant care

Apply a general fertilizer and mulch in spring, to benefit plant growth. New growth may be damaged by slugs and snails. If growth is particularly fulsome and congested, thin it out in early summer by cutting back the weakest stems to ground level.

Do not allow plants to dry out in late summer, when they are putting on a growth spurt before they flower. Stake tall, late-flowering varieties securely (see "Supporting plants", page 41), because by the time they come into flower buffeting autumn rain and winds will be a problem.

Deadheading

There is little to be gained by the deadheading of chrysanthemums.

Overwintering

Chrysanthemums are totally hardy and therefore need no winter protection.

Propagation

This is best done by division, in spring or autumn (see page 44). Cuttings can also be taken in midsummer (see page 45).

It is also worth mentioning here that those pots of chrysanthemums sold with massed flowerheads for indoor display in winter in fact consist of several individual small plants of florist's chrysanthemums that have been grown together closely and forced into flower under glass. If the flower colour is to your liking, you can carefully separate the plantlets, cut them back a little, and grow them on in pots of John Innes No 2 in a cool greenhouse or cold frame. Plant out the best of the young plants in a border in spring. Before flowering, they will develop into very much taller plants than they were in their forced state in the pots. Their hardiness, however, cannot be taken for granted.

Recommended varieties

C. 'Clara Curtis'
Flower centres turn from green to yellow, as the flowers age, on this tallish variety bearing many long-lasting, lightly scented, single, pink flowerheads from late summer onwards. H: 75cm (30in); S: 45cm (18in).

C. 'Nantyderry Sunshine' ♈
Compact dark green-leaved 'Nantyderry Sunshine' carries lemon-yellow, button-like flowers, shaded with deeper yellow/orange, late in the season – from midautumn to early winter. H: 40-70cm (16-28in); S: 50cm (20in).

C. 'Mary Stoker'
This late-flowering chrysanthemum (to late autumn) of medium height carries apricot-yellow flowers, which perfectly harmonize with the changing colours of autumn leaves. H: 70cm (28in); S: 50cm (20in).

C. 'Mrs Jessie Cooper'
The large, single, deep red flowers are a good colour for an autumn garden. H: 60-75cm (24-30in); S: 50cm (20in).

Clematis

Herbaceous – non-climbing, non-clinging – clematis are the no-nonsense, easy-to-grow members of this slightly intimidating plant tribe. They may be less glamourous, perhaps, than their climbing, clinging relations, but they do perform the function of useful and charming border plants, nonetheless. Herbaceous clematis are, in themselves, a pretty diverse group. Some are more or less like other border perennials but with slender stems that benefit from simple staking, to keep their heads above the floral throng. Other herbaceous clematis will do their best to scramble among other plants or, in a big border, can be allowed to make untidy masses that may hide or disguise other, earlier-performing border plants that may have become untidy.

Site and soil

All herbaceous clematis have one thing in common: they do best in well-enriched, well-drained soil that is preferably (but not essentially) slightly alkaline. They must have their roots shaded by other plants or by large stones (take note: small shards of broken pots perform little function) or by a deep, spring-applied mulch.

Before planting herbaceous clematis, prepare the ground meticulously, adding a substantial amount of compost and bone meal to the soil. Set each clematis deeply in the planting hole, with its lowest 10cm (4in) of growth below soil level, as you would with climbing clematis plants.

Buying guide

All clematis specialists carry plants of herbaceous clematis species. At garden centres they should be among the other herbaceous plants, but if you fail to track them down there try looking for them among the climbers. Choose plants that have several strong shoots appearing from soil level in the pot.

The best plants will probably be available to buy in spring, and it is worth remembering that they will probably have been kept under cover, to start them growing slightly prematurely. New shoots, which are brittle anyway, may therefore also be vulnerable to late frosts and cold wind, so cover plants with horticultural fleece if cold or very windy weather is forecast.

HERBACEOUS CLEMATIS ARE perhaps the unsung heroes of their genus – pretty and subtle border plants that don't give you a crick in your neck or a nightmares with their pruning.

ROOM FOR MORE?

There's always room for another clematis. Take a slow-growing hedge, such as yew or holly, and allow late-flowering clematis to scramble up the side. In midautumn, you can cut down the clematis to 60cm (2ft) and trim the hedge – a perfect partnership. Alternatively, secure a post 3m (10ft) high in a border and tie up a clematis into previously unused space.

Plant care

The attention of slugs and snails is a constant threat to delicate stems, so protect new plants (see page 215).

Water new plants deeply once every two weeks for the first few weeks while they establish new roots.

Provide new growth with twiggy sticks to grow into. Eventually remove the bamboo cane that is normally provided with a new clematis and which gives totally inadequate and unsuitable support for the growing number of brittle shoots. Pinching out the shoot tips in midspring of those species that tend to sprawl may create slightly bushier plants.

Shade roots and apply a thick organic mulch each spring, or at least before the drier months of mid- and late summer.

Although not overly susceptible to clematis wilt, towards the end of a dry summer plants may succumb to powdery mildew (see page 215).

Deadheading

Flowers of several herbaceous clematis give way to attractive seedheads so deadheading is not appropriate. It is also not particularly productive on the other varieties of herbaceous clematis.

Overwintering

All herbaceous clematis are hardy. They can be cut down to the ground during winter, and their bases covered with a mulch.

Propagation

Although it is possible to grow clematis from seed, division in spring or autumn is a less troublesome option (see page 44).

Recommended varieties

C. integrifolia

This fairly erect clematis has markedly veined leaves and small, nodding, bell-shaped, pale lavender-blue flowers between early and late summer. After the flowers come silky seedheads. H: 75–100cm (30–39in); S: 75cm (30in).

C. heracleifolia 'Roundway Blue Bird'

Flowers are dark blue and scented on this clematis, which will tolerate a considerable amount of shade. It has coarse leaves and almost shrubby growth. Cut back in late spring. H&S: to 1m (3ft).

C. recta 'Purpurea'

Masses of scented, ivory-white flowers are produced from early summer onwards, and the distinctly purple leaves gradually fade to slate grey-green. The numerous slender stems need supporting with fine twiggy sticks. H: 1.5m (5ft); S: 1m (3ft).

C. x durandii ♀

This sparsely stemmed clematis likes to drape over neighbouring plants – its indigo-blue flowers look particularly fetching among the variegated leaves of Cornus alba 'Elegantissima', for example. The lax and lanky growth may occasionally need tying to the host plant. H: 2m (6½ft); S: indefinite.

Convallaria *Lily-of-the-valley*

An absolute favourite as a cut flower is lily-of-the-valley. There are three species of this rhizomatous perennial, with its deliciously scented, small, bell-shaped, white flowers carried in late spring and early summer on short, arching racemes over wide, pointed leaves. Each plant then gradually dies down, and by late summer there may be very little trace of it until the following spring. When happy, lily-of-the-valley will spread about freely and make a sizeable colony, classically grown in combination with Solomon's seal (*Polygonatum*) – one of the great delights of the spring garden.

Site and soil

Lily-of-the-valley grows well in partial or complete shade, in leafy, fertile, moist soil, and is happy on the margins of a deciduous woodland garden or at the front of a shady border. It also thrives along the edges of shaded garden paths, tucking its rhizomes into the cool, damp soil under bricks and paving stones.

Growing lily-of-the-valley where there is competition for space will mean they are less likely to become (mildly) invasive, and their early dormancy will not be noticed. Intersperse them with easy, clump-forming perennials such as lady's mantle (*Alchemilla mollis*), which will come into leaf and flower as the lily-of-the-valley finishes flowering.

Growing convallaria from seed, although possible, is a long-winded process. The resulting plants need painstaking management and it may be four years before they flower.

Buying guide

Lily-of-the-valley is most often available in spring, when it is flower in small pot. As soon as the flowers fade, plant it out in soil improved with copious amounts of leafmould. At the same time, remove the dead flowers so the plant's energies are put into root growth, not seed production.

Rhizomes can also be bought dry and dormant in bundles, loose, or in packet, during autumn, but these may be less easy to establish.

Plant care

Take care of newly planted rhizomes, watering them during dry spells in their first year as they become

THESE SHADE LOVING, easy-going colonizers bear perfect, little sprigs of white, scented flowers. Surely every garden has a corner where lily-of-the-valley can be allowed to do its own thing.

established. There will be little or no debris to clear up in autumn, but apply a mulch of leafmould to the site where the lily-of-the-valley are spreading around each year. Slugs and snails do not seem to be at all interested in this plant.

Deadheading

Pick and enjoy – and there will be nothing to deadhead.

Overwintering

These totally hardy plants need no winter protection.

Propagation

By far the easiest way to propagate lily-of-the-valley is to separate rhizomes in autumn and replant them straight away (see page 45). It is probably easier, and more tempting to carry out this slightly delicate operation in spring, when the new shoot tips are just visible coming up through the ground, although this might cause a slight disruption to their growth. Whenever the job is attempted, ensure that the rhizomes remain moist while they are out of the ground. If there is likely to be a delay – for example, if you are giving some to a friend – pot the rhizomes up temporarily in leafy compost to prevent them drying.

Lily-of-the-valley can also be grown from seed sown as soon as it is ripe. Do this in a cold frame in the garden and remove the flesh from the seeds before sowing.

HEAVEN SCENT

Lily-of-the-valley is an enduringly popular scent, and a flower that carries a wide range of symbolism. In the Victorian Language of Flowers, a gift of the blooms reflected sweetness; return to happiness; humility; and perfect purity. These ideas pick up on religious allegory. One Christian story says that lily-of-the-valley represents Mary's tears from the crucifixion of Jesus. Another legend says the plant came into being from Eve's tears after she and Adam were driven out of the Garden of Eden. In France and Germany, lily-of-the-valley flowers are still exchanged on May Day to reflect joy in the fact that spring has sprung.

Recommended varieties

C. majalis ♀
The old favourite and most often seen lily-of-the-valley is *C. majalis*, which is the easiest to grow – and to find in garden centres. H: 15cm (6in); S: indefinite.

C. majalis var. rosea
Similar to the above is this variety, with its pale pink flowers. H: 20cm (8in); S: 30cm (12in).

C. majalis 'Hardwick Hall'
This variety has broad, green leaves edged very narrowly with pale green, and produces slightly larger flowers than the species. H: 25cm (10in); S: 30cm (12in).

C. majalis 'Albostriata'
Broadly striped, creamy gold leaves are produced by this new and rare plant, although they tend to turn greener if grown in total shade. It is less vigorous (in this case, spreads less quickly) than its plain green-leaved relations. H: 25cm (10in); S: 30cm (12in).

Cosmos

Cosmos originates from meadows and scrubland of southern USA and Central America and is grown chiefly for its large and spectacular, crimson, pink, or white, long-stemmed, daisy-like flowers. The foliage is fine and feathery. Tall annual cultivars of *C. bipinnatus* are useful fillers for the back of a sunny mixed border and will grow to about 1.5m (5ft). Shorter and altogether stockier *C.* 'Sonata' (to 45cm/18in) is suitable for mixed annual planting. Slightly tender and often rather leggy *C. atrosanguineus* (45cm/18in) is best grown in a container and given winter protection, except in the most sheltered gardens where it can be planted in a warm site and overwintered under a dry mulch.

Site and soil

Cosmos does best in moderately fertile soil in full sun. When given the right conditions, tall varieties can become almost tree-like by the end of a warm summer and will go on flowering until the first autumnal frosts.

Seedlings of *C. bipinnatus* grow tall surprisingly quickly, so don't start them off too early (that is, not before late spring) or they will become unmanageably leggy.

Sow cosmos seed on the surface of a loam-based seed and cutting compost, such as John Innes No 1, cover them with vermiculite, and seal in a plastic bag. Place the pot somewhere warm and light until germination, which can take place in as little as seven days. Before planting outside, harden off young plants carefully, as cosmos dislikes cold nights and cold winds.

Alternatively sow cosmos seed *in situ* in late spring.

Buying guide

The short annual *C.* 'Sonata' is now often sold as seedlings in strips in garden centres, frequently already in flower, in early summer. Young plants of taller annual *C. bipinnatus* varieties are harder to find, but it is relatively easy to grow them from seed sown in midspring under glass. Tender *C. atrosanguineus* can be found as young plants coming into flower in nurseries and garden centres in midsummer.

Plant care

When they are about 60cm (24in) high, pinch out the shoot tips of tall varieties to encourage bushier growth.

THE PLEATED PETALS of tall *Cosmos bipinnatus* 'Seashells' and *C.b.* 'Psyche White' seem to float above the abundant, frothy foliage. These daisies, perfect for picking, flower until the frosts.

If allowed to grow tall they may also need to have their main stems supported by a substantial stake, as cosmos is relatively shallow rooted and becomes slightly top-heavy, despite its feathery foliage and graceful growth.

Deadheading

Cosmos makes exceptionally good cut flowers that last well in water, so picking them is a natural way of prolonging its flowering period – as is deadheading any fading flowers that were superfluous to your needs. Towards the end of the flowering season let some seedheads ripen. They will self-seed *in situ*, or you can save some for sowing the following spring (see page 46).

Overwintering

Although perennial, *C. atrosanguineus* is not hardy in cool-temperate climates and should be kept quite dry at the roots and overwintered under glass.

Propagation

In spring, take basal cuttings of tender perennial *C. atrosanguineus* (see page 45).

Grow annual cosmos from seed that has been saved (see page 46) or purchased. Self-sown seedlings of *C. bipinnatus* will germinate quite late – early summer – so will flower later than those sown in pots indoors. If they are a result of a mixed-coloured population the previous year, most of the seedlings will have midpink flowers. You can tell the future flower colour of seedlings by the colour of the stem: plain green = white flowers; pale rose pink = pink flowers; and dark pink = red flowers. Seedlings can be moved around once they are a manageable size to handle by their leaves.

SUNSHINE SHADES

While cosmos are pretty in pink, there is a range of fiery shades from the Mexican *C. sulphureus*. In the wild, it is a tall species reaching up to 2m (6½ft), creating a substantial blaze along roadsides. Garden cultivars have been considerably tamed, with many now reaching only 45cm (18in) high. The breeders have also managed to increase the array of colours: there is yellow 'Ladybird Lemon', rusty-red 'Ladybird Scarlet', and a mix of all colours in-between in 'Polidor'.

Recommended varieties

C. bipinnatus
This cosmos is seriously tall, reaching almost tree-like proportions by late summer, with abundant pink or white, yellow-centred flowers. H: 1.5m (5ft); S: 50cm (1½ft).

C. bipinnatus 'Psyche White'
This tall plant produces semi-double, glistening white flowers and ferny foliage. H: to 1.2m (4ft); S: 50cm (1½ft).

C. bipinnatus 'Double Click'
Very double, pompon flowers in shades of white, pink, and rosy red are borne on slightly shorter and sturdier plants. H: 90cm (36in); S: 45cm (18in).

C. bipinnatus 'Seashells'
'Seashells' is another tall variety of cosmos, and it has pink, white, or red flowers with petals that are curiously tubular. H: to 90cm (36in); S: 45cm (18in).

Crocosmia

The sword-like, bright green leaves of montbretia – the most common crocosmia now more or less treated as a weed – are familiar to those who inherit old and unkempt gardens, where there may be a clump that has virtually stopped flowering. But these bright-flowered South African plants have moved on in recent years and now numerous cultivars provide gardeners with a wide array of colours, sizes, and even shapes of flowers. All are welcome in the border in the second half of summer.

Site and soil

Despite their African origins, crocosmia tolerates a cool-temperate climate well, although it needs soil that has been improved with organic matter and full sun to flower best. It does particularly well if it receives plenty of moisture in summer.

Short cultivars can be grown as clumps near the front of a border, where their bright, upright foliage, even before they flower, makes a good foil for more hummock-forming, front-of-border plants. Taller crocosmias, such as *C. masonorum* and *C.* 'Lucifer', need careful siting as they flower less well if buried at the back of a border in the shade of earlier-flowering, tall perennials. Darker-leaved crocosmia varieties are far less vigorous than green-leaved ones.

Plant corms about 15cm (6in) deep. Crocosmias flower rather better if they are grown in a close-ish group, and they form thick clumps.

Buying guide

Buy as corms and plant straight away, in early autumn if at all possible.

Plant care

Make sure that plants receive adequate water in the hotter months of summer, otherwise they flower less well. Also spider mites can become a problem, making the leaves go bronze and sandy-looking, and curling up (see page 216). This will completely ruin the look of the entire group just as it is about to flower.

Remove old foliage in late autumn by pulling it gently away from the underground corms.

THE TERRACOTTA FLOWERS of C. 'Severn Sunrise' are perfectly partnered here in a late summer garden by the scarlet spikes of *Persicaria amplexicaulis* 'Blotau'.

Divide clumps every three years in autumn. New corms will have developed on top of the old ones, and will eventually have formed vertical stacks, the lower ones rotting down and providing a source of food for the newer, upper ones. When dividing a clump, lift all the corms out of the ground, keep the uppermost and discard the lower ones, and re-energize the soil with compost before replanting.

Some of the tall crocosmias have long-lasting and attractive seedheads. If not divided regularly, tall varieties become liable to topple and may need a subtle restraining circlet of canes and string to keep them upright in autumn (see "Supporting plants", page 41).

FRENCH REVOLUTION

Today montbretia (*C. x crocosmiiflora*) is considered ubiquitous, growing in many gardens and as an escapee in the countryside of south-west England. It is hard to recapture the original excitement with which the plant must have been received in the UK when it arrived in the 1880s. Yet, its easy-growing nature and fiery flowers ensured that, by 1898, one writer was noting enthusiastically that it was "grown in hundreds of gardens". The original hybrid came from France and was bred by Messrs Lemoine, a noted nurserymen. They went on to produce many popular cultivars, including 'Aurora' and 'Solfatare', which are still available in many nurseries today.

Deadheading and cutting back
Deadheading is unnecessary.

Overwintering
Crocosmia is fully hardy and generally needs no winter protection, although winter mulching with compost is beneficial in colder gardens.

Propagation
Increase your stock of crocosmia by division, when thinning out congested colonies (see above).

Recommended varieties

C. x *crocosmiiflora* 'Solfatare' ♀
Extremely attractive 'Solfatare' is alas less prolific and hardy than other varieties. This crocosmia has lovely, bronze foliage and open-faced, apricot-yellow flowers. H: 40-60cm (16-24in); S: 45cm (18in).

C. 'Severn Sunrise' ♀
This midheight variety produces pale orange flowers that fade to terracotta-pink. They appear from late summer to midautumn. H: 75cm (30in); S: 45cm (18in).

C. x *crocosmiiflora* 'Star of the East' ♀
The wide-open flowers on this beautiful crocosmia are apricot-yellow, with slightly paler centres, opening from dark buds. H: 60-70cm (24-28in); S: 30cm (12in).

C. x *crocosmiiflora* 'George Davison'
Fine, star-shaped, yellow flowers over midgreen foliage are produced slightly earlier than those of other cultivars – between early and late summer. H: 60-75cm (24-30in); S: 30cm (12in).

Dahlia

Dahlias are South American razzle-dazzlers for sunny, warm positions. They have moisture-laden tubers, rather like potatoes, and this water-storage system allows them to perform well even in the driest of summers. The best varieties, however, are versatile enough also to flourish in summers that are cool and damp. As they are frost tender, you need to protect dahlias in winter in cool-temperate climates.

Site and soil

Grow in full sun and fertile, well-drained soil. Don't let dahlias sulk in shady areas of a bed or border.

In midspring, plant the tubers in pots of seed or cutting compost. Water them only when new shoots emerge, as still-dormant tubers tend to rot in wet conditions. Once the shoots are 5cm (2in) tall and there is little risk of frost, remove them from their pots and plant them out.

Sow dahlia seed in pots in spring. Germination usually takes 7-21 days, and seedlings will be variable.

Buying guide

The most economical way to buy dahlias is to purchase dry, dormant tubers from a reputable nursery in late winter, and store them in a light, frost-free place until it is time to start them off in pots. Do not be in too much of a hurry to get them going – later sprouting tubers will form stocker plants that will flower later and for longer.

The commercially available strains of dahlia seeds produce plants with a maximum height of 40cm (16in).

Dahlias can also be bought as potted tubers already starting to flower in summer. These make useful but slightly expensive, last-minute gap fillers.

DAHLIA DECISIONS

Don't see a dahlia you like? Keep looking! There are nine distinct flower forms, plus a tenth group of miscellaneous. They range from tiny pompons to giant cactus and elegant waterlily-flowered types. Similarly, the colours range from deep purples to white, reds to acid yellows. In fact there are over 1700 in the British National Collection to choose from.

DAHLIAS NEED A SHELTERED, sunny site in order to put on their best show. Remember their Mexican origins when deciding where to place them in the garden.

Plant care

At the same time as planting tall dahlias, put substantial stakes in place (see page 41). This will avoid the possibility of damaging the tubers later.

Water plants during periods of drought, to prevent their lower leaves becoming yellow and unsightly.

The main enemies of dahlias are snails, which climb up into the foliage and do a lot of damage, particularly to young plants (see page 215). Earwigs like to hide within double flowers and feast on the petals (see page 216).

If you particularly like a dahlia that you have grown from seed, in autumn lift their small tubers, overwinter them dry and frost-free, and replant them the following year.

Deadheading

If they are to flower non-stop, dahlias need deadheading. The pointed seedheads (which feel soggy to the touch) can look very similar to the bun-shaped buds when you're a novice, so get your eye in before you start.

Single-flowered forms have a mass of smaller flowers that last only a day, whereas fuller-flowered forms have weather-resistant blooms that last a full week and are much easier to deadhead.

Overwintering

Many gardeners now leave the tubers in the ground from one year to the next. However, in a severe winter the tubers will probably be reduced to useless mush.

If you prefer to lift them from the soil and store them in a cool, dry shed, it's best to wait until the foliage is already blackened. Cut the stems to 15cm (6in) in height and upend them on a frost-free bench, so that the hollow stems drain and dry. Then store in dry peat, checking the tubers regularly. When checking, remove immediately any that are rotting.

Propagation

In addition to being grown from seed (see left), mature dahlia tubers can be easily propagated by division just before they are potted up in spring (see page 44). Remove individual fingers from the tuber, ensuring that each has a very visible growing point and pot them up individually. Alternatively, take basal cuttings in spring (see page 45).

Recommended varieties

D. 'David Howard' ♀
The strong-stemmed, purple cactus-flowers seem to explode like fireworks as each sharply quilled petal radiates outwards. H: 75cm (30in); S: 60cm (24in).

D. 'Hillcrest Royal' ♀
This strong, easy-to-grow dahlia has semi-double, butterscotch–orange flowers and dark, smouldering foliage. It is the perfect addition to an exotic, fiery border containing crocosmias, cannas, and kniphofias. H: 1m (3ft); S: 60cm (2ft).

D. 'Bishop of Llandaff' ♀
Probably still the best garden dahlia, this 1920 vintage variety performs whatever the weather, producing an abundance of warm-red, peony-shaped blooms set against dark, divided foliage. H: 1m (3ft); S: 45cm (18in).

D. 'Magenta Star'
Clear-cut, bright-pink, single flowers and dark foliage, together with a pristinely neat habit, make this new variety a show stopper in the garden. Being single, the flowers attract butterflies and bees. H: 40-100cm (16-39in); S: 30cm (12in).

Delphinium

There can be few finer sights in a big, sunny garden than the massed stems of perfectly grown delphiniums in full flower. These exotic-looking border perennials in various shades of blue, purple, and white, are stately relations of cottage-garden larkspur (*Consolida*). Some of them, such as the Pacific Hybrids, are grown chiefly for exhibition. They are, however, rather too tall and overblown for most garden planting schemes. Of the many delphinium hybrids to choose from, easiest to accommodate and look after are those that are more refined and shorter, with a more branching habit, such as Belladonna Hybrids. These are simpler to support than the taller hybrids, although they don't have quite the same vertical majesty as Elatum or Pacific Hybrids.

Site and soil

Delphiniums need a sunny site with well-cultivated soil that has been enriched with well-rotted garden compost before planting. Avoid growing very lush and tall varieties in a windy site.

Buying guide

Plants - barely more than seedlings - bought in squashy, little, plastic pots in spring at garden centres are best potted on and grown for a season (and ideally not permitted to flower) until they are more viable.

Larger delphiniums sold seductively in flower may do slightly better but should not be allowed to set seed, which will take their energy away from vital root production. It may be a year or two before they alter their stride and start to make really good, sturdy growth.

Named varieties can be grown from seed in spring. Chill the seed for a week in a refrigerator before sowing in trays of seed and cutting compost under glass in a warm place.

Plant care

Give delphiniums an annual spring feeding with a balanced fertilizer and a midseason mulch after they have flowered.

In spring, put twiggy sticks or other stakes in position to support plants as they develop.

Cut plants back in autumn, and remember that they will start growing as soon as early spring, so renew slug defences early (see page 215).

THAT DELPHINIUMS SUCH as these are tricky to grow is indisputable. But all the slug protection and careful staking can bring stunning, 1.5m (5ft) high rewards.

STAKING

Once delphinium stems are about 75cm (30in) high they need careful support (see "Supporting plants", page 41). Beware of using simple metal rings, however, as once the plants are in flower they become very top-heavy after rain and the stems can break off at the point where they lean against the unyielding metal. Plants fare best, it seems, if grown up through a forest of twiggy sticks, which becomes invisible once flowers open. When plants are young, and produce only a few spires, it might be practical to support each spire individually with a cane, tying it in every 15cm (6in) or so. Staking correctly is definitely worthwhile.

Deadheading

By cutting down their spent flower stems by about two-thirds and mulching and feeding the plants – possibly with a soluble fertilizer if the summer is hot and dry – you can persuade many delphiniums to flower a second time, generally in early autumn. Protect the base of the plant from slugs and snails (with copper, grit, or pellets), and when new shoots appear cut the remainder of the old foliage right down, making way for new stems to power upwards. Second spires will not be as tall or lush as the midsummer originals.

Overwintering

Plants are hardy and need no special winter protection.

Propagation

Take basal cuttings (see page 45) or divide plants in spring (see page 44).

Refrigerate any saved seed and sow it in spring. It may not produce plants that share the same characteristics as the parent plants.

Recommended varieties

D. 'Blue Nile' ♀
Good bright blue flowers, each with a white "eye" (known as a "bee" in delphinium-speak), are borne on this magnificent, large-flowered hybrid. H: to 1.8m (6ft); S: 75cm (2½ft).

D. 'Sungleam' ♀
This medium-height delphinium produces creamy white, double flowers. H: 1.2-1.5m (4-5ft); S: 75cm (2½ft).

D. 'Vespers'
The more delicate-looking flowers are part sky-blue, part dusky mauve, with a white "bee". H: 1.2m (4ft); S: 75cm (2½ft).

D. 'Amadeus'
Spectacular, deep blue-purple flowers have a dark brown "bee". H: 1.2-1.5m (4-5ft); S: 75cm (2½ft).

Dianthus

This large genus of mostly low-growing plants includes many familiar, cottage-garden staples such as the old-fashioned pinks (which flower in early summer), modern pinks (which are very similar but have a slightly longer flowering period), taller hardy and half-hardy carnations (often grown just for cutting and for exhibition), and the much-loved biennial bedding plant sweet William (*D. barbatus*). Pinks carry sweetly clove-scented flowers above generally fairly compact mounds of grey-green, pointed leaves. There are numerous cultivars with single and double blooms, in striking colours and variously marked and/or fringed petals. Carthusian pinks (*D. carthusianorum*) have flat, single, deep magenta-pink flowers carried over a long period well above the green, grassy foliage. Pinks are useful plants for the front of a sunny border, and are effective when grown in a dry garden, where they associate well with low-growing grasses. They make good cut flowers.

Site and soil

Dianthus do best in slightly alkaline, well-drained soil in an open, very sunny site. They grow well in gravel and even in a seaside garden with strong, salt-laden winds. Add coarse-textured compost and grit to heavy soil or even create a raised bed, because these plants – many of them native to the rocky limestone hillsides in southern Europe – are extremely fussy about drainage.

Grow Carthusian pinks from seed sown in gritty compost in early spring, which will provide plants suitable for planting out in late summer.

Sow sweet William in late spring, for flowering the following season.

ON THE SCENT

If you are looking for a pink with an exquisite fragrance, there is more to the art of sniffing one out than you might expect. Common sense suggests that you just breathe deeply. However, you may be scuppering your chances. There's only so much a nose can take before the olfactory receptors are overloaded – typically less than five plants' worth. This number goes down further if you start with a heavy scent, such as the intoxicating clove fragrance of *D.* 'Mrs Sinkins'. Instead, start with

GARDEN PINKS NEED sun and sharp drainage to produce their beautifully marked and scented flowers. They will then grow happily for week after week throughout summer.

a light-fragranced cultivar, and then try others. This way you'll be able to spot the differences and choose a scent you really like.

Buying guide

Buy and plant dianthus in spring or autumn. The selection of plants in local garden centres may be fairly limited, but there are nurseries that specialize in dianthus, where you will be able to find numerous interesting varieties. A cheat's way of getting more than you pay for is to buy untidy plants in spring and then propagate from the wayward shoots a few weeks later (see below).

Plant care

Sprinkle a general fertilizer around the plants in spring to help them grow vigorously. On no account should you mulch heavily around the lower shoots of dianthus, which might encourage them to rot.

Deadheading

Tidy up and trim back low-growing pinks as they finish flowering or they rapidly become straggly. Trimmings can be used to propagate new plants.

Carthusian pinks have attractive seedheads, so can be left to the very end of the season or beyond before being cut down.

Overwintering

As long as they are grown in perfectly draining soil, dianthus are frost hardy.

Propagation

Take cuttings from short, non-flowering shoots in summer. Trim them just below a leaf node, remove the lower leaves, and put several together in a pot of cuttings compost mixed 50/50 with horticultural grit. Seal the pot in a plastic bag and place it somewhere warm and light until you see signs of growth.

Increase Carthusian pinks and sweet William plants from seed (see left).

Recommended varieties

D. carthusianorum
Deep magenta-red, single flowers on tall, slightly wafting stems over green grassy foliage make this a very special plant for a dry garden. H: to 40cm (16in); S: 20cm (8in).

D. 'Elizabethan'
This short variety of modern pink produces very neat, single, magenta-fringed, white flowers with maroon centres. H: 25cm (10in); S: 20cm (8in).

D. 'Mrs Sinkins'
White, fringed, slightly untidy, beautifully scented flowers are borne on this old-fashioned pink. H: 60cm (24in); S: 40cm (16in).

D. 'Gran's Favourite' ♡
This modern pink has heavily scented, double, white flowers laced with deep mauve-pink, carried on short stems. H&S: 40cm (16in).

Dicentra

Dicentra is a useful genus of plants, of which the smaller, fine-leaved perennial members are extremely happy spreading around in the dappled shade of a woodland garden – although all will grow in some sun, too. Taller and altogether more substantial *D. spectabilis* is a perennial that needs careful placing, so the large, pendent flowers on elegant, arching stems can be appreciated in early summer, but where its absence will not be missed when it dies completely back later in the season. Leaves of the small woodland varieties are soft, sometimes slate-grey, and, for plants that are essentially quite robust, they have stems that are alarmingly fragile. The small flowers, which can be roughly described as heart-shaped, are delicate-looking and vary in colour from deep red through to soft pink and white and cream; they are carried just above the pretty foliage.

Site and soil

The small woodland dicentras have shallow, rhizomatous root systems that grow well in the humus-rich soil of a deciduous woodland floor, which is just moist enough during spring, but dries out when the plants go dormant in later summer.

A TALL, STATUESQUE member of this tribe of little woodlanders is *D. spectabilis*, which produces strings of elegant flowers on arching, leafy stems for weeks at the start of summer.

D. spectabilis will grow well in full sun as long as its fleshy roots are tucked well into reliably moist soil. Because of the brittleness of its stems, this species does not cope well with a windy site, yet providing support tends to somewhat spoil the elegant outline of the plant.

If growing small dicentras at the front of a shady border, where they look very fetching, it is worth remembering that as a colony expands with age there will be a considerable gap in late summer and autumn, when the dicentras die back.

Mark the spot where the dicentras will reappear in spring if you are likely to forget the geography of your borders.

Sow dicentra seed in trays of seed and cutting compost in an open cold frame in autumn.

Buying guide

Somewhat inevitably, these dicentra are always sold when in leaf and flower in spring. Plant at once.

WHAT'S IN A NAME?

While the botanical name *Dicentra* rather boringly means "two spurs", there is a startling selection of vividly descriptive common names. Bleeding hearts relates to the white drip from the base of *D. spectabilis* blooms; then turn the same bloom upside-down to find the lady in the bath. There are also Chinaman's breeches, Dutchman's breeches, locks and keys, lyre flower, and finally seal flower.

Plant care

In their first year, ensure the roots of young plants do not dry out while they become established.

Protect new shoots from slugs (see page 215).

Once growth becomes tired and increasingly unsightly after midsummer, cut the whole plant to the ground.

Deadheading

Deadheading of dicentras is unproductive. In the case of *D. spectabilis* the removal of short stems of spent flowers and a few upper leaves will tidy the plant up and reveal a few smaller, fresher flowers beneath.

Overwintering

In winter, apply a layer of leafmould mulch over and around all dicentras.

Propagation

Divide plants in spring or when they become dormant (see page 44).

Woodland hybrids self-seed and produce seedlings that vary considerably in leaf and flower characteristics.

Take root cuttings of *D. spectabilis* in winter (see page 105).

Recommended varieties

D. 'Bacchanal' ♀
Rich maroon-red flowers hover over bright green, feathery leaves on this very eye-catching dicentra, suitable for a woodland planting scheme. H: 50cm (1½ft); S: 1m (3ft).

D. spectabilis 'Alba' ♀
Korea and north China are the source of this distinctive plant, which is more refined-looking than its more often seen, pink-and-white flowered relation, known as lady in the bath or bleeding heart. H: 60-75cm (24-30in); S: 60cm (24in).

D. formosa alba
Despite its name, this is in fact an American species. It will flower longer than other dicentra, if the soil remains moist enough. H: 50cm (20in); S: 50cm (20in).

D. 'King of Hearts'
This is a newish, compact hybrid, with pinky red flowers over slightly glaucous leaves. Like *D. formosa* (above), 'King of Hearts' will flower longer if the soil stays moist, but will die back as soon as it becomes droughted. H&S: 50cm (20in).

Dierama

Much admired dieramas, which are also known as angel's fishing rods because of their graceful, arching growth, are not particularly easy to grow. However, they are well worth the extra care and attention that they need to perform successfully. In midsummer, they produce long stems, each with a succession of pendent, slim, bell-shaped flowers. Their semi-evergreen leaves – somewhat rather reminiscent of coarse grass – appear from gladiolus-like corms.

Site and soil

Dieramas look best if they are grown in a wide-open space where their arching stems can be best appreciated. They look particularly effective in a gravel garden or near water, as their common name suggests. However, originating in the mountainous grasslands of various parts of Africa, the corms are not tolerant of winter-waterlogged soil, so any attempt to establish them in the damp ground on a pond margin will end in failure.

They prefer fertile, loamy soil improved with organic matter, which doesn't dry out in summer.

Plant corms in spring, 5-7.5cm (2-3in) deep. If bought already potted and in leaf, make sure that the corms are planted out so the surrounding soil is at the same level as when the plant was container-grown. New acquisitions of dieramas seem inevitably to take some time to settle down and start flowering.

Buying guide

Dry corms are sometimes sold, but these should be avoided as they rarely grow well. Buy plants already potted and in leaf in spring and plant them immediately in soil improved with plenty of organic matter, taking care to set the pot's contents at the right level in the soil. Plants, even those bought later in the season already in flower, may take two years or more to settle down and flower properly.

Plant care

Feed dieramas with a balanced fertilizer every spring and keep them well watered while in growth.

Remove old, brown leaves in spring, to smarten up the plants considerably.

Deadheading

The removal of dying flowers and stems is unproductive.

Overwintering

Once the plants have become established, dieramas are winter-hardy.

Propagation

Divide established plants in spring, taking care not to damage fragile roots; cut the leaves down by half at the same time. It may take a year or two before the divisions settle down and flower.

Dierama can be grown from seed sown as soon as ripe in a frost-free cold frame, but the resulting plants will take five years to flower.

Recommended varieties

D. pulcherrimum 'Blackbird'
Deep wine-red flowers, 4-5cm (1½-2in) long, on widely arching stems, make this a spectacular addition to the flower garden. H: 1m (3ft); S: 50cm (20in).

D. dracomontanum
Bell-shaped flowers in various shades of pink are produced on this slightly smaller plant, which is suitable for a small garden. H: 75cm (30in); S: 30cm (12in).

Digitalis *Foxglove*

Graceful and imposing, these are lofty biennials and short-lived perennials that colonize freely if allowed to. It is hard to imagine a woodland garden without them. The common foxglove (*D. purpurea*) is a very variable European native wild flower, producing rosettes of soft, silky leaves in its first year and flowers in its second (and occasionally third) year. The native plant carries mid-mauve-pink flowers on only one side of the stem. Hybrids and other species from the Mediterranean region and central Europe are more reliably perennial than common foxglove. Some have upward-facing flowers (Excelsior Hybrids) or slightly frilled ones.

Site and soil

Foxgloves prefer to be grown in leafy, well-drained soil that doesn't dry out completely, in the dappled shade of woodland margins. However, small groups can create a strong, vertical presence in a mixed border, or they can be planted - or allowed to seed around - as singletons, so they add a relaxed air to a cottage garden.

In spring, sow seed *in situ* or in a seed tray in an open cold frame. Plant out in autumn or the following spring.

Buying guide

Small plants (year-old seedlings) are most often available in spring. Even those plants sold as perennials are not reliably so, so it is worth buying young seedlings two years running in order to establish a self-seeding colony.

To establish a single-colour colony of common foxgloves (other than the wild pink), weed out any unwanted-coloured varieties before they flower (this can be reliably established early on from the colour of leafstalks).

Plant care

These are easy plants to grow, and despite their height need no staking.

Leaf hoppers (see page 216) and fungal disease (see page 214) attack older, exhausted plants.

Deadheading

By cutting back the main flower spire before it has completely finished flowering, you can ensure that the secondary spires will be substantial.

Overwintering

First-year seedlings are totally hardy and need no winter protection. Some plants may behave like (very) short-lived perennials so don't be in too much of a hurry to rip them up once they have flowered - check if there is some newly produced foliage at the base of the stem, which may indicate that they will survive another year - probably producing several rather shorter stems.

Propagation

Allow foxgloves to self-seed or collect the seed, save it, and sow it in spring (see page 46). Despite the millions of seeds produced, foxgloves seldom become invasive.

Recommended varieties

D. purpurea 'Sutton's Apricot' ♥
This lovely form bears soft apricot-yellow flowers in early summer. H: 1m (3ft); S: 50cm (20in).

D. ferruginea ♥
Curiously squashed-looking leaves adorn this variety, as do its bronzy flowers, each with a paler lip. H: 1-1.2m (3-4ft); S: 30cm (1ft).

Echinacea *Coneflower*

Not a plant for those who like their borders to be soft, billowy, and tactile, this perennial prairie plant from the gravelly hills of central and eastern North America has dark green, rough, tough, bristly basal leaves. Its tall, hairy stems, which in some species can grow 1m (3ft) or more high, are topped in mid- to late summer by strong-coloured, daisy-like flowers in white or various quite subtle shades of reddish or purplish pink. Many have slightly turned-down petals, and each has a large, cone-shaped, yellow, orange, or bronze central disc. Cultivars of *E. purpurea* make statuesque, colourful, and trouble-free border plants, some of them suitable for a small border, although they are more impressive planted *en masse*, particularly in a prairie setting. They provide a long season of interest, flowers giving way to bold seedheads. *E. pallida* is slightly more refined with spidery, droopy petals.

Site and soil

Plant coneflowers in well-prepared, compost-enriched, well-drained soil that never becomes waterlogged in full sun, although they are tolerant of some shade.

Coneflowers can be grown from seed under glass in spring and will often flower a little in their first year. Seedlings may be variable, however.

The clumps expand slowly, and plants die right back in winter. They are quite late to produce foliage in spring.

Buying guide

Buy and plant container-grown coneflowers in spring or, to be sure of exact flower colour since plants propagated by nurseries can be variable, buy them in flower in mid- to late summer. Pot them on and keep them in a cold frame until the following spring.

New pink/orange-flowered coneflowers are much sought after, and many nurseries and garden centres also offer one or two shorter hybrids of *E. purpurea* (*E.p.* 'White Swan' and *E.p.* 'Kim's Knee High', for example), which are easy to accommodate in a smaller garden.

Plant care

Apply an annual spring mulch.

Plants deeply resent disturbance and should be left well alone to become established.

IT IS EASY to see why echinaceas have become so popular. Robust yet subtly coloured daisies, they hold their own in both traditional borders and in grassy prairie gardens in late summer.

Support coneflower stems if plants are grown in a slightly shaded position; in an open site in full sun, they are usually self-supporting.

Protect coneflowers from snails (see page 215).

Deadheading

Removal of faded flowers will encourage plants to produce a second flush, on shorter stems, later in the season.

Overwintering

Although the plants are quite frost hardy, protect plants in colder areas with a dry winter mulch. Long, wet winters can take their toll and may even kill coneflowers.

Propagation

Increase coneflowers by seed in spring. The subsequent variable plants will often flower a little in their first year.

Divide mature plants in spring (see page 44).

Take root cuttings in winter, when plants are dormant. Cut a robust-looking root into sections 5cm (2in) long. Lay them flat on some seed and cutting compost in a seed tray and cover with more compost. They should be ready for potting on a few weeks later.

JUST WHAT THE DOCTOR ORDERED?

The botanical name *Echinacea* means hedgehog and it is something of a prickly customer when it comes to health benefits. Native Americans have long used it to help increase the body's resistance to infection – an effect that *Echinacea* products often proclaim. In truth, the medical jury is undecided. No sooner has one study concluded that there is a definite effect (such as cutting the chance of catching a cold by 50 per cent), than another study says this is hogwash. While the scientists battle it out, there are more *Echinacea* than ever to enjoy growing in the garden. Once it was the gorgeous pink blooms of *E. purpurea*, *E. pallida*, and *E. angustifolia* that were usually seen in the UK. Now, thanks to recent breeding work at the Chicago Botanic Garden, there are yellows, reds, oranges, and pinky-oranges, such as *E. 'Art's Pride'*. These greatly add to the coneflower's versatility, particularly when creating a trendy prairie-style planting.

Recommended varieties

E. purpurea 'White Swan'
White flowers, each with a prominent, golden-yellow disc, typify this garden-border plant. H: 90cm (36in); S: 50cm (20in).

E. purpurea 'Fatal Attraction'
This variety produces deep pink flowers and bronze discs. H: 80cm (32in); S: 60cm (24in).

E. purpurea 'Kim's Knee High'
As the name suggests, this is a somewhat dwarf form. It produces soft pink, slightly drooping petals and orange/bronze discs. H: to 60cm (24in); S: 40cm (16in).

E. pallida
A very tall coneflower is *E. pallida*. With its thin and spidery, drooping, white petals that are shaded slightly pink, it is somewhat more refined looking than other species. H: 1m (3ft) or more; S: 45cm (18in).

Echinops

The sight of a mass of prickly, steely-blue-grey, spherical echinops flowerheads being intensely worked over by numerous bees is one of the most wonderful in the flower garden. Also known as globe thistles, these sturdy plants belong to the daisy family and bear rather unpleasantly spiny leaves that are grey-green or greyish white. They originate from dry and gravelly hills in southern Europe, Asia, and India, and from the mountains of tropical Africa. Echinops are undemanding and, like many grey-leaved plants, are tolerant of drought. They make good cut flowers and also dry well.

Site and soil

Echinops are best grown in poor, well-drained soil in full sun, although they will tolerate a little shade. When cultivated in rich, moisture-retentive soil, they become more leafy and flower less well. Tall varieties are suitable for growing at the back of a big border, or even in a wilder area of the garden. Shorter varieties suit small gardens.

Sow echinops seed in spring under glass.

Buying guide

Source substantial-sized plants in autumn, and you can then split them up before planting them 30cm (12in) apart. This is easier than dividing up an established clump which in time develops a very thick, branching taproot.

THE BUDS OF sun-loving echinops look strange and other-worldly. The moment these big, sunny-border thistle-relations open their myriad tiny flowers they become irresistible to bees.

Plant care

Apply an annual feed with a general fertilizer.

Stake echinops if they are growing in very rich soil (see "Supporting plants", page 41).

Aphids can severely disfigure leaves, so take remedial measures (see page 216).

Deadheading

Echinops can often be persuaded to flower twice in a season if old stems are cut down by about half once the first flowers have tailed off. Subsequent flowers will be smaller, on shorter stems.

Seedheads are extremely attractive to birds, so unless they become unsightly, you can leave plants standing in winter, finally cutting them down and cleaning them up only in spring.

Overwintering

Echinops is hardy and needs no special winter protection.

Propagation

Divide echinops in autumn or spring (see page 44), although this might prove difficult once plants have become very congested because of the thickness of the plants' roots.

Root cuttings taken in winter (see page 105) might be a better option, as might allowing plants to self-seed and subsequently relocating the young plants.

Echinops may also seed itself around mildly if seedheads are left intact over winter, but this is not a particularly reliable method of propagation.

FINDING THE BUZZ

Echinops flowers create a real buzz for insects. They readily fly in to groom the heads for food, an activity that is not just for the daytime. Renowned gardener Edward Bowles wrote of this species in 1914: "I have often recommended them for entomologists' gardens where plants are wished for that can be visited after dark with a lantern, to surprise a supper party of noctuid moths." As well as fitting well into the wildlife garden, they look splendid in cottage gardens and herbaceous borders.

Recommended varieties

E. bannaticus 'Taplow Blue' ♀
This tall variety bears blue-grey flowerheads. H: 1.2m (4ft); S: 1m (3ft).

E. ritro ♀
The most compact echinops is E. ritro, with its flowerheads that are metallic-blue before opening. H: 60cm (24in); S: 50cm (20in).

E. sphaerocephalus 'Arctic Glow'
Vigorous 'Arctic Glow' carries silvery grey flowerheads on distinctly grey stems. H: to 2m (6½ft); S: 1m (3ft).

E. ritro 'Veitch's Blue'
This bold blue-flowered E. ritro cultivar is suitable for a small garden, and is particularly good for cutting. It is one of the best second-flowerers. H: 1-1.2m (3-4ft); S: 75cm (2½ft).

Epimedium

Epimediums are subtle, rather than show-stopping, plants. These diminutive members of the *Berberis* family are found in woodland, scrub, and shady rocky places in a wide geographical area running from the Mediterranean to eastern Asia. All epimediums bear delicate-looking, saucer-shaped flowers in soft colours – creamy yellow, pink, red, white, or lilac – from spring to autumn. All are essentially ground-hugging, have roughly heart-shaped, leathery leaves sometimes bronze-tinted in spring, and often take on good colour in autumn. Some species form neat clumps, while others spread themselves around via shallow, creeping underground runners. Some species are deciduous in autumn, yet others retain their leaves through the winter until new ones are produced in spring.

Site and soil

All epimediums require leafy and humus-rich, well-drained soil, and shady conditions. Particularly in the case of the evergreens, they need some protection from cold, winter winds. They are thus ideally suited to growing on a woodland floor. Furthermore, epimediums can cope – and will even spread mildly – where the underlying soil is full of tree roots. Well in advance of planting in autumn or spring, prepare the ground by incorporating leafmould and a little bone meal. After planting and watering well, mulch around the new plant with more leafmould.

DELICATE FLOWERS AND mottled leaves are produced by *Epimedium* 'Amber Queen' in spring. This is one of the first flowers to go looking for when a woodland garden stirs at the start of the year.

You can also sow epimedium seed in pots placed in a cold frame, as soon as it is ripe and while still green. Once there is little risk of frost, and they are large enough to handle by their first true leaves, plant them out.

Buying guide

Buy epimediums in spring or autumn. These plants are not particularly eye-catching when seen growing in a 1 litre pot in a garden centre and are thus not easy to find, but *E. grandiflorum* 'Lilafee' is one that is most often spotted. Nurseries specializing in shade-tolerant plants should carry a larger number of epimedium species.

Plant care

As with all new additions in a woodland planting, take care of new epimediums during their first year, scraping back mulch and watering the plants slowly once or twice during the driest months.

Apply an annual leafmould mulch in spring.

Remove all the old foliage from evergreen epimediums in spring, just before new growth starts.

Cut back deciduous plants in late autumn, when they have died back.

Notched leaf margins will indicate that vine weevils are at work, so treat these promptly (see page 216). Otherwise, epimediums are hardy, robust, and pest free once established.

Deadheading

There is nothing to be gained by deadheading epimediums, and indeed it would be a very fiddly job.

Overwintering

Epimediums look their best if they are thoroughly groomed – generally cleaned up and any remains of old foliage snipped away – in late winter, before the new leaves and flowers appear. This job may be somewhat impractical for plants that have spread over a large area.

Propagation

Divide plants in autumn, or just after they have flowered, in late spring.

They can also be propagated by seed sown as soon as it is ripe in pots in a cold frame (see above).

Recommended varieties

E. x *versicolor* 'Sulphureum' ♀
Strong yellow, long-spurred flowers are borne from mid- to late spring on this clump-forming evergreen. Its leaves are veined coppery red and brown when young, but turn green. H: 30cm (1ft); S: 1m (3ft).

E. x *perralchicum* ♀
This robust, clump-forming evergreen is slightly taller than most, and has leaves that are bronze when young. It produces pendent, yellow flowers from mid- to late spring. H: 45cm (18in); S: 30cm (12in).

E. 'Amber Queen'
The leaves are flushed bronze when young on this evergreen epimedium, with pale bronze-apricot, long-spurred flowers. H&S: 60cm (24in).

E. *grandiflorum* 'Lilafee'
Also known as lilac fairy, this evergreen epimedium has purple-tinted, young leaves and violet-purple flowers with long spurs. H&S: 30cm (12in).

Eryngium

Within this striking genus of thistle-like perennials, biennials, and annuals are two distinct types. There are those that are generally lumped together under the name of sea holly, which is actually the name of the native *E. maritimum*, which grows in dry, shingly ground along the coasts of the British Isles, but includes other species, several of which are to be found on dry, rocky coastland around the Mediterranean. They have tough taproots, ovate, heart-shaped, or divided leaves (sometimes attractively veined), and curious, thistle-like flowerheads, each with an attractive ruff. This ruff is composed of spiny bracts often coloured inky-steely blue or silver. The other type of eryngium comes from wet and marshy grasslands of North, Central, and South America. These are evergreen, with sword-like foliage and greenish flowers.

Site and soil

Grow taprooted eryngiums in dry, well-drained soil and full sun. The bracts do not take on good colour if plants are positioned in a site that is shady. These plants are ideally suited to a gravel garden, and they make an eye-catching statement and give a strong backbone to a mid- to late-summer, hot border.

American eryngiums also need full sun, but they require much more moisture around their roots. They look best growing on their own or when forming part of an exotic planting scheme.

Sow eryngium seed in autumn in trays in an open cold frame or even *in situ*.

Buying guide

Young taprooted eryngium, in small pots, may establish better than older, larger plants, because, like all plants with taproots, Mediterranean-type eryngiums resent disturbance. Buy and plant them in spring.

You may need to go to a nursery that specializes in exotic plants to find American eryngiums. They should also be bought as leafy, young plants in spring.

Plant care

Perennial eryngiums are trouble-free plants, given the correct growing conditions and full sun.

WITH THEIR METALLIC sheen and thistly flowers, eryngiums such as this *E. alpinum* pictured at Wisley, Surrey, UK, look totally at home in the arid, sunny places that suit them so well.

Cut them to the ground when they eventually lose their silver/blue colouring and become beige and unattractive. Some will produce a rosette of basal leaves thereafter.

Pull up biennials and leave them lying somewhere out of sight, so that the seeds spread themselves around.

Deadheading

Because of the spiny nature of the plants, deadheading is an uncomfortable and not very fruitful procedure and furthermore not much in the way of new flowering growth will result.

Overwintering

Perennial eryngiums and first-year seedlings of biennial eryngiums are hardy as long as they are grown in well-drained soil. American ones may be slow to come round after a hard winter.

Propagation

Collect seed and sow it in the ground as soon as it is ripe, or in trays in a cold frame. If allowed to do so, short-lived, cottage-garden perennials such as *E. giganteum*, normally grown as a biennial, self-seed prolifically, seedlings turning up in all sorts of odd places, hence the common name Miss Willmott's ghost. (The 19th-century gardener was apparently known to cast seeds of this, one of her favourite plants, around her acquaintances' gardens without telling them.) Thin out seedlings rigorously while they are young, where they appear in congested crowds, so that just a few individual plants are retained here and there and can grow to majestic maturity the following year. Seedlings transplanted to new sites may resent the upheaval and die.

Divided plants will be slow to re-establish (see page 44). Taking root cuttings in late winter is probably a more reliable method (see page 105).

CANDIED CONFESSIONS

Candied fruits are a common Christmas treat, but I am yet to spot candied eryngium among the cherries and citrus peel. However, this was a traditional use. The candied roots of *E. maritimum* are said to be sweet and aromatic, and they were once thought to be a nerve tonic and an aphrodisiac.

Recommended varieties

E. giganteum 'Silver Ghost' ♀
On this refined form of Miss Willmott's ghost, stout, branched stems carry thimble-shaped inflorescences that turn from pale green to silvery blue, each with intensely silver bracts. H: 60cm (2ft); S: 30cm (1ft).

E. x oliverianum ♀
Attractive, veined basal leaves are produced on this clump-forming perennial, with blue stems and small, blue flowers that tend to fade to purple-blue as they age. H: 60-90cm (24-36in); S: 45-60cm (18-24in).

E. bourgatii 'Oxford Blue' ♀
This clump-forming eryngium has dark green, silver-veined basal leaves in spring. Numerous small, dark blue flowerheads, with fine pointed bracts, are carried above the foliage in midsummer. H&S: 45cm (18in).

E. pandanifolium ♀
Quite unlike the above is this huge eryngium from South America – a clump-forming evergreen with tufts of long, roughly sword-shaped, slightly spiny-edged, silvery green leaves. In late summer it produces lofty stems of brownish flowers with purple bracts. H: to 4m (13ft); S: 2m (6½ft).

Erysimum *Wallflower*

Having fallen out of favour at the end of the 20th century, when fashionable garden colours became dominated by tasteful pastels, a group of bright and colourful annuals, biennials, and evergreen perennials native to Europe, Africa, Asia, and North America are now on their way back. They are wallflowers. Historically biennial wallflowers were used as nose-gays to disguise the foul odours of Elizabethan England, because of their lovely, delicate scent. They then became a staple of vibrantly coloured Victorian bedding schemes. Perennial wallflowers – some of them almost shrubby – are useful for their long flowering season, and recent years have seen the introduction of more subtly coloured biennial varieties. These are frequently sold in single colours (rather dizzy, rather variable mixtures).

Site and soil

Grow both perennial and biennial wallflowers in sun and moderately fertile, well-drained soil. In very rich soil, wallflowers tend to make a lot of leaf at the expense of flowers. Like all members of this broad plant family that includes cabbages, honesty, and rape, wallflowers grow best in soil that is slightly limy. They do very well when planted in containers.

ON THE UP

Wallflowers are all too often the preserve of bedding displays, which is quite different from their origins. The plant was probably introduced to Britain centuries ago and it was said to have been planted on the walls of castles to help scent the bedchambers. Whether this is true or not, wallflowers are found on many ancient landmarks, such as the Roman walls of Colchester and Oxford colleges. The lightweight seed easily blows to a new home, even if it is many metres off the ground.

Buying guide

Small biennial wallflower plants can be found for sale from early autumn, and they will flower the following spring. They are frequently sold in bundles, their roots either almost bare or protected by a ball of clay soil. If bought this way, make sure that the leaves are a good

WALLFLOWERS SUCH AS this yellow-flowered biennial *E. Citrona* Yellow have a powerful scent and a wonderfully long flowering season during late spring.

healthy green, and soak the roots before planting. More often, biennial wallflowers are now sold as seedlings in strips or pots with their roots in moist compost.

Buy perennial wallflowers as young plants singly in pots. Such plants start to flower really well only in their second year. The maturity of plants offered for sale can be judged by the woodiness of the stem.

Wallflower seeds can be available as colour mixes (such as 'Persian Carpet') and as single colours (such as Sunset Series). There are short and tall varieties. Sow seed of biennials in a seedbed outdoors in late spring, and thin out seedlings as they grow. Plant them out where they are to flower in early autumn, pinching out shoot tips to make them bushier. The earlier in autumn you plant such seedlings of biennial wallflowers, the more time they have to establish good roots before winter, and the better they will grow away in spring.

Sow seed of perennial wallflowers in trays in a cold frame in spring.

Plant care

In summer, regularly cut back the untidiest elongated flower shoots on perennials, to keep the overall appearance acceptably neat. Some become almost shrub-like, and may need to have wayward branches cut out as well.

At the end of the flowering season, discard biennials or cut them down to within 15cm (6in) of the ground and they will grow and flower (albeit rather untidily) the following year.

Deadheading

Deadhead wallflowers to prolong flowering considerably.

Overwintering

Wallflowers are completely hardy.

Propagation

Sow saved seed in late spring (see above). Biennial wallflowers will seed themselves around a little, but flower colours of such plants will be very unpredictable.

Take softwood cuttings in late spring or early summer from trimmings of mature biennials that have finished flowering (see page 46). Do this from non-flowering shoots of perennial wallflowers.

Recommended varieties

E. 'Bowles's Mauve' ♀
The most well-known and well-loved of the wallflowers is 'Bowles's Mauve', which can flower for 11 months of the year for three years or more. Its rich mauve flowers appear above a mound of slate-grey foliage. H: to 75cm (30in); S: 45cm (18in).

E. 'Constant Cheer'
In early summer, the dusky orange flowers of 'Constant Cheer' fade to smoky purple. It is one of several varieties that carries flowers that change colour as they age. It is less woody and robust than 'Bowles's Mauve'. H: 35cm (14in); S: 60cm (24in).

E. 'Parish's'
This dramatic, colour-changing perennial produces almost black buds that open to deep red flowers. These eventually fade to a softer red. H: 60cm (24in); S: 90cm (36in).

E. chieri Sunset Series
Plants described as Sunset Series are relatively new, soft-coloured biennials that can be bought as seeds or now often as plug plants. H: 60cm (24in); S: 30cm (12in).

Euphorbia

There are vast numbers of euphorbias, and they grow in all parts of the world. Those that are suitable for gardens are, it would seem, very much love-them-or-hate-them plants. They are indeed curious-looking when viewed at close quarters, the so-called flowers, for the most part, being showy and often colourful bracts in which the true, extremely small and often insignificant cyathia nestle. Many, but not all, garden euphorbias have bracts that are at their best in late spring and early summer, while some also have leaves that colour well in autumn. The house plant poinsettia, with its large, scarlet, pink, or cream bracts, is in fact a woody-stemmed euphorbia (*E. pulcherrima*) from Central America.

Site and soil

This is a very diverse group of plants. There are clump-forming herbaceous euphorbias – short and tall – that are suitable for a border, and evergreen, almost shrubby euphorbias that thrive in a hot, gravelly garden with light soil and full sun. Other softer evergreens thrive in shady, moist sites, and some will grow in dappled, dry woodland.

Some euphorbias are clump-forming and will self-seed; some have rhizomes that spread about tolerably, while others such as *E. cyparissias*, a front-of-border dwarf with delicate foliage, can be seriously invasive. Evergreen *E. amygdaloides* var. *robbiae* is only really suitable for (and therefore extremely useful for) dry shade – when given moist, rich soil and good sunlight it will readily run amok. However, soft-stemmed perennials such as *E.a.* 'Purpurea' appreciate moisture-retentive soil and are prone to mildew if grown in hot, dry situations.

Sow seed of hardy euphorbias in spring in small pots, two seeds in each and thin them to one. Sow annual euphorbia *in situ*, also in spring.

Buying guide

Buy and plant euphorbia in autumn. Bearing in mind their diversity, it pays to do some research before you buy. Some of the larger euphorbias (such as *E. characias*) make a year-round architectural feature in the garden, while others (such as *E. polychroma* and *E. palustris*) are herbaceous. The biennial caper spurge or mole spurge (*E. lathyris*) is quite architectural.

THE SOFT LIME-GREEN bracts of euphorbias – here *E. polychroma major* – light up a spring garden, whether it is situated in sun or in dappled shade.

Plant care

Once the bracts become dull and brown on shrubby, evergreen euphorbias (*E. characias* and relations and also the virtually prostrate *E. myrsinitis*) cut their fading flowering shoots right out. If self-seeding is desired, one flower shoot should be left intact to do so. On hot days in late summer, seed are audibly, explosively expelled. The new shoots should be left alone to flower next year.

Cut down clump-forming herbaceous varieties (*E. polychroma*, *E. palustris*) in autumn once the leaf colour has faded. Apply a rich organic mulch in spring, and they may need twiggy sticks to support them.

Cut down rhizomatous, spreading, deciduous herbaceous euphorbias (such as *E. griffithii*) in autumn. If necessary, in spring control them by using a spade to sever and remove shoots that appear where they are not wanted.

Cut down herbaceous euphorbia to the ground in winter.

Deadheading

Deadheading euphorbias will not prolong flowering.

Overwintering

All the recommended euphorbias (see right) are frost hardy and need no special winter protection. Despite their exotic looks, shrubby evergreen garden euphorbias are quite hardy (with the exception, perhaps, of the honey-scented giant, *E. mellifera*, which needs the protection of a warm wall). Stems may wilt in frosty weather.

Propagation

Collect and sow seeds immediately they are ripe, putting them in pots of gritty compost in a cold frame. Plants of shrubby euphorbias and biennial *E. lathyris* self-seed; if necessary, move seedlings to their permanent positions, since mature plants intensely dislike root disturbance. Alternatively, take softwood cuttings from shrubby euphorbias in summer.

Divide clump-forming perennials (see page 44) or take basal cuttings (see page 45), in spring. Cuts may bleed white (slightly irritant) sap, so stem the flow by dipping the cuttings in lukewarm water or charcoal before inserting them in the potting compost.

Sever sections of rhizomatous euphorbias and pot them up in spring.

Recommended varieties

E. amygdaloides 'Craigieburn'
This soft-stemmed evergreen, for a cool spot, produces brownish purple leaves and bright lime-yellow-green bracts in spring. H&S: 35cm (14in).

E. griffithii 'Dixter' ♀
Dark green, red-ribbed leaves and dramatic, golden-scarlet bracts are carried by this tall herbaceous perennial with a somewhat running habit. H&S: 1m (3ft).

E. polychroma ♀
This is a neat, clump-forming euphorbia that makes an attractive dome of green foliage topped with bright lime-green bracts in early summer. The whole plant takes on orange/red autumn colours when grown in full sun. H&S: 40cm (16in).

E. characias
The tiny flowers are distinctly black and yellow, and the bracts are soft pale green on this majestic shrubby euphorbia. There are numerous closely related shrubby varieties with flowers that are yellow/red, or yellow/green, and bracts that vary from dull green to lime-yellow. H&S: 1.2m (4ft).

Geranium *Cranesbill*

It is the perennials in this large plant family that form the mainstay of many a flower garden. They should not, however, be confused with tender pelargoniums, which are grown as pot and bedding plants and have the common name geranium. Cranesbill is the common name of the *Geranium* genus, which has pretty, blue, pink, magenta, or white, saucer-shaped flowers. There are small, more or less ground-hugging cranesbills suitable for shoehorning into generous crevices in paving or for the front of a border. Rhizomatous cranesbills spread gently sideways and form useful, flowery ground cover. Other, slightly larger, lax, and spreading varieties clamber up through neighbouring plants in a soft and billowy planting scheme, while taller, clump-forming varieties are suitable as main players in a more structured mixed border or on the edge of a woodland garden.

Site and soil

Most cranesbills appreciate well-prepared, fertile, moisture-retentive soil. They grow best in sun but are quite undemanding, and some (*G. macrorrhizum*, *G. endressii*, *G. x cantabrigiense*, and *G. phaeum*) are especially drought and shade tolerant.

Plant sprawlers such as *G.* 'Ann Folkard', *G. wallichianum* 'Buxton's Variety', and *G.* Rozanne among perennials of stouter stature or even near lowish-growing shrubs so that they can ramble around at will: flowers of *G.* 'Ann Folkard', for example, will appear as much as 1m (3ft) away from home.

Many cranesbills, apart from sterile hybrids such as *G.* 'Ann Folkard' and double-flowered forms, can be grown from seed, which should be sown in spring under glass. It may be two years before plants flower well.

Buying guide

Buy and plant cranesbill in spring or autumn. Generally, only one or two varieties are served up as standard fare at garden centres. It pays, therefore, to be more adventurous and go to nurseries that make a point of specializing in cranesbills. Also, do your research and read labels carefully. Some cranesbills flower only once and rather briefly, or, like *G. endressii*, are overenthusiastic colonizers – not particularly rewarding, therefore, for those with a small garden. Others may seem deceptively

A TINY HUMMOCK-FORMING plant a few centimetres high, *Geranium subcaulescens* 'Splendens' is one of the smallest of the cranesbills – all of which are fine and easy-to-grow garden plants.

compact when in the pot, but really do sprawl around, so will need some sort of support.

Take particular care when buying potted plants of the popular G. 'Johnson's Blue' (distinctive, luminous silvery blue flowers), which is too often confused with G. himalayense 'Gravetye' (distinctly magenta-blue flowers). Buy these plants when they are in growth. The former is clump-forming, the latter rhizomatous – the difference should be clear to see when you remove the plant from its pot.

Plant care

Apply a general fertilizer in spring.

Support tall, clump-forming varieties such as G. maculatum, G. pratense, and G. psilostemon with twiggy sticks or grids if grown as border plants.

With experience you will learn which cranesbills benefit from a midseason tidy up or cut back – some, but not all of them, will repeat flower after such a prune. You should, for example, cut right back large, determinedly once-flowering cranesbills – most notably G. x magnificum – after flowering in early summer. This will release space in the border for planting annuals, perhaps, although you need to bear in mind that such cranesbills will produce some new leaves.

If groomed carefully after flowering, G. phaeum var. phaeum 'Samobor' will repeat flower and produce fresh, handsome leaves, as will G. 'Johnson's Blue'.

Deadheading

Deadheading is not necessary nor particularly productive, although in some cases cutting plants back (see above) may encourage further flowers.

Overwintering

All the recommended herbaceous cranesbills (see right) are hardy and they die right back to the ground in winter.

Propagation

Increase cranesbills by division in spring (see page 44). Some such as G. 'Ann Folkard' can also be propagated by basal cuttings (see page 45). Others will self-seed (for example, G. pratense, G. pyrenaicum, and G. palmatum) (see page 47).

Recommended varieties

G. maculatum 'Elizabeth Ann' ♛
Intensely dark slate-purple foliage enhances the pale lilac-blue flowers of this cranesbill. H: 45cm (18in); S: 45cm (18in).

G. maculatum 'Beth Chatto'
'Beth Chatto' is a beautiful, clump-forming, blue cranesbill. H: 60cm (24in); S: 45cm (18in).

G. phaeum var. phaeum 'Samobor'
The brown-maroon splashed leaves add an interesting dimension to this drought-tolerant shade-lover, which bears dusky-mauve flowers. H: 80cm (32in); S: 45cm (18in).

G. 'Ann Folkard' ♛
The lime-green, spring foliage is an attractive advance guard for vigorous, scrambling growth that can wander through a border bearing a succession of black-centred, vivid magenta flowers over a long period in high summer. H: 50cm (1½ft); S: 1m (3ft).

Geum

These lovely. cottage-garden perennials have fallen somewhat out of fashion and are often undervalued by gardeners. They are tolerant of sun and light shade and flower mainly in early summer, but will continue to do so off and on over a long period if they are deadheaded. Most geums produce flowers that are bowl-shaped, either single or double and almost like single roses (geums belong to the same family as roses), or flowers that are slightly droopy, nodding bells. Colours are in the yellow, apricot, orange, soft red, or scarlet spectrum. All are carried on thin stems well above rosettes of slightly hairy, wrinkled leaves.

Site and soil

Grow tall border geums (such as G. 'Lady Stratheden' and G. 'Mrs J Bradshaw') in fertile, well-drained soil in full sun. Their somewhat transparent growth habit (low leaves, high flowers, with slim stems, and not much else in between) makes them good plants for the front of a border or thereabouts.

Plant shorter-statured G. rivale and its cultivars in light shade in moist, but not waterlogged, soil, where it will form more of a spreading clump. This useful perennial produces its nodding, bell-like flowers well before a lot of the main summer border players.

Sow seed under glass in spring. Geums hybridize readily so saved seed may not come true.

Buying guide

G. 'Mrs H Bradshaw' and G. 'Lady Stratheden' are quite easy to find at garden centres in spring or autumn. G. rivale is more likely to be found in a specialist herbaceous nursery, along with other interesting relations. Plant them straight away.

Plant care

Apart from G. rivale (when grown in moist soil), these are not very leafy or prolific-looking plants. Foliage becomes extremely tatty over the winter, and the whole plant is therefore best if it is cut right back and fed in spring so that it can make a fresh start.

Deadheading

To encourage flowering for a longer period, deadhead geums, although their quite spiky seedheads (particularly of G. rivale) are in themselves attractive.

Overwintering

Geums are hardy and need no extra winter protection.

Propagation

By division in autumn or spring (see page 44). G. 'Lady Stratheden' will self-seed if allowed to do so. Its seedlings may be variable.

Recommended varieties

G. rivale 'Leonard's Variety'
The delicate, nodding, downward-facing flowers on fine stems are a rather intriguing, dull raspberry-red, slightly paler within. Spiky, blackish seedheads follow. H: 45cm (18in); S: 20-60cm (8-24in).

G. 'Lady Stratheden' ♀
This semi-double, rich-yellow geum is traditionally partnered by bright scarlet G. 'Mrs J Bradshaw', and they make an impressive, airy duo in a hot planting scheme. H: 45-60cm (18-24in); S: 45cm (18in).

Helenium

Helen's flower (of Troy, that is) is one common name for these perennials, annuals, and biennials. Their name in America is sneezeweed, because the plant was apparently used by North American Indians to prevent hayfever – heleniums being native to North and Central America, where they grow wild in damp, swampy meadows or at woodland margins. Heleniums are almost indispensable in autumn, when their appealing, daisy-like flowers in yellows, oranges, russets, and browns are produced over a long period, when the sunlight is low and golden. The flowers have a conical central disc and lightly frilled petals that turn slightly downwards as they age.

Site and soil

Heleniums do best in moist soil, or soil that has been well prepared and quantities of moisture-retaining organic matter added. They are best positioned in full sun. Many hybrids of 1.2m (4ft) high *H. autumnale* are back-of-the-border plants, or else are suitable for growing in large swathes in wild, soft, and grassy gardens.

Buying guide

Heleniums are often seen for sale and making a big splash, in full flower, at plant fairs in high, dry, summer. The advantage of this is that you can choose varieties (of which there are numerous) by colour, but it may be

LATE SUMMER DAISIES don't get much better than these, a swathe of heleniums in the RHS Wisley garden, Surrey, UK.

Recommended varieties

H. 'Sahin's Early Flowerer' ♡

As the name suggests, this is one of the first to flower, starting in early summer, when it has yellow flowers that become streaked with red, before maturing to burnt orange. H: 90cm (36in); S: 50cm (20in).

H. 'Waltraut' ♡

This hybrid starts flowering in late summer, and produces yellow, orange-smeared flowers with brown discs. H: 90cm (36in); S: 60cm (24in).

H. 'Feuersiegel' ♡

Tall and upright 'Feuersiegel' carries golden-brown-red petals and brown discs. H: 1.2m (4ft); S: 60cm (2ft).

H. 'Blütentisch' ♡

Well-branched stems carry bright yellow flowers, from late summer, on this tall hybrid. H: 1-1.5m (3-5ft); S: 50cm (1½ft).

best to pot them on at once and plant them out later, in autumn or even the following spring, rather than plant them out immediately.

Plant care

Lay a protective encircling strip of grit around each clump of heleniums to deter slugs from doing a lot of damage to early spring growth (see page 215). Slugs will reinvade later, and eat completely through flower stems after summer rainstorms, so vigilance is crucial.

Stake tall varieties or grow them through a metal grid support (see page 41) as helenium stems are quite brittle, sappy, and congested.

To make tall varieties flower slightly later and on shorter stems, cut them down in mid- to late-spring (the so-called "Chelsea chop", see page 42).

Cut down heleniums late in autumn. They may retain a few basal leaves throughout winter; these invariably attract slugs in mild weather.

Lift heleniums every two or three years in spring or autumn, once they have run out of steam. Either simply replant them in soil that has been reinvigorated with the addition of organic matter, or else split the rootstock, discarding the central part, before replanting.

Deadheading

Remove summer flowers as they fade to prolong the flowering season considerably, into early autumn.

Overwintering

Heleniums are frost hardy and need no special protection during winter.

Propagation

In spring, once the plant has started to grow, divide heleniums into small sections, teasing their roots away from the outside part of the original plant (see page 44).

Take softwood cuttings from shoot tips in midspring, when the plant is growing vigorously (see page 46).

Helianthus *Sunflower*

Native to North and Central America and parts of South America, the familiar, giant, annual sunflower is grown widely in Europe and elsewhere for seed and oil crops, as well as for its dramatic, cheerful, decorative flowers. The somewhat smaller-flowered perennials are less well known, however, and although still rather coarse and tall, they are a lot more subtle than their annual relations and form a useful addition to the flower garden in late summer. They are good for cutting.

Site and soil

Grow in moderately fertile, well-drained, neutral to alkaline soil that has been enriched with organic matter. They flourish in full sun and flower most prolifically during long, hot summers.

Plant sunflowers at the back of a large border. Use spreading varieties, which given ideal conditions can be slightly invasive in a border, in difficult areas of a sunny, wild, and grassy garden. Although these sunflowers make good cut flowers, those with sensitive skin should avoid contact with their coarse and slightly abrasive foliage.

Recommended varieties

H. 'Lemon Queen' ♀
Perhaps this is the least coarse of the perennial sunflowers, with its pale yellow flowers that are darker in the centre. It spreads sideways, via its rhizomatous roots. H: 1.7m (5½ft); S: 1m (3ft).

H. 'Capenoch Star' ♀
Clump-forming, non-invasive 'Capenoch Star' is slightly less imposing than 'Lemon Queen'. Its pale yellow flowers are some of the best for cutting. H: 1.5m (5ft); S: 60cm (2ft).

Perennial sunflowers can be grown from seed sown in pots in a cold frame in spring.

Buying guide

Perennial sunflower plants can be hard to find in run-of-the-mill garden centres, which seem determined to sell dwarf, annual sunflowers already in flower. Source them instead online or by mail order, in autumn.

Plant care

Apply an annual feed in spring, to make these plants perform even better.

In midspring, shorten tall varieties by one-third (the so-called "Chelsea chop", see page 42) , which will make them flower at a slightly shorter height and slightly later.

To maintain their vigour, lift sunflowers every three or four years and replant in re-enriched soil.

Deadheading

Sunflowers make good cut flowers, and by cutting them (or deadheading them) you will persuade them to flower over a longer period.

Overwintering

The recommended varieties (see left) are all frost hardy.

Propagation

Divide plants in spring or autumn (see page 44). Left *in situ*, annual sunflowers will self-seed. You can also collect and store seed for sowing in spring under glass or late spring in the ground (see page 46).

Helleborus

Hellebores are natives of the grasslands and woodlands of southern and south-eastern Europe and western Asia. All species are spring-flowering and have become an almost essential feature of the northern European, deciduous woodland garden. Some are clump-forming and deciduous, others are almost shrub-like, producing stout leafy stems that bear clusters of greenish flowers the following year. Their groundcovering, leathery foliage remains attractive in dappled shade in summer.

Site and soil

Although an ideal site will have slightly alkaline soil, hellebores will grow more or less anywhere as long as the site is slightly shady and the soil moisture retentive and leafy. Avoid exposed situations in harsh sunlight or drying winds.

Sow seed *in situ* or in pots in a cold frame in late summer. They will germinate the following spring. Seedlings somewhat resent being moved around.

Before planting hellebores in spring or autumn, improve the soil with leafmould and a little bone meal.

Buying guide

Hellebores are most often to be found for sale during spring when they are in flower and at their most

attractive. All have become somewhat collectable, but particularly the hybrids (often referred to as Oriental Hybrids) with the darkest leaden-maroon flowers. Several nurseries specialize in selling the numerous named varieties with ever more unusual (lurid, some say) flower colours and forms.

If you are choosing plants yourself (as opposed to buying them online) make sure the pots feel heavy when picked up. Hellebores are often grown in peat or peat-substitute-based composts that too easily dry out. Once this has happened you will need to submerge the pot in water to rewet the compost properly before planting.

Plant care

Keep an eye on spring-planted hellebores, watering them in dry weather while they get established – particularly if they are planted under deciduous trees, the canopies of which will thicken up as the season advances.

In spring, apply a thick mulch of leafmould, to help to keep moisture in the soil during the drier months, as well as a fistful of a general fertilizer, spread around each plant when it is making new leaf growth.

In midsummer, as the new stems grow upwards, prune out the tired shoots on taller hellebores with biennial stems right down to ground level.

In winter, support stems of the more shrub-like species, such as *H. foetidus* and *H. argutifolius*, with canes and twine, when they become heavy with flower buds. This will prevent wind or snow damage.

Also in winter, cut out the old leaves and leaf stems on hybrid hellebores. Although technically herbaceous, the

THE EXQUISITE BEAUTY of the flowers of *H. orientalis* is revealed when you look inside them. A colony of these lovely things is a woodland-garden essential.

hybrids hang on to their old leaves from year to year and the older ones become distinctly unattractive – a favourite place for slugs and snails to hide, too.

Deadheading

Hellebore flowers generally last for weeks on end, but wilt almost the instant they are picked and refuse to revive in water. However, flowerheads floating face-upwards in a shallow dish look stunning. Deadheading does not encourage further flowering, but if you don't want to encourage the hybrids to self-seed, deadhead them before they drop their seed (check by looking into the slightly annoyingly, downward-facing flowers).

Overwintering

Hellebores are frost hardy, need no special winter protection, and some will send up early flowering shoots through snow. They flower later and less well after a long cold winter. Protect the stems of shrubbier species from snow or wind damage (see left).

Propagation

Hellebore hybrids are promiscuous breeders and set seed easily, producing numerous seedlings some of which will survive and carry variously coloured flowers – generally a dilution of the originals. It is possible to recognize dark flower-coloured seedlings by the colour of their stems. Transplant seedlings with care if they are needed elsewhere in the garden.

The roots of clump-forming hybrids can also be divided (see page 44), although they may take a year to settle down and flower well again.

Increase shrubby species by seed, as their roots are not suitable for division. Collect it as soon as it is ripe and sow straight away in a seed tray or pot. Protect the container in a cold frame while the germination and subsequent growth take place.

Recommended varieties

H. x hybridus
In this very varied group are flowers ranging from greenish and speckled through nondescript, muddy pink to dark rose-maroon and almost black. There are even orange-tinted and double varieties. H&S: 45cm (18in).

H. foetidus ♔
This comparative giant of a hellebore has finely cut leaves and clusters of bell-shaped, green flowers. It is one of the species with biennial stems, which produce flowers in their second year. H: 80cm (32in); S: 45cm (18in).

H. x ericsmithii
In this cross between two biennial-stemmed species (H. x sternii and H. x corsicus) and clump-forming H. x niger, can be seen some of the characteristics of all of them. It has particularly beautiful leaves. H: 35cm (14in); S: 45cm (18in).

H. x hybridus 'Black Swan'
One of the sought-after named varieties is 'Black Swan', with its deeply slate-grey-maroon flowers. H&S: 45cm (18in).

Hemerocallis *Day lily*

Day lilies from mountains, forest margins, and marshy valleys in eastern Asia are so-called because each flower lasts only one day. On the face of it, therefore, they do not sound particularly suitable for a garden dedicated to prolonged floral abundance. However, these striking, upright, clump-forming plants, with their arching, strap-like, sometimes evergreen or semi-evergreen leaves, produce numerous stems in midsummer, with several buds on each. These open up as trumpets of various forms, some fine and spidery, some double and almost artificial-looking, others sweetly scented, day after day over quite a long period of time from midsummer onwards. The bigger and more mature the clump, therefore, the longer the flowering season.

Site and soil

Grow in a warm position in sun or in very light shade, and very damp soil.

It is possible to acquire from specialists the seeds of named varieties of day lily that will have been hand pollinated and stratified (subjected to low temperatures, which some seeds need in order to induce germination). In spring, sow seeds in pots filled with a mix of seed and cutting compost and leave in a cool greenhouse.

Buying guide

Buy and plant them in spring or autumn.

Day lilies are often on sale when in flower, so that the subtleties of shape and colour of the more glamorous garden hybrids can be observed. However, many garden centres only offer a few very popular varieties. They may also be found at water-garden centres among the bog-garden plants, because of their preference for damp soil. There are also nurseries that specialize in day lilies.

Plant care

In autumn or spring, apply an organic mulch.

Protect new leaves in spring, when they are attractive to slugs and snails (see page 215).

When the flower stems start to grow, give an occasional liquid feed. This will help keep the roots moist as well.

Remove the rigid stems once the last flower has faded.

FRESH FLOWERS OF the appropriately named day lily open every morning and fade that night. A mature plant is so prolific, however, that it may flower non-stop for a month or more.

Day lily leaves will stay looking relatively good for a few weeks longer before turning yellow and dying back.

Replace old clumps of the common-or-garden, dull orange variety that flower poorly because they have become congested and too shaded by overhanging trees and shrubs. However, digging them out may prove arduous, to say the least.

Hemerocallis gall midge lays eggs on the surface of buds. Grubs develop inside the buds, which become very obviously swollen and wrinkled, and pupate in the soil beneath the plants before hatching. Therefore, remove swollen buds and destroy them before the larvae are able to complete their feeding. This will reduce damage in the following year.

LITTLE-KNOWN FACTS

This plant has a great following in the United States, where each year around 1000 new hybrids are registered and there are already 30,000 named cultivars, some changing hands for as much as $500. The Chinese regard the wilted flowers as a bit of a gastronomic treat and apparently the buds can be eaten, too (though you may wonder why anyone would forgo the flowers to do so, but apparently they have a pleasant nutty flavour). The leaves have long been used to treat medical and psychological disorders. Day lilies are also an antidote for arsenic poisoning.

Deadheading

Brush away or tweak off by hand any spent flowers, which have an annoying habit of clinging to the stems. This considerably improves the look of the whole plant.

Overwintering

Plants are completely hardy and need no protection. They vanish from view during winter.

Propagation

Divide plants in autumn or spring (see page 44). Day lilies can also be grown from seed. Plants can be increased by seed collected and saved (see page 46) but it will not have the same characteristics as the parent plants.

Recommended varieties

H. 'Golden Chimes' ♀
This smallish and quite refined day lily flowers (deep yellow) particularly prolifically once it is well established. It is ideal for a small garden. H: 75cm (30in); S: 60cm (24in).

H. 'Stafford'
'Stafford' is a handsome, relatively stocky, evergreen day lily and one of the most readily available. It carries deep russet-red flowers that have yellow midribs and throats. H: 75cm (2½ft); S: 1m (3ft).

H. 'Whichford' ♀
Tall 'Whichford' bears pale yellow flowers with lime-green throats. This day lily has a beautiful fragrance. H: 1m (3ft); S: 50cm (1½ft).

H. 'Joan Senior'
White flowers slightly flushed pink, with greenish-yellow throats, adorn this free-flowering day lily of short stature. H: 60cm (2ft); S: 1m (3ft).

Heuchera

These are dainty plants from North America that form, from slightly woody-based clumps, loose domes, 30cm (12in) high, of mainly evergreen, rounded but slightly jagged leaves. In midsummer, they bear thin stems, around 45cm/18in high, clothed with lots of small, bell flowers in pinks, strong reds, creams, and even green. Many of the numerous heuchera hybrids that seem to have been flooding onto the market in recent years appear to have been bred for their attractive leaf colouring and markings rather than their flowers. Too many of them seem to be remarkably alike. Despite this, they have certainly caught the public eye – when shown in massed displays at plant shows and fairs, for example – and they have become almost collectors' items for some gardeners.

Site and soil

Grow in soil that has been enriched with organic matter. Heucheras need some moisture around their roots, particularly if they are expected to do well in full sun. However, they dislike unrelenting winter wet.

Heuchera light needs vary considerably. Those with dark leaves require at least a couple of hours of direct sunlight each day, to colour up well. Grow pale- and bright-leaved hybrids in light shade, as full sun will scorch their leaves.

Plant heucheras with pretty-coloured leaves at the front of a border. Grow shade-lovers (and their close relations the heucherellas, tiarellas, and tellimas) in swathes in a woodland garden or as flowering ground cover.

If you plant too many of the bright, coloured-leaved varieties, you run the risk of making your garden look somewhat spotty (a word of great derision when used in horticulturally élite circles).

Commercial seed (often supplied as hybrid mixes and therefore slightly variable) should be sown in spring in pots or trays of seed and cutting compost in a warm greenhouse, scattered on the surface of the compost.

Buying guide

Buy heucheras when they are starting to grow well in spring – either as mature plants or as small plug plants. Foliage heucheras are often found on sale in mid- to late summer, when they are at their most beautiful. Plant them straight away; they will flower the following year.

THE DECORATIVE LEAVES of many modern heucheras are well loved. The delicate flowers, held attractively above the foliage on fine stems, come as a bit of a bonus.

Plant care

Once the new leaves start to be produced in spring, carefully cut away the old foliage, to smarten up the plant. Also in spring, apply a mulch of well-rotted garden compost or leafmould.

Cut down old flower stems and remove the oldest leaves after flowering. This considerably tidies up the plant for the remainder of the summer.

Tackle vine weevils, which will delight in laying their eggs around the base of heucheras (see page 216). The grubs can completely destroy plants in a single season. The first you may know about this problem is when the plant wilts and collapses.

Dig up the whole plant once the woody base of the plant starts to protrude from the ground. This will occur after a few years. Replant the rootstock more deeply or else discard it. Cutting off the woody protrusions will result in the plant going rapidly downhill and scarcely leafing up or flowering.

Deadheading

Removing individual flowers from heuchera as they die is not practical or necessary.

Overwintering

Heucheras are hardy, and keep some of their foliage during winter.

Propagation

Divide heucheras in autumn (see page 44). If allowed to do so, they will self-seed mildly (see page 47), but seedlings will very rarely come true.

Heucheras grown for their coloured leaves do not produce viable seed, so they are always propagated vegetatively (by division).

HEUCHERA PLUS POINTS

- Slugs and snails are not interested in heucheras – unlike hostas, with which they often share territory.
- Heucheras make good container plants, although this frequently makes them even more likely to attract vine weevils, it would seem.

Recommended varieties

x *Heucherella* 'Kimono' ♥
One of the newest, this heuchera has narrow-fingered, rich green leaves with dark central markings. Silvery pink flowers are borne in spring. H: 45cm (18in); S: 35cm (14in).

H. 'Obsidian'
Tiny, white flowers on red stems are carried above really dark, purple-black, glossy leaves – darker even than original dark-leaved *H.* 'Palace Purple'. H: 50cm (20in); S: 40cm (16in).

H. 'Green Spice'
The attractively marked foliage is green margined with silvery centres and strong, deep burgundy veins. The flowers are white. H&S: 50cm (20in).

H. 'Rave On'
Masses of small, pinkish red flowers seem to hover over the silvery plum-marked foliage of 'Rave On'. H&S: 35cm (14in).

Hosta

Also known as plantain lilies, hostas come from East Asia, particularly Japan. They come in many shapes and sizes, and the foliage is very variable, but all hostas have strong veining of the leaves and similar clump-forming growth. The delicately perfumed flowers are borne on tallish stems above the leaves and are roughly bell- or trumpet-shaped and either white or dull mauve. Most people grow hostas for the beauty of their leaves, many of which colour yellow in autumn. You could certainly never mistake these highly distinctive plants for anything else in the garden. Indeed, it could be said that no flower garden is complete without at least one, even if it serves only as a hefty gauntlet thrown down before the gardener. It takes not a little effort and much dogged persistence to get a hosta right through from spring to autumn without the leaves being shredded by snails.

Site and soil

Hostas like shade and moisture, and grow particularly lush and fulsome when sited near water or in a damp and shady gravel garden. If well mulched in spring, they will also thrive in a deciduous woodland garden.

Plant golden-leaved hostas in a site that receives at least some direct morning or evening sunlight, so they take on a better colour. All hostas will in fact perform satisfactorily in a fairly sunny site as long as they are not growing in dry soil. Avoid sites that are buffeted by drying winds – this stipulation applies particularly to hostas with thinner leaves.

Hostas grow well and look handsome in a large container filled with a nutrient-rich, loam-based compost (John Innes No 3) lightened with plenty of leafmould.

Hostas can be grown from seed sold commercially, frequently as mixtures, which can make the whole adventure a bit of a lucky dip. Sow hosta seeds in trays of potting compost in a cold frame outdoors in spring.

Buying guide

Cultivars with thick, crepy leaves are far less likely to suffer from snail damage. It can be a little disconcerting buying hostas in early spring when there may be absolutely no sign of life in the pot. Very gentle investigation with an index finger will reassuringly reveal some strong pointed shoots just under the surface of the

THE FOLIAGE OF *H. undulata* **is still fresh and unblemished as the flowers start to emerge in midsummer. Keeping the snails away from young growth was clearly worth the effort.**

compost – there should be several of these, at least three, perhaps, in a 1 litre pot. Plant the new purchases out in the garden soon after bringing them home.

PICK OF THE CROP

Hostas are one of the flower arrangers' favourites. The leaves are long-lasting and sculptural, and they come in a range of greens, greys, and golds, as well as variegated forms. There are large cultivars, such as *H.* 'Snowdon', which are ideal for hefty church pedestals, while tiny hostas such as *H.* 'Baby Bunting' are just about big enough for a buttonhole.

Plant care

In spring, spread a leafy mulch around each hosta plant, to conserve moisture around their roots.

Protecting plants from snails is vital, not just in early spring, but also all through the growing season, particularly as hostas become hemmed in by other plants. A thick covering of fine grit is the simplest protection, followed by extreme vigilance (see page 215). Protect container-grown hostas with copper adhesive tape – two rows are better than one. Ensure that hosta leaves do not touch walls and other plants, thus making the entire plant vulnerable, as snails are adept climbers.

In late summer, remove the old flower stems, for aesthetic reasons – they will have become singularly unattractive by this stage.

In autumn, cut away hosta foliage once it has flopped.

Deadheading

Removing individual flowers from hosta as they fade is not necessary.

Overwintering

Hostas are completely hardy.

Propagation

Increase plants by division in spring, when you can see the pointed shoots clearly (see page 44). Roots are tough and almost woody and may need to be cut with a saw or old serrated knife.

Recommended varieties

H. 'Sum and Substance' ♛
Tall and imposing 'Sum and Substance' produces shiny, heart-shaped, yellow-green leaves, which are 20cm (8in) long. The flowers are dull pale mauve. H&S: 75cm (30in).

H. 'Frances Williams' ♛
The tough, thick, glaucous, blue-green leaves, about 20cm (8in) long, have irregular cream/yellow margins. This variety is one of the more snail-resistant hostas. H: 60cm (24in); S: 1m (3ft).

H. sieboldii 'Paxton's Original' ♛
Deep violet-purple flowers and flat, matt, olive-green leaves that are irregularly edged white typify this vigorous hybrid. H: 30cm (12in); S: 60cm (24in).

H. undulata var. undulata ♛
This tall and vigorous hosta has leathery, slightly shiny, bright green leaves that are deeply veined and cream-splashed with wavy margins. H: 1m (3ft); S: 50cm (1½ft).

Iris

The *Iris* genus is named after the Greek goddess of the rainbow and is a huge family of some 250 species and innumerable named cultivars containing some wonderfully colourful members. Iris flowers are distinctive, extraordinary, and warrant close inspection: they have six apparent petals. In many varieties, three of these are borne upright (standards) and three curve outwards and downwards (falls). Some have little patches of hairs on the falls (beards). In other varieties, all six petals are carried more or less horizontally. Irises mentioned here all flower between late spring and midsummer, with the exception of *I. unguicularis*, which blooms in late winter. Irises are divided into several distinct groups, each needing different soil requirements and cultural care. Growing information for just three of these groups – bearded, Siberian, and Unguiculares – is given below.

Site and soil

Grow bearded irises in full sun, so their slowly spreading rhizomes receive a thorough summer baking to ensure that the plants flower well the following year. They also require free-draining, neutral to alkaline soil improved with a little bone meal, in a situation where they are not hemmed in by other plants. For this reason, many gardeners choose to grow them on their own – flanking a path, or at the base of a sunny wall, for example. Bearded irises are somewhat dreary to look at when not in flower and in overfilled, modern mixed borders they are hard to accommodate and to keep flowering well.

Among the beardless rhizomatous irises are Siberian irises, which form a gradually spreading clump. These are suitable for a cool, damp border or for wet, bog-garden soil, in sun or light shade. The foliage becomes untidy, but the seedheads are attractive.

Another grouping within the beardless rhizomatous irises is the winter-flowering Unguiculares irises. Plant these at the base of a sunny wall in dry, slightly poor soil. This essentially untidy iris resents root disturbance and competition from other plants. The beautiful out-of-season flowers make up for the shortcomings.

Buying guide

The best selection of bearded irises is without doubt offered by specialist nurseries, who sell by mail order

THIS LITTLE BULBOUS IRIS – *I. reticulata* – is one of the very first joys of spring, producing brilliant blue flowers barely 15cm (6in) high in mild weather soon after the turn of the year.

in late summer or early autumn, which is the best time to plant them. Interesting cultivars of *I. sibirica* and *I. unguicularis* are found at more adventurous herbaceous plant nurseries.

Plant bearded irises in autumn, more or less horizontally, with the top of each rhizome (from which leaves will appear) at soil level and preferably to the north of the bottom of the rhizome (the root end) so that the leaves do not shade the rhizome when in growth. After planting, cut the leaves down (slanting cuts look better than straight ones) to within 15cm (6in) of the base.

Plant beardless rhizomatous irises in spring or autumn.

Plant care

In spring, apply a general fertilizer to bearded irises. In midsummer, cut back their leaves. Every three years or so, lift their matted, exhausted rhizomes and discard the central part and then replant (see below).

Each spring, give Siberian irises a moisture-retaining mulch. Directly after flowering, in midsummer, cut back the untidy foliage. The seedheads will provide long-lasting structure in the winter border. Cut away the leaves in winter, after they have died down.

In autumn, if it looks really appalling, remove all the untidy foliage completely on Unguiculares irises. Snails can be a problem so take protective measures.

Deadheading

Nip off soggy, old flowers between finger and thumb. If the seedheads are attractive, leave them until they are no longer so, in late winter.

Overwintering

All those irises mentioned here are hardy.

Propagation

Increase bearded irises by division when plants are lifted in late summer (see page 44). Having discarded the central part of the rhizome, separate the outer sections into individual fingers, each with a growing tip and a root. Shorten the leaves to within 15cm (6in) of the base and replant (about 25cm/10in apart) in re-invigorated soil, or pot each one up into gritty compost and plant out later in the autumn.

Recommended varieties

I. 'High Roller' ♀
Lilac/apricot, slightly frilled flowers with distinct, golden yellow beards are carried by this gorgeous tall bearded iris.
H: 90-120cm (3-4ft);
S: indefinite.

I. 'Langport Wren' ♀
This intermediate bearded iris produces dramatic deep purple flowers, with brown beards. H: 1m (3ft); S: 50cm (1½ft).

I. unguicularis ♀
The ethereal, pale blue, scented flowers on this beardless iris appear a few at a time during late winter, among untidy, grassy foliage. H: 20cm (8in); S: indefinite.

I. 'Toucan Tango'
This tall bearded iris produces creamy yellow flowers that are splashed and finely lined with violet purple. H: 90cm (36in); S: indefinite.

Knautia

Knautias (the "k" is silent) are scabious-like, clump-forming perennials that grow in alkaline scrub and grasslands in their native Balkans. They flower prettily over a long period from early summer onwards. The numerous slim flower stems rise from jagged, dark green basal leaves in late spring. A succession of small, light green, pincushion buds, each with a ruff of slightly furry, green bracts, open to 5cm (2in) wide flowers in deep rich maroon red, or in shades of pink.

Site and soil

Grow in full sun and slightly alkaline, moisture-retentive soil. If the soil is constantly dry around knautia roots, the crowded leaves and stems may succumb to powdery mildew in midseason.

In spring, sow seed in containers in a cold frame.

Because knautias have a soft outline, they look best if grown with taller, slightly bulkier neighbours – the plentiful, button flowers showing up well, for example, as a haze of maroon against the leafy stems of tall, pale blue campanulas. Another good companion, of similar height and scale, is a pale cream scabious: *Scabiosa columbaria* subsp. *ochroleuca*.

Buying guide

Buy and plant pot-grown knautias in spring. They are generally available at many garden centres.

Plant care

Apply a moisture-retentive organic mulch in spring.

To hold mildew at bay, spray with a systemic fungicide during late spring (see page 215).

Knautia is essentially a blowsy, insubstantial plant that will always manage to escape from supports given to its rising stems in late spring.

Deadheading

Deadheading of the slightly furry, green, spent flowers (which, confusingly, rather resemble unopened buds) is somewhat fruitless on a plant that is so prolific, although it does make it look a bit tidier. However, in midsummer you should cut down the whole plant by half and give it a soluble feed. It will then perform very well for a second time in late summer and early autumn.

Overwintering

Knautias die right back in winter, and are totally hardy.

Propagation

The easiest way is from seed, in spring. However, this plant will do it all by itself, and seedlings will always be found close by, the first few leaves of which have slightly toothed edges – jagged leaves developing later.

Basal cuttings can be taken from mature plants in spring (see page 45).

Recommended varieties

K. macedonica
The species most often to be found in nurseries and garden centres is *K. macedonica*. It bears deep rich maroon flowers. H: 60-90cm (24-36in); S: 60cm (24in).

K. macedonica Melton pastels
These slightly loftier perennials in mixed shades of pink and red create a softer impression altogether. H: 1.2m (4ft); S: 50cm (1½ft).

Kniphofia *Red hot poker*

Finding exotic-looking plants that are hardy enough to plant out permanently in the ground and leave to fend for themselves in a cool-temperate climate can be difficult, but these dramatic and trouble-free hardy kniphofias (with a silent "k") - red hot pokers, or torch lilies - from southern and tropical Africa fit the bill for many gardeners. They are not to everyone's taste, it has to be said. Some gardeners find them altogether too alien-looking and thus hard to accommodate in more staid and traditional planting schemes. Over time the rhizomatous roots of red hot pokers form extremely dense clumps of arching, strap-shaped leaves with distinct ridges (keels) on their undersides. Some are truly herbaceous, while others keep most of their leaves throughout winter. Flower-bearing stems - pokers - can vary in height, and they carry numerous closely packed flowers ranging from cream through yellow, orange to glowing red well above the foliage. Some flower as early as late spring, while others will provide glowing colour from late summer and into early autumn.

Site and soil

All red hot pokers need full sun and deep, fertile, humus-rich, moist but well-drained, preferably sandy soil.

They eventually take up a considerable amount of space, and look rather better as stand-alone plants in an exotic garden. Red hot pokers look particularly good when seen against a dark backdrop or when teamed with late summer daises in a softly grassy garden.

Sow commercial seed under glass in spring or autumn.

TURN UP THE HEAT

Although red hot pokers are often talked about as late-flowering plants, many actually begin sooner. Cultivars such as *K*. 'Early Yellow Buttercup' can start flowering as early as midspring, then have a rest, and bloom again in fits and starts between late summer and the first frosts of autumn. For a mid- and late summer display choose *K*. 'Sunningdale Yellow' and *K*. 'Prince Igor'. And for true late colour try *K. linearifolia* and *K*. 'Wisley Whiskers', which don't get going until early autumn. Thankfully they have good foliage and so make an unusual alternative to the leafy bergenia, wood sedges, and stachys often grown in dry spots.

HERE THE ORANGE pokers of *K. triangularis* subsp. *triangularis* form a radiant, fiery combination with equally vivid, crimson-flowered penstemons.

Recommended varieties

K. 'Tawny King'

This deciduous red hot poker has bronze stems and brownish buds opening to soft bronze-orange flowers from mid- to late summer. H: 1.2m (4ft); S: 1m (3ft).

K. 'Prince Igor'

Glowing, orange-red flowers are produced in early and midautumn on this giant, deciduous perennial. H: 1.8m (6ft); S: 1m (3ft).

K. 'Brimstone' ♧

In late summer, tall and imposing 'Brimstone' produces pokers that are lime-green and yellow. The foliage is more or less evergreen. H: 75cm (30in); S: 50cm (20in).

K. 'Wol's Red Seedling'

The narrow, red flowers are carried very prolifically on erect pokers. H: 60cm (24in); S: 30cm (12in).

Buying guide

Buy and plant in spring or autumn. For a good selection of varieties, you will probably have to visit a herbaceous plants specialist.

Plant care

For their first winter, protect young red hot poker clumps with a dry winter mulch of straw or bracken. Thereafter, apply a spring mulch of well-rotted manure or compost, spread around, but not over, their crowns. Also in spring, clear out the old foliage, which often harbours hibernating snails, as well as any tatty leaves.

In dry summers plants may need to be watered.

Deadheading

Once a poker stem has finished flowering, cut it right out at the base, to encourage new ones to form.

Overwintering

Old foliage stays on the plants in winter and looks extremely untidy, but should be left as light protection over the crowns until spring.

Propagation

Increase plants by division in autumn (see page 44). As an established clump develops an extremely woody and impenetrable root, it may be necessary just to slice off sections from one side, keeping the sections in pots until they start to regrow. New plants created this way may not flower for two or three years.

Red hot poker can be propagated by saved seed in spring or autumn, but cultivars seldom come true.

Lathyrus *Sweet pea*

The most familiar member of this family is undoubtedly the strongly scented and colourful climbing annual sweet pea (*L. odoratus*), but there are other pretty plants in the genus – perennials that deserve inclusion in the garden. Some are, like the sweet pea, climbers with tendrils that enable them to scramble somewhat untidily over nearby shrubs or climb up more formal supports. Others are simply herbaceous, suitable for a border or woodland garden. Most of these other sweet peas are unscented.

Site and soil

Grow in fertile, humus-rich well-drained soil and full sun or light dappled shade. In order to flower well over a long period, annual sweet peas in particular need soil that is deeply enriched with well-rotted manure or garden compost during the autumn before they are planted out.

Annual sweet peas can be sown in containers in autumn or spring. Soak or chip the seeds beforehand. Or they can be sown *in situ* in late spring.

If grown in containers, these should be large, deep, and non-porous and filled with loam-based (John Innes No 2) potting compost bulked out and enriched with additional manure or garden compost. Position pots away from the midday sun.

Buying guide

After buying sweet peas growing all together in crowded little pots in early spring, be sure to harden them off carefully. If necessary, separate them, pot them on individually or in pairs, pinching out the shoot tips to encourage them to bush out before planting them out in their permanent sites when chilly spring winds are definitely over.

Perennial pea *L. latifolius* 'Albus' is frequently missold as *L.* 'White Pearl'.

Plant care

All sweet peas need adequate water throughout the growing season.

In winter, cut old stems on perennial peas right down off their supports.

PICKING BUNCHES OF fragrant sweet peas for the house is one of the most pleasurable jobs in the summer garden. But it must be done every day if the flowers are to continue appearing.

Recommended varieties

L. odoratus 'Gwendoline'
The petals on this soft pink, highly scented sweet pea darken towards their edges. H: 2m (6½ft); S: 50cm (1½ft).

L. odoratus 'Oxford Blue'
Large, sweetly scented, wavy-edged blooms are in a rich purplish blue that darkens as each flower ages. H: 1.2m (4ft); S: 30cm (1ft).

L. vernus purple-flowered
This is a pretty, clump-forming herbaceous perennial carrying racemes of small, deep purple-blue, unscented flowers in early spring. H&S: 45cm (18in).

L. latifolius 'Albus' ♡
Beautiful, wildly scrambling 'Albus' is far more attractive than the usual, rather raggedy pink variety. Alas, its white flowers are not scented. H: 2.5m (8ft); S: 1m (3ft).

ANNUAL SWEET PEA TIPS FOR SUCCESS

Mid- to late autumn-sown seeds will overwinter in a cold frame, cold greenhouse, or porch, and if they are pinched out (the shoot tip simply removed between finger and thumb) once or twice as their stems lengthen, they make sturdier plants than those germinated in spring.

Sweet pea tendrils do not cling easily to bamboo canes or other smooth surfaces, particularly when the plants are tiny. Chicken wire or plant protection mesh can be wrapped around supports to provide a more suitable surface. Protection from wind may also help the plants to grow away better.

Don't crowd sweet peas together too closely. Even annual climbers need plenty of root space to do well, and congestion both above and below ground – competition for space and water – will render plants vulnerable to powdery mildew.

Once they have started to flower, a liquid feed (tomato food, for example) will ensure a long flowering season.

Deadheading

Daily picking or deadheading will ensure that the plants continue to go on flowering for a long period.

Overwintering

Perennial sweet peas are totally hardy, but die right back to ground level each winter.

Propagation

Divide perennial peas in spring (see page 44). New plants may take two seasons to start flowering well.

Lavandula *Lavender*

A sunny flower garden would be incomplete without lavender, and for that reason this much-loved, aromatic, evergreen flowering shrub has been included here. While the base of lavender is essentially woody, young growth produced each year is grey-green, fragrant, and soft, with the spikes of scented, tiny flowers of most varieties held on long stems high above the foliage for a long period in midsummer. The flowers are irresistible to bees. Stature varies, and some lavender varieties are hardier than others, while the flower colours of most vary subtly from pale lavender-blue to deep inky purple. There are also pink-, white-, and cream-flowered varieties. Lavender comes mainly from the dry and rocky hills around the Mediterranean, and some varieties struggle in damp cool-temperate climates and rich soil.

HISTORY AND FOLKLORE

The Romans, who introduced lavender to Britain, used it to scent their communal baths. The Greeks used it medicinally to alleviate throat and chest complaints, and in the Middle Ages lavender was used to treat head lice. The Elizabethans disguised foul smells with it, and during the Plague in 1665 bunches of lavender were hung around to cloak the stench of decay.

Old wives' tales about lavender include the fact that it provided protection, peace, and happiness. Planting lavender around a house would deter evil and protect the people within. Flowers placed between bed sheets would ensure that a couple would never quarrel – and both its calming and stress-relieving qualities are valued by many today.

Site and soil

Grow in a dry and sunny spot in light, only moderately fertile, free-draining soil that is slightly alkaline. Badly drained, heavy soil and humid conditions can render plants more susceptible to disease. If necessary to ensure good drainage, open up the texture of your soil with coarse-textured organic matter, sand, or grit and do not bury the roots of the plant too deeply. Adding a little bone meal to the soil at the time of planting in spring

FRENCH LAVENDER, WITH its curious purple flowers, requires a really sunny spot to do well. This type of French lavender is *L. pedunculata* subsp. *pedunculata*.

Recommended varieties

L. *angustifolia* 'Hidcote' ♀
Moderately compact 'Hidcote' is one of the most popular and reliable varieties. It has rich purple flowers and silvery grey leaves. H: 60cm (24in); S: 75cm (30in).

L. x *intermedia* 'Seal'
Taller and more lax is this so-called English lavender, with its very silvery leaves and purple flowers. H: 75cm (30in); S: 60cm (24in).

L. 'Regal Splendour'
This French lavender has deep purple flowers borne on short stems each with a top frill of purple bracts. It is earlier flowering (from early summer) and slightly less hardy than lavender that does not produce bracts. H: 75cm (30in); S: 90cm (36in).

L. *pedunculata* subsp. *pedunculata* ♀
Pale purple flowers with characteristic, conspicuous bracts are carried well above the foliage on this early flowering French lavender type. H&S: 60cm (24in).

is helpful for long-term feeding needs, even though lavender does not require richly fertilized soil.

Lavender dislikes being crowded by other plants, so site it at the front or corner of a border or flanking a path.

Where you cannot provide adequate conditions in the ground, consider growing lavender in a large pot of free-draining, loam-based compost, into which a little grit or perlite has been added.

Buying guide

Most garden centres offer several different varieties. Be aware that *L.* x *intermedia* is surprisingly wide-spreading when in full flower. The smaller varieties are much better for lining a path, and are easier to keep in good shape.

Plant care

After their first year, prune plants annually to ensure that they stay shapely. In late summer, shear off flowerheads and stems together with 5-10cm (2-4in) of foliage.

If a plant needs to be kept particularly compact, in late winter cut off slightly more stem (again with shears), but make sure that you do not cut into the old wood and that there are plenty of tiny, new, grey leaves in evidence.

Deadheading

Removing flowers does not encourage a second crop.

LAVENDER FOR DRYING

Stems should be cut early in the day, just as the first few tiny flowers are opening. This is when the lavender oil is at its most powerful. Dry stems by hanging them upside down (bunched together using rubber bands not twine, since the stems shrink) for about two weeks.

Overwintering

Most lavenders are pretty hardy if grown in full sun and free-draining soil. However, French lavender is noticeably more temperamental and only reliably hardy in an extremely sheltered garden.

Propagation

Take semi-ripe cuttings in summer (see page 46).

Leucanthemum

This is a genus that contains many robust, useful border daisies, also sometimes known loosely as shasta daisies. They are natives of Europe and temperate Asia, where they are to be found in rough grassland and on wasteland. There are now numerous varieties with double and semidouble flowers in white, creamy white, or yellow. The plants vary in stature from relatively squat, suitable for the front of a border, to tall substantial plants (with slightly fleshy, toothed, dark green leaves and stems) that spread rapidly and make an attractive, simple statement in mid- and late summer. All leucanthemum make good and long-lasting cut flowers.

Site and soil

Grow in moderately fertile, moist but well-drained, slightly alkaline soil and sun or partial shade.

In spring, sow seeds in containers in a cold frame. Plants grown from commercial seed may be short-stemmed in their first year of flowering, becoming taller thereafter.

Buying guide

Buy and plant leucanthemum in spring or autumn.

Recommended varieties

L. 'Goldrausch'
Short flower stems carry flowers comprising masses of fine petals that are white at the outer edges and golden-yellow where they meet the yellow central button of the daisy flower. H: 30cm (12in); S: 40cm (16in).

L. 'Aglaia' ♛
This tall, border daisy bears white flowers that are neat, frilly, almost double, and yellow centred. H: 1m (3ft); S: 60cm (2ft).

Garden centres tend to stock only dwarf varieties. Try herbaceous specialists for taller varieties.

Plant care

Be extra vigilant for slugs and snails, which can present a problem in early spring (see page 215). Aphids can be troublesome, too – they cluster around at the top of stems around flower buds (see page 216).

Stake taller varieties, with stems that become top-heavy under the weight of the stout daisies. Plants can also be chopped back in late spring (the so-called "Chelsea chop", see page 42) to make them bushier and shorter.

Although some varieties are difficult to get going, clumps of larger, coarser cultivars, once established, will spread sideways rapidly. Every three years, lift and divide them, to stop them becoming invasive.

Deadheading

The first stems to flower will have secondary shoots carrying flowers at a slightly lower level. Deadheading – or picking – the tallest flowers once they have faded will encourage the production of more flowers on this lower level in later summer, making sure the plant looks better for longer.

Overwintering

Leucanthemum plants die right back in winter, but are completely hardy.

Propagation

Propagate by division in spring or autumn (see page 44), or by seed in spring (see above).

Lobelia

Flowers of all lobelias are very recognizable – having two upper and three larger, downturned lobes. Cancel from your mind any visions of the little, blue, white, or purple bedding and basket plants. There are members of the *Lobelia* genus (also known as cardinal flowers) that are altogether different – magnificent, brightly coloured, moisture-loving, slightly tricky herbaceous perennials that are well worth the effort of growing, despite the possibility of loss from a hard winter and from massive slug and snail attacks. The tall and imposing herbaceous perennials mentioned here come from marshes, wet meadows, and river banks in North America.

Site and soil

The stature and colouring of lobelia might lend it to inclusion in a late-summer-spectacular planting scheme complete with grasses and hot colours. However, it should be borne in mind that lobelia will not perform well in dry conditions. It needs deep, moist soil to grow and flower well. It prefers a site that is in full sun, but its flowering season is lengthened if it is grown in light or dappled shade.

Recommended varieties

L. cardinalis 'Queen Victoria' ♛
In late summer, vivid scarlet flowers are produced on rich brownish purple-red stems, with foliage of a similar hue underneath. H: 90cm (36in); S: 30cm (12in).

L. x speciosa 'Hadspen Purple'
'Hadspen Purple' is a lush green-leaved lobelia bearing vivid purple flowers. It flowers from midsummer onwards. H: 70cm (28in); S: 40cm (16in).

Buying guide

Green-leaved lobelias are quite hard to find, whereas *L. cardinalis* 'Queen Victoria', with its eye-catching red foliage, is relatively common. Buy and plant in spring.

Plant care

Whether you can get lobelia to work for you depends on your vigilance. If you can provide it with the moist soil it demands, the real problem will then be the mollusc menace. Therefore, after planting, immediately protect plants from slugs and snails (see page 215). Spread a wide mulch of fine grit as a deterrent. The mulch will also help retain moisture in the soil.

Deadheading

Cut back old flowering stems as well as any that get damaged, to encourage a small second crop of flowers – slugs and snails permitting.

Overwintering

Cut down the stems and protect the crown with a dry mulch in winter.

Propagation

Increase by division in spring (see page 44).

In case of a cold winter, it is wise to take cuttings each year in mid- to late summer. Lobelia is one of only relatively few plants (such as basil) whose stems can be induced to develop roots by simply putting them in a glass of water. Once roots have formed (but well before they have filled the glass), pot up the cuttings in a loam-based potting compost.

Lunaria *Honesty*

Biennial honesty or satin flower, a European native, is grown almost as much for its scented, white or purple racemes of four-petalled, early summer flowers, as it is for its flat, circular seed capsules that become white, papery, and translucent as they ripen and drop their flat black seeds in autumn. The seed pods are also excellent in dried flower arrangements. Clump-forming perennial honesty has smaller, pale lilac flowers and elliptical rather than circular seedheads.

Site and soil

Grow in sun or light shade and fertile soil to achieve quite lofty proportions (90cm/3ft high). White biennial honesty is particularly effective at lighting up a woodland garden just as the leaf canopy starts to close overhead, in early summer. Perennial honesty makes a gentle, early-season statement in a shady border, where few other plants will flower well.

Both perennial and biennial honesty can be either sown in pots or directly in the ground in spring.

Buying guide

You may find young seedlings of special varieties (with variegated leaves, for example, or *L. annua* 'Munstead Purple') at plant fairs and specialist nurseries in late spring and summer. Plant them out in autumn.

Plant care

Keep thinning plants so they are not overcrowded and thus more susceptible to mildew.

After flowering, thin out plants that are to be kept for the beauty of their seed pods, leaving a few in strategic places where their translucency shows up well in autumn and early winter.

Perennial honesty is a trouble-free plant and should simply be cut down completely at the end of the season.

Deadheading

To prolong flowering, remove flowers of biennial honesty as they fade; plants will then go on flowering until they exhaust themselves or succumb to mildew – but you will then forgo their attractive seed pods.

Perennial honesty, the seeds of which are not so spectacular, will go on flowering intermittently for a little longer if old flowers are removed.

Overwintering

Honesty is extremely hardy and neither young seedlings of biennials nor perennial plants need winter protection.

Propagation

Biennial honesty self-seeds almost rampantly. From early autumn onwards, you can relocate seedlings and cull unwanted plants at the same time.

Divide mature perennial honesty in spring (see page 44).

Recommended varieties

L. rediviva
This clump-forming perennial is invaluable for growing in a shady border or woodland setting. Flowers are lilac-mauve in bud, but almost white when opened. H: 60–90cm (24–36in); S: 30cm (12in).

L. annua
Purple or white forms of this biennial are easy to grow and will develop into a permanent, shifting colony. *L. annua* 'Munstead Purple' has the darkest flowers of the species and violet-tinged stems. H: 75cm (30in); S: 30cm (12in).

Lupinus *Lupin*

It is the distinctive, peppery-sweet scent of these imposing, early-season perennials that is, for some people, the very essence of remembered childhood summer days. There are numerous perennial lupin hybrids that form clumps of slightly hairy, palmate basal leaves, which hold a drop of dew in the centre. They also have stout, torch-like, tall stems bearing abundant pea-flowers, some that are of a single colour, others that are eye-catchingly bicoloured. Flowers give way to hairy-silky, upright pods of peas that are mildly poisonous if ingested. Such hybrid lupins are derived from those growing wild in grassy meadows and banks in North America.

Site and soil

Lupins thrive in sun or light shade and light, sandy, moderately fertile, slightly acid soil in a border. They are not easy to keep going on heavy clay soil.

In spring or autumn, soak lupin seed for 24 hours before sowing. Pot seedlings on frequently and plant them in a garden when they have made substantial growth, by the following spring. Seed sown *in situ* will be vulnerable to slug and snail damage.

Recommended varieties

L. 'Manhattan Lights'
The name says it all in this bicoloured lupin, with its dramatic flower stems in summer and dark green leaves. H: 90cm (36in); S: 75cm (30in).

L. 'Red Rum'
Bright coral-red flowers start putting in an appearance above midgreen foliage during late spring. H: 90cm (36in); S: 50cm (20in).

Buying guide

If you purchase tiny, first-year plug plants, pot them on at once. Then leave them in an open cold frame to plump out, before moving them to the open ground, in autumn or the following spring.

Plant care

Lupins flower extremely early in summer and then become somewhat unsightly and pest prone. Protect them from slugs and snails with barriers - grit or copper, for example. Keep a watch out for extremely plump and vigorous lupin aphids, which have become a problem in recent years and can completely destroy entire plants.

In spring, feed with a general fertilizer. Support individual stems with slim canes. Water plants in dry weather, to prevent mildew.

Once the flowers have finished, cut down their stems - the seeds are poisonous, and furthermore fascinating to children. Also remove any really untidy leaves. Then give plants a soluble feed. To cover the new gap, plant around lupins with tall annuals or late-flowering perennials.

Deadheading

Lupins do not reliably produce a lush second flush of flowers even when the main flowering stem is cut off.

Overwintering

Lupins are hardy, can be cut down completely in autumn, and will then disappear until spring.

Propagation

In midspring, take basal cuttings (see page 45).

Meconopsis

The cheerful, little, yellow- or orange-flowered Welsh poppy (*M. cambrica*) is perhaps the least spectacular – and least fussy – of this genus of woodlanders, all of which are capable of illuminating patches of cool shade with their clear colours. Apart from that one Western European native, all others are from the wooded mountainous regions of the Himalayas, Myanmar, and China. All share certain characteristics: distinctive, hairy buds that open into papery, cup-shaped, slightly pendent flowers with numerous prominent, yellow stamens; and slightly softly bristly stems rising from basal leaf rosettes. Those featured here are mostly perennials – albeit quite short-lived ones. *M. napaulensis*, however, is monocarpic – taking two or more years to flower – after which it dies.

Site and soil

The Asian species all need perfect conditions in a cool-temperate climate in order to thrive and be truly perennial. Therefore, grow them in light shade and damp but not sodden soil that is neutral or slightly acid. They do altogether better, furthermore, during summers that are generally cool and rainy.

Before planting Asian species, prepare the soil well, incorporating as much well-rotted leafmould into the soil as possible, to improve moisture retention. Sow seeds in spring or autumn in a sheltered and shaded cold frame in a loamless compost.

Welsh poppy will grow anywhere, and frequently everywhere, except in very dry soil.

Buying guide

Young seedlings of the much admired, blue Asian species are invariably offered for sale in high summer by more ambitious herbaceous nurseries and at plant fairs. It pays to nurture them before planting them out at this time, even potting them on (using ericaceous or loam-free compost) and keeping them in an open, shaded cold frame; do not to let them flower in their first year.

There should never be any need to buy Welsh poppy seed, since without a shadow of doubt you will have an acquaintance that will be only too happy to give you seed from their own population, which you can simply cast about in suitable sites as soon as it is ripe.

LITTLE, ORANGE AND yellow Welsh poppies (*M. cambrica*) will grow absolutely anywhere if you let them, producing masses of papery flowers, which is particularly welcome in a shady place.

Recommended varieties

M. cambrica
Easy to grow *M. cambrica* is a short-lived, self-seeding, shade-tolerant perennial with brittle, bright green stems and leaves. Papery, yellow or orange flowers appear in early summer. H: 30–45cm (12–18in); S: 30cm (12in).

M. napaulensis
Numerous dull pink, dusty red, or purple flowers are borne in early and midsummer on this monocarpic, evergreen perennial with olive-green, bristly leaves. H: 1m (3ft) or more; S: 60cm (2ft).

M. betonicifolia 🏆
This deciduous, short-lived perennial has rosettes of bluish leaves. Its sometimes single, sometimes clustered flowers, borne in early summer, are generally clear, pale blue but occasionally white with white stamens. H: 1–1.2m (3–4ft); S: 50cm (1½ft).

M. punicea
It is well worth collecting the seeds regularly from this much sought-after, red-flowered Himalayan poppy, because it has a tendency to die after flowering. H: to 75cm (30in); S: 30cm (12in).

Plant care

Mulch Asian species with well-rotted leafmould, in spring, and protect them from slugs and snails.

For their first year, monitor perennials planted in a woodland garden extra carefully and water them as necessary. Also remove any buds, to prevent flowering while they are getting established in their first summer and developing a good root system.

Deadheading

To concentrate the plant's energy into bulking itself up, deadhead slightly tricky Asian poppies – unless you want to grow some from your own saved seed (see page 46).

Counter the invasive tendencies of Welsh poppies by prompt deadheading and do a complete cutback of the leaves and stems in early or midsummer. The subsequent regrowth of leaves and a few flowers is a refreshing sight in a late-summer garden.

Overwintering

Welsh poppy is totally hardy, but dies right back in winter. The Asian poppies are somewhat less reliable until they are well-established.

Propagation

Increasing all these poppies is relatively easy by seed sown either when just ripe or in spring. Asian species can also be divided after flowering (see page 44).

Welsh poppy self-seeds prolifically, and it has to be said, with great charm, but its taproots are surprisingly persistent and the plant can be invasive.

TRUE BLUE

The rich hues of the big blue poppies have often proved electrifying for gardeners and botanists alike. The mystique is further enhanced by tales about George Mallory collecting herbarium specimens of meconopsis on the Reconnaissance 1921 Expedition of Everest. He sadly died in an attempt to reach the summit of Mount Everest in 1924.

Monarda *Bergamot*

Also known as bergamot and bee balm, these tall perennials with aromatic leaves and bright flowers come from North America, where they are to be found in scrubby land and in light woodlands. Plants spread rapidly by underground stems and are somewhat prone to powdery mildew – old varieties more so than recent introductions. Flowers – in various shades of red, pink, or purple, and white – are borne in mid- to late summer and are both extraordinary and eye-catching. They consist of numerous upright, curving, tubular blooms around a central disc, and sit *en masse* on top of colourful bracts. Bergamot flowers are extremely attractive to bees and butterflies.

Site and soil

Grow in moderately fertile, moderately moist soil and full sun. Avoid sites likely to be waterlogged in winter as well as those that dry out rapidly in summer, which will make the plants more likely to develop mildew.

Bergamots spread sideways rapidly and their most vigorous, outer, new stems may invade the crowns of other plants, so allow them plenty of space.

Buying guide

Presumably because of their spreading habit, these plants are not happy in pots and are not commonly seen in garden centres. However, they are often found for sale very showily in flower at summer plant fairs. Otherwise grow them from seed in spring.

Plant care

Apply a moisture-retaining mulch in spring.

Powdery mildew may be a serious problem with some varieties. To an extent you can keep this at bay with a preventative spray of a systemic fungicide when the shoots are in the early stages of growth, and again a few weeks later.

To retain the vigour in a bergamot plant, lift it every other year in spring and remove the old, unproductive central section. In the gap thus created, improve the soil with a little, well-rotted organic matter and then replant some outer sections of underground stem. At all costs, avoid simply cutting away the invasive outside of the plant or

THE CURIOUSLY SHAGGY flowerheads of moisture-loving bergamot (*Monarda*) are irresistible to bees, hence its other common name of bee balm.

Recommended varieties

M. 'Gardenview Scarlet' ♔
One of the varieties known to be relatively mildew-proof is 'Gardenview Scarlet'. It produces bright green leaves and bright red flowers carried over pale green, pink-tipped bracts. H: 80cm (32in); S: 50cm (20in).

M. 'Violet Queen'
As the name suggests, this variety carries violet flowers over dull purple bracts and purple-tinged foliage. H: 90cm (36in); S: 75cm (30in).

M. 'Jacob Cline'
'Jacob Cline' is another relatively mildew-resistant variety. It has particularly large, tubular flowers held over deep red bracts and very dark green/red foliage. H: 90cm (36in); S: 75cm (30in).

M. 'Croftway Pink'
This is an older, taller variety of bergamot and one that is somewhat mildew-prone. Rose-pink flowers are surrounded by darker, pink-tinged bracts. H: 1.2m (4ft); S: 50cm (1½ft).

else you will end up with very little in the way of flowering shoots as you will have discarded the best bits.

Deadheading
Deadheading is definitely advantageous and will prolong the flowering period of the plant, although subsequent flowers will be smaller than the originals.

Overwintering
Bergamot is hardy as long as it is not growing in ground that becomes regularly waterlogged in winter.

Propagation
Increase bergamots from seed in spring.

Take small vigorous sections of underground stems (see above) in spring and transplant them immediately or else do this in autumn, potting them up and keeping them in a cold frame for replanting the following spring.

TEA TIME
It's something of an urban myth that bergamot (*Monarda* species) is used to make Earl Grey tea. While it is true that it smells so when the leaves are crushed, the real scent (or the one artificially substituted) is bergamot orange (*Citrus bergamia*). This is literally related to oranges and lemons, so quite different from the herbaceous perennial from North America. However, if you grow bergamot you can still make a refreshing cuppa. Put a few fresh leaves into a tea pot, add a light tea such as Darjeeling, pour on boiling water, and allow to brew. Even if this version of Earl Grey isn't quite to your taste, herbalists say that it can help treat colds and bronchial complaints.

Nepeta *Catmint*

Broadly referred to as catmints by gardeners, these aromatic-leaved, clump-forming, easy-to-grow perennials come mainly from rocky places in Europe and northern Africa, although some are from damper woodland and mountain regions in Asia. Flowers are extremely attractive to bees, and are usually blue-purple, white, or mauve-pink. *N. govaniana* has soft creamy yellow flowers. All catmints flower over a long period from midsummer.

CAT CONTENTMENT

From experience, eight out of 10 cats prefer rolling in catmint (the other two like a good chew)! Of course, what this frenzied activity is doing is releasing the pungent scent. For cats, this is now known to be more than just a pleasing smell. It contains a chemical called nepetalactone, which is a feline pheromone. So, excited by the sensation, it's not unusual to see other reactions such as meowing, purring, and biting. Curiously, the sensitivity to catmint has been found to be hereditary and not all cats respond. Australian moggies, in particular, are known to turn their noses up at it.

Site and soil

The more well-known catmints need a site that is in full sun and has well-drained soil. However, *N. govaniana* and *N. subsessilis* are fundamentally different, and they appreciate some light or dappled shade unless grown in moist soil.

Some of the clumpier, blue-flowered nepetas act as extremely effective stand-ins for lavender. The smaller varieties make good front-of-border plants, but larger ones can be irritatingly floppy.

Buying guide

N. x *faassenii* and *N.* 'Six Hills Giant' are easy to find at many garden centres in spring or autumn. For other varieties you will almost certainly need to visit a herbaceous plant specialist. Plant catmint as soon as you have acquired the new plants.

MASSED, MISTY FLOWERS of catmint (*Nepeta*) are a magnificent sight in high summer. If you take the shears to the whole plant when the blooms fade, it will flower all over again.

Recommended varieties

N. 'Six Hills Giant'
This is one of the best tall, strong-growing, blue catmints, although it is likely to flop. It produces dense spikes of lavender-blue flowers. H: 90cm (36in); S: 60cm (24in).

N. x faassenii ♀
Often confused with and sold as N. mussinii, this neat, pale lavender blue front-of-border nepeta is one that is most beloved by cats. It thrives after a midseason trim. H&S: 40cm (16in).

N. govaniana
Slightly less robust than other garden nepetas is this softly blowsy, elegant, perennial from the Himalayas, with its very pale green leaves and numerous loosely carried small, creamy yellow flowers. H: 90cm (36in); S: 60cm (24in).

N. subsessilis Nimbus
Loose, blue flower spikes and large leaves typify this stiffly upright plant, which flowers over a long period - through to late summer - if regularly deadheaded. H: 25cm (10in); S: 25cm (10in).

Plant care

The new shoots start to grow surprisingly early in spring, and it is these that are attractive to cats, which can destroy young aromatic leaves by nibbling at them. Cats also enjoy rolling in the middle of unsupported clumps later in the summer. To deter cats, place a disused upside down hanging basket over the crown of each vulnerable plant. This may also provide a modicum of support for the stems, which - particularly with the taller varieties - eventually become top-heavy and untidy. Catmints defy all attempts to stake them efficiently, and such limitation, anyway, makes them look somewhat unnatural.

In a hot dry site, catmint foliage frequently becomes infested with leaf hoppers (see page 216) as the flowers age (showing as pale dots all over the leaves - the insects hide on the undersides). It is aesthetically and practically beneficial, therefore, to rejuvenate the plants by shearing them to within a few centimetres of their crowns around midsummer, after which a surprisingly good second flush of foliage and flowers will be rapidly produced.

Cut old growth down once it has died back completely in winter. To reinvigorate catmint rootstock, divide clumps every two or three years in autumn (see page 44).

Deadheading

It is not necessary to remove individual flowers.

Overwintering

N. govaniana is slightly less hardy than other catmints, and dislikes winter-wet soil.

Propagation

Increase plants by division in autumn or by taking softwood cuttings in summer (see page 46).

Nicotiana *Tobacco plant*

All of the popular sweet-scented flowering tobacco plants grown as annuals in cool-temperate gardens are in fact biennials or short-lived perennials that flower well in their first year. They principally come from South America. Many open their flowers only late in the day, and most are night-scented, with tubular or trumpet-shaped flowers and slightly sticky stems and leaves. Some new, shorter, colourful bedding plants have virtually unscented flowers that are open all day.

Site and soil

Grow in well-drained, moisture-retentive soil that does not become too hot and dry in summer, in a site that gets a degree of shade during the day. Tobacco plants make good container plants – plant three or four in a large trough filled with John Innes No 3 potting compost mixed with a little organic matter.

Sow seed under glass in spring. Do not start seeds off too early as tobacco plant seed germinates extremely fast and seedlings become lanky and unmanageable. Before sowing, mix the fine seed with dry sand to ensure more even distribution. Harden off and plant out young seedlings and plug plants only once the nights warm up.

Buying guide

Some varieties can be bought as plug plants in spring. If you set your heart on tall, scented plants, look for white *N. alata* (also known as *N. affinis*) or pink-, red-, and white-flowered 'Sensation' (mixed), or even go for *N. sylvestris* (a shade-tolerant, heavily scented late flowerer with leaves the size of dinner plates). 'Domino Series' plants, universally available, are colourful unscented dwarfs.

Plant care

Protect young plants from slug and snail attacks (see page 215), also leaf hoppers (see page 216). Pinch out growing tips when the young plants are about 30cm (12in) high, if you want stockier, bushier plants. Water the plants in dry weather especially if they are grown in strong midday sun. Support tall varieties – a single cane for the main stem is usually sufficient.

Deadheading

Cut back lanky shoots in midsummer, when they have almost finished flowering, and feed the plants. They may then continue to flower until midautumn.

Overwintering

In a very sheltered garden some annuals may survive the winter. Cut them back the following late spring and they will regrow and flower within a few weeks, but may burn themselves out by late summer.

Propagation

Tobacco plant self-seeds, but the seedlings will germinate and flower very late in the season.

Recommended varieties

N. alata
The white flowers are deliciously night-scented over a very long period. If you grow only a few plants, this is the one to go for. It is offered in a range of named varieties. H: to 1m (3ft); S: 30cm (1ft).

N. 'Tinkerbell'
Each unscented but extremely delicate and pretty flower is lime-green on the outside and varying shades of terracotta inside on this relatively recently produced variety to grow from seed. H: 75cm (30in); S: 50cm (20in).

Nigella *Love-in-a-mist*

More often known by its English common name love-in-a-mist, *Nigella* is for many a cottage-garden essential. It is hard to believe, therefore, that it is a foreigner and that its natural habitat is wasteland around the Mediterranean. Upward-facing flowers are carried singly on top of and amid a froth of delicate, feathery foliage. As well as the familiar, blue-flowered varieties, there are now white varieties and some in darker shades of blue or pink. Love-in-a-mist lasts well as a cut flower.

Site and soil

Grow in full sun and well-drained soil that need not be particularly fertile. The delicate growth of love-in-a-mist can be overwhelmed if grown singly or in twos and threes and where it has to compete with stouter neighbours. It, therefore, looks best when grown in large swathes.

Sow seed *in situ* in autumn or spring in a weed-free patch near the front of a border. Thin out the seedlings as they grow, so that plants are eventually 15cm (6in) apart. Give autumn-sown seedlings some winter protection, or start off seeds in a pot or seed tray in a cold frame. Protect spring sowings with a cloche to start with.

Autumn-sown seedlings that survive the winter make the best and most robust plants the following year, flowering from early summer. Seed sown in the spring will be shorter in stature and may not flower until late summer.

Buying guide

All the major seed companies carry good ranges of seed - named varieties in individual colours as well as interesting mixtures.

Plant care

Love-in-a-mist is easy to grow and trouble-free, and not particularly attractive to slugs and snails once it is past the seedling stage.

Pull out and dispose of the dried stems and seed pods when they eventually collapse.

Deadheading

Live-heading - cutting for the house - will induce more flowering. However, many gardeners value the dried beige seedheads, which are very decorative in the garden once flowering has finished. Leaving seedheads also enables the plant to disperse its seed, which will germinate in early autumn and grow into plants that will flower the following year.

Overwintering

Not all autumn-germinated seedlings (for example, *N. papillosa*) will get through the winter, so if in doubt put a cloche over a patch of them.

Propagation

Once you have love-in-a-mist in your garden, you will never be without it as it self-seeds happily.

Recommended varieties

N. damascena 'Miss Jekyll'
The most popular and reliable love-in-the-mist bears open, sky-blue flowers that darken as they age. H: 50cm (20in); S: 20cm (8in).

N. papillosa 'African Bride'
For something slightly different and even more refined, try 'African Bride', which has black-centred, white flowers. H: 90cm (36in); S: 75cm (30in).

Oenothera *Evening primrose*

There are about 80 species of evening primrose. These annuals, biennials, and perennials, with flowers that are often scented, come from the meadows and prairies of North America. A rough, scrubby, bright yellow biennial has naturalized on roadsides and wasteland in the UK and occasionally it finds its way into gardens. Generally, after a year or two, any interest in it gives way to the delights of more refined perennial hybrids of evening primrose, which offer much more. Tall species will add a bit of zest to the back of the border, while shorter ones will flower in untidy profusion in the front row for several weeks in summer.

Site and soil

Grow in full sun or light shade and soil that is fairly rich and well drained. Evening primroses are relatively drought tolerant, flowering well in their first year.

Evening primroses can be grown from seed sown under glass in spring and will flower in their first year.

Plants tend not to expand rapidly, so set them fairly closely (30cm/12in apart) in threes (this particularly applies to back-of-the-border varieties) to achieve a good showing in the first year.

Buying guide

Evening primroses can be bought in garden centres as small, first-year plants in spring, the front-of-border types being easier to find than taller varieties.

Plant care

Protect young foliage from damage by slugs and snails (see page 215). In spring, apply a general fertilizer.

Provide support for tall evening primroses (such as fragrant *O. stricta*), which can become extremely lanky and floppy.

Cut stems down at the end of autumn.

Deadheading

All evening primroses are tricky to deadhead until you have learned to distinguish the developing seed pods from the flower buds. Unless you are sure, it is best to leave the plants to their own devices and just shorten stems once they have stopped producing flowers, cutting to just above an obviously emerging lower shoot.

Overwintering

Constant winter wet is the main enemy and may even kill evening primrose plants.

Propagation

Plants self-sow freely. Seedlings discovered in a bed or border re-establish themselves quickly if they are moved once they are large enough to handle. Divide *O. macrocarpa* in spring (see page 44).

Recommended varieties

O. 'Apricot Delight'
The reddish stems carry scented, very pale yellow flowers that fade to apricot then darken to salmon-pink, from midsummer to early autumn. H: 75cm (30in); S: 30cm (12in).

O. macrocarpa ♀
This is a sprawling, front-of-border evening primrose with masses of large, pale yellow flowers in summer. H: 10cm (4in); S: 40cm (16in).

Paeonia

Gardeners are divided on the subject of herbaceous peonies (there are shrubby ones as well, but not in this story). Some regard them as flower garden essentials, while to others they are space hungry and somewhat boring when not in flower. Indeed, their flowering season is short – species peonies such as the delicate, single-flowered Molly the witch (*P. mlokosewitschii*) flowering as early as midspring. The numerous peonies available to gardeners are cultivars of *P. lactiflora*, hybrids between a few Chinese cultivars that were introduced in the 19th century, and flower slightly later, in late spring and early summer. Stems are reddish; leaves dark green; and flowers, some of which are highly fragrant, are generally semidouble and double, in colours ranging from white to various shades of pink. The most recently introduced cultivars have stronger stems than the older ones.

Site and soil

Peonies grow best in full sun and well-drained soil enriched with organic matter and cannot cope with waterlogging. Most prefer soil that is neutral to alkaline, and need plenty of sun in order to flower well. They do not thrive in containers.

Site and plant peonies with considerable care, since they will need to be left alone for several years to get completely established and they do not respond well to being moved around.

Dig a deep planting hole, and incorporate plenty of organic matter into the soil at the bottom. Position the plant in the hole so its crown is about 10cm (4in) below ground level. Then carefully backfill around the plant. Water the plant well, and mulch around but not over the crown so it is not buried too deeply.

Buying guide

Peonies are often sold in pots but are also available as bare-rooted plants. Either way, they should all be planted during mild weather in winter, when they are dormant. Plants bought in spring will need extra care and watering during their first year.

Popular varieties such as *P. lactiflora* 'Bowl of Beauty' are widely available, but if you are looking for unusual peony cultivars you will need to go to a nursery that specializes in them.

THE HUGE AND exotic blooms of peony hybrids (in this picture, *P. suffruticosa* 'Duchess of Kent') are a relatively fleeting pleasure, but one of unparalleled beauty in the flower kingdom.

Plant care

It takes a peony about three years from the time of planting to get properly into its stride.

In spring, apply an organic mulch, in a circle 15-20cm (6-8in) wide, to inhibit weed growth and retain moisture around the roots of each plant.

Support peonies, particularly the heavy-headed, double-flowered varieties, with a metal grid, which can be placed high enough to support the flowerheads yet will largely be hidden by the plentiful foliage.

Leave foliage intact after flowering, and those of some varieties colour well in autumn. Then cut back all old leaves and feed the plant with a general fertilizer.

CAN YOU MOVE PEONIES?

The answer is yes, as long as they don't notice you have done it. Move them in autumn, when they are dormant, watering them well so that as much soil sticks to their rather coarse roots as possible, and also giving their roots a wide berth with your spade. Add organic matter to the soil where they are to be planted, and ensure that the crown of the plant is at the right depth (see left). Apply a general fertilizer. Moved plants may miss out on flowering the following spring.

Deadheading

To improve the look of the plant, remove fading flowers.

Overwintering

Peonies are extremely hardy.

Propagation

Peonies are most reliably propagated by division in autumn, but it is not simply a question of digging up the plant and slicing it with a spade. You should remove all soil from the roots so you can see what you are doing, and carefully cut the plant cleanly into sections, each of which must have a good root and four or five obvious growing points. Replant each with the growing points 10cm (4in) below the surface of the soil. New divisions may take two or three years to become fully established flowering plants.

Recommended varieties

P. lactiflora 'Duchesse de Nemours' ♀
Very fragrant, very double, white flowers are borne in early summer on this herbaceous perennial. H&S: 80cm (32in).

P. 'Buckeye Belle'
This early-flowering peony produces russet-red flowers during late spring and early summer. H: 90cm (36in); S: 85cm (34in).

P. lactiflora 'Festiva Maxima' ♀
In early summer, fragrant, double flowers open pale pink but fade to white with some red shading on the inner petals. H&S: 1m (3ft).

P. lactiflora 'White Wings'
The very beautiful, pure white, single flowers, held on reddish stems, are slightly fragrant and are produced in midsummer. H&S: 80cm (32in).

Papaver *Poppy*

All poppies share the same characteristics – ovoid, hairy flower buds that open to reveal short-lived flowers with papery, fluttery petals that are slightly crinkled at first, followed by pepperpot seedheads that are an attractive feature in a bed or border for weeks. Both annual and perennial poppies have a huge place in the hearts of most flower gardeners. Some annuals, including various forms of opium poppy (*P. somniferum*) and relations of the delicate field poppy (*P. rhoeas*), thrive in dry, scrubby places and need little or no nurturing to persuade them to produce a profusion of midsummer blooms. Others, such as the stately, tall, hairy-leaved and enormous-flowered perennial Oriental poppies, require a little more in the way of annual fussing and grooming, yet can become invasive. These poppies are in the same plant family as, but should not be confused with, *Meconopsis*.

Site and soil

Annual poppies will grow well in full sun and do not need very rich soil. Indeed, the combination of rich soil and an exposed site will produce tall, unstable plants that may keel over untidily and unattractively when in full flower after rain. Acid soil does not suit them.

Perennial Oriental poppies also need a lot of sun, and do best in moderately fertile, well-drained soil that is slightly alkaline. Very rich soil encourages the production of too much of their coarse hairy foliage. Mature plants tend to be somewhat invasive, so those with a really small garden should perhaps be wary of growing such poppies.

Buying guide

Many forms of annual poppy can be grown from seed sown *in situ* in spring, and several are cultivars of *P. rhoeas*. For example, *P.r.* 'Fairy Wings' (also known as 'Mother of Pearl') has mixed flowers that are principally soft pink and grey. For poppies in the red/yellow/orange colour spectrum seek out *P.r.* Shirley Group.

Perennial Oriental poppies are most often sold as named varieties in pots. You will find them at most garden centres in spring and autumn, or buy them online.

Plant care

Annual poppies need little in the way of care, apart from the thinning out of crowded, self-sown seedlings. Cutting

PRETTY BIENNIAL ARCTIC poppies (*P. croceum*), such as these in poster-paint shades of oranges and reds, make a particularly fine spectacle of themselves in early summer when planted *en masse*.

plants back in late spring will result in stockier plants that look slightly unnaturally bushy, with more flowers but also a lot of untidy foliage. Remove rogue, plain scarlet-flowering plants of *P.r.* 'Fairy Wings' if you intend to let them self-seed, otherwise red will gradually become dominant in the colony.

After flowering, cut back the unsightly foliage on perennial Oriental poppies. They may then snap back into action in early autumn and produce new leaves that may persist through a mild winter. In spring, groom these as more new growth starts, and also mulch the plant.

Support tall Oriental poppies with a grid of some sort, which can then be completely removed and used elsewhere when you cut back the plants in midsummer.

Deadheading

Remove the attractive seedheads on perennials before they disperse their seed, as unwanted seedlings become deep rooted quickly and are thus potentially invasive.

Snipping off immature seedheads and stems on annual poppies, with scissors, is a tedious but probably worthwhile, daily job that will prolong flowering. After midsummer, to rejuvenate the plants a little and encourage a few more flowers, cut out some of the flagging stems and give plants a soluble feed.

Overwintering

Some seeds of annual poppies may germinate randomly in autumn and, in a sheltered site, may be tough enough to get through winter.

Perennial poppies need no special care in winter.

Propagation

Allow some seedheads of annual poppies to form and let them disperse naturally, and also save some seed for spring sowing *in situ* (see page 46). Self-sown seedlings make very good, early, and profusely-flowering plants as long as they are not disturbed or moved around.

Propagate perennial poppies by basal cuttings in spring (see page 45). It is not a good idea to let them disperse their seed. It will not come true. Digging up, dividing the crowns, or moving Oriental poppies to a new site are jobs fraught with difficulty; it is virtually impossible not to leave invasive bits behind in the soil.

Recommended varieties

P. orientale 'Karine' ♀
The shell-pink petals are slightly pleated and shaded purplish red towards the centre of each flower on this relatively short Oriental poppy. H: 70cm (28in); S: 1m (3ft).

P. 'Türkenlouis'
This is a striking hybrid with large, fiery orange-red flowers that have fluttering, dramatically frilled petals. H: 90cm (36in); S: 60cm (24in).

P. commutatum 'Ladybird'
For something slightly different grow this annual poppy with its deep scarlet flowers, each petal boldly blotched with black on the outside as well as inside. H&S: 45cm (18in).

P. rhoeas 'Fairy Wings'
This delicate, fluttery, easy-to-grow annual poppy bears flowers in soft, misty colours enhanced by the odd enlivening touch of red in the mix. H: 90cm (36in); S: 30cm (12in).

Penstemon

There are few flowers that are harder to beat for sheer exuberance in the border than perennial penstemons, beloved by the Victorians and now, after a brief hiatus, again very much in fashion. Innumerable garden hybrids are available, and in the hands of dedicated plant breeders the number is growing. Coming originally from Central and North America, penstemons are not known for their reliable hardiness, nor for their longevity, so if you want to grow them successfully you really have to learn how to propagate them each year, as insurance against their winter demise. Most garden hybrids are evergreen and have a more or less woody base from which new green stems grow. Each stem bears thinnish, pointed leaves and is topped by short, vertical flower spikes. Individual flowers slightly resemble small foxgloves, and often have pale and attractively spotted throats.

Site and soil

Grow penstemons in really rich, perfectly draining soil that has had plenty of well-rotted organic matter dug into it. Position them in an open, sunny site and plant in small groups away from taller plants.

Buying guide

Penstemons are frequently sold in flower in high summer. Pot on such newly purchased plants and plant out the following spring. Cuttings can and should be taken from them at this stage (see right). It is worth remembering that the hardiest penstemon varieties tend to have the narrowest leaves – with the exception of *P. heterophyllus*.

Plant care

In mid- or even late spring (in a cold garden), snip away the old top growth – none of which is destined to flower that year, taking great care not to damage the new shoots beneath. These are particularly susceptible to damage from slugs and snails so give them ample protection (see page 215).

Also in spring, apply a mulch of organic matter around the base of the plant. Put in place supports for taller plants, using twiggy sticks or a metal grid.

By the end of summer in the border, penstemons will have developed a mass of rather untidy, soft green shoots, most of which will not have flowered. These

THIS, THEN, IS the real *P.* 'Sour Grapes'. If you want to grow the plant you thought was 'Sour Grapes', go on a hunt for *P.* 'Stapleford Gem' (see right).

must be left as protection for the new shoots, which will start to grow the following early spring. Never cut them down during autumn or winter.

Deadheading

Check plants every few days and snip away the top few centimetres of each spent flower shoot. Unless regularly deadheaded, penstemons will gradually run out of steam and stop flowering prematurely.

Overwintering

Winter damp is far more damaging to these marginally tender plants than winter cold, which is why good drainage is essential. It is not possible to protect plants from frost with a dry mulch, as penstemon are evergreen.

Propagation

Take softwood cuttings in midsummer (see page 46) or semi-hardwood cuttings in late summer to midautumn. Protect resulting new plants in a cold frame or unheated greenhouse during winter, and plant out survivors (with ample slug protection) in late spring.

A CASE OF SOUR GRAPES?

Back in the early 1990s, one penstemon was riding high in the public imagination and its name was 'Sour Grapes'. Or was it? The favoured plant had lilac and white flowers. And, indeed, this was the plant entered in the RHS's Trial, which ran between 1990 and 1992. However, doubts began to creep into the committee's minds as to whether it matched the original description from 1948 for "metallic blue and violet" flowers. Thankfully, one of the experts knew and grew the real plant and, after careful deliberation, a decision was made... the lilac penstemon really should be called 'Stapleford Gem', and the relatively unknown, inky violet penstemon took on the now-familiar name of 'Sour Grapes'. This has had one curious effect: 'Sour Grapes' has continued to remain the firm favourite with gardeners, despite being a different plant! The once-loved 'Stapleford Gem' is now definitely in second place with seven fewer suppliers in *RHS Plant Finder 2010-2011*. Both received the RHS's Award of Garden Merit from the trial.

Recommended varieties

P. 'Andenken an Friedrich Hahn' ♀
Often known as *P.* 'Garnet', this is one of the hardiest penstemons. It has rich red flowers. H: 75-90cm (30-36in); S: 60cm (24in).

P. 'Alice Hindley' ♀
'Alice Hindley' carries particularly pretty, mauve-and-white flowers from midsummer to midautumn. H: 90cm (36in); S: 45cm (18in).

P. heterophyllus 'Catherine de la Mare' ♀
This very eye-catching penstemon has bluish leaves and masses of dense sprays of small, blue-purple flowers in summer. H: 50cm (20in); S: 50cm (20in).

P. 'Raven' ♀
The darkest maroon-black flowers are somewhat relieved by their pale throats. H: 1-1.2m (3-4ft); S: 60cm (2ft).

Persicaria

To give this group of plants one of its other names, knotweed, might frighten some people off. However, some members of the genus stay where they are put – if you allow for relatively orderly expansion – and are extremely useful even in a fairly modest-sized garden. Of these, many are from China and the Himalayas, where they grow in damp, grassy, wooded places. The group is diverse, but many persicarias share certain obvious characteristics: taller perennials such as *P. amplexicaulis* form dense clumps of dock-like foliage and, in late summer, have leafy stems carrying tight, thin spikes of minute flowers. Others are even lusher, with softer, paler, fuller flower spikes. There are also ground-hugging persicarias, with flowers that are miniatures of those of their bolder cousins and with more or less evergreen foliage; some have leaves that colour rusty red in autumn.

Site and soil

Persicarias need a lot of moisture in the soil to do well. *P. amplexicaulis*, in particular, likes a cool site and dappled shade, and is especially happy when planted near water.

Plant persicaria in spring. Prepare the ground for the larger varieties well, adding masses of leafmould or garden compost to the soil. If, when you dig out a planting hole for a large persicaria, you find that the soil is bone dry 30cm (1ft) down, you should probably look for an alternative site. When grown in such dry soil and full sun, the lower leaves tend to become brown and unattractive.

Sow seed in a cold frame in spring. Small plants can be potted on in autumn and will be ready to be planted out singly the following spring.

Buying guide

Botanists have reorganized the names of these plants and other close relations, which has led to some confusion. You may still find plants labelled "Polygonum" or "Bistort" rather than *Persicaria*.

Being mild spreaders, these plants do not grow happily – nor do they look particularly fetching for long – in black plastic nursery pots. Therefore, only the small, low-growing varieties are easy to find at garden centres, and often they are in among the alpines. Buy the other varieties at specialist nurseries, online or by mail order.

THE METRE-HIGH red tails and lush leaves of *P. amplexicaulis* 'Atrosanguinea' are superb on a big scale. There are smaller varieties, some of them a mere 20cm (8in) high.

THE CALL OF THE NEW

Persicaria has a rising reputation. Once known as thugs that annexed large swathes of border, they are now proving just the thing for modern-style herbaceous plantings. There are new selections, such as tapering, rose-red *P. amplexicaulis* 'Firedance' from the Dutch perennial specialist Piet Oudolf and dark ruby *P.a.* 'Blotau' (see right) from British breeding legend Alan Bloom. For a sizable and long-lasting display, plant them with the tall *Eupatorium maculatum* Atropurpureum Group, the rusty orange *Helenium* 'Moerheim Beauty', and towering, willowy grass *Stipa gigantea*.

Plant care

In spring, trim back ground-hugging varieties and generally groom and tidy them up.

In spring, feed all persicarias with a general fertilizer, and mulch *P. amplexicaulis* and *P. bistorta* with a moisture-retentive organic mulch.

When they start to form flower buds, in midsummer, make sure plants get adequate water.

Cut down all stems in late autumn, when they have become unattractive.

Every two years or so, lift and divide the whole clump in spring or autumn (see page 44), throwing out the weaker centre and replanting the edges in reinvigorated soil. As with all moderately spreading plants, resist the temptation to reduce its sideways incursions by simply chopping away the outer edges of the plant each year – or you will end up with just the weaker, older core.

Deadheading

There is no need to deadhead these plants. Old flowerheads remain attractive for some time.

Overwintering

Persicarias are totally hardy and therefore need no frost protection.

Propagation

Divide plants in spring or autumn. They can also be propagated from seed sown in spring.

Recommended varieties

P. bistorta 'Superba' ♕
Bold, fattish, pale pink flower spikes adorn this lush plant, which looks good in a big border.
H: 75-90cm (30-36in);
S: 60cm (24in).

P. vacciniifolia ♕
This tiny, deep pink-flowered groundcover persicaria flowers in late summer and early autumn.
H: 15-20cm (6-8in);
S: 30cm (12in).

P. amplexicaulis 'Blotau'
Also known as 'Taurus', this is the best and boldest, true deep red persicaria for a cool, moist site in dappled shade. It has particularly bright green leaves. H&S: 1.2m (4ft).

P. affinis 'Darjeeling Red' ♕
Mildly spreading 'Darjeeling Red' forms an evergreen mat in a couple of seasons. The late summer, pink flowers darken as they age – as do the leaves.
H: 20-25cm 8-10in);
S: 60cm (24in).

Phlomis

Gardeners may be familiar with the relatively common shrubby phlomises such as Jerusalem sage (*P. fruticosa*) that light up the rocky hills around the Medterranean in spring and bear egg-yolk yellow flowers and felty, young leaves. They may be less aware, however, of their useful perennial relations – some of them from the Himalayas and China. These are tough, easy-to-grow plants, and some are in fact subshrubs, with distinctly woody bases beneath their soft herbaceous stems. All phlomis share certain characteristics. Their leaves are generally grey-green, leathery, and slightly hairy – certainly not refined. The pale or darker yellow or soft lilac pink flowers are similar to those of their relations, the deadnettles, being hooded and carried in dense whorls at intervals up the flower stems. Phlomis seedheads remain attractive and make a strong visual statement in winter.

Site and soil

Grow in well-drained soil and full sun, although as long as drainage is absolutely perfect *P. russeliana* will tolerate some shade.

Buying guide

Buy and plant phlomis in spring. Container-grown plants of yellow-flowered phlomis are generally easy to find, although there is occasional confusion as to whether they should be described as shrubs or perennials. Also labelling is sometimes erratic: subshrubby P. 'Edward Bowles', for example, is occasionally sold as herbaceous *P. russeliana*, yet their growth and flowering habits are ultimately quite different. If in doubt, delve among the lower leaves and look at the base of the plant.

Pink-flowered phlomis are inexplicably harder to source.

Plant care

Naturally lean-limbed phlomis, being a native of sunny, dry, scrubby places, is transformed into something quite substantial when grown in a cool-temperate climate and nutrient-rich soil. There is no need, therefore, to feed these plants.

After flowering, prune woody-based species that have become lax, to keep them in bounds.

Cut back the lofty flower stems of *P. tuberosa* only when they are no longer attractive. *P. cashmeriana* tends to die

DISTINCTIVE PHLOMIS FLOWERS – these ones belong to the familiar Mediterranean shrub, Jerusalem sage (*P. fruticosa*) – give way to long-lasting, attractive seedheads.

back by the end of summer, to reappear in spring, so needs no special care.

At the end of winter, cut back the flower stems of *P. russeliana*, which is virtually evergreen. If necessary, as it spreads rapidly, in spring lift and discard the weakest, central part of the clump, then replant it. Otherwise, in late spring, grub out and spruce up its spreading, untidy foliage as growth begins in earnest.

WHAT IS A SUBSHRUB?

Herbaceous plants are defined as those that produce new, soft, green growth from ground level each growing season, while shrubs are plants that quickly develop a substantial framework of woody growth, from which they produce new growth each year. A subshrub is one that has a very low, even ground-hugging woody base from which substantial amounts of greenery grow. Many herbs and aromatic plants fall into this category, including lavender, sage and its relations such as some species of *Phlomis*.

Deadheading

Removal of flowers is unnecessary and somewhat inappropriate, as the stems and long-lasting seedheads create quite a large part of the impact of these plants.

Overwintering

Phlomis shrubs, subshrubs, and herbaceous perennials need no winter protection.

Propagation

Divide herbaceous species in spring (see page 44). Increase shrubs and subshrubs from softwood cuttings taken in summer, using a sandy compost and keeping them in a cold frame (see page 46).

Recommended varieties

P. russeliana ♈
With large leaves and two-tone yellow flowers, this phlomis is exceptionally easy to grow and has a long season of interest. It does spread, however. H: 100cm (39in); S: 80cm (32in).

P. 'Edward Bowles'
This rather spreading subshrub has soft grey, woolly shoots and leaves. It will not produce many of its yellow flowers unless grown in full sun. H&S: 75cm (30in).

P. tuberosa 'Amazone'
Each year this tuberous perennial produces numerous long stems bearing darkish, serrated-edged leaves and purple-pink flowers. H: 1.5m (5ft); S: 75cm (2½ft).

P. cashmeriana
Beautiful and rather more refined *P. cashmeriana* has silver-backed and edged, slightly pointed, green leaves and dense, pink flowers. H: 90cm (36in); S: 60cm (24in).

Phlox

This is a glamorous genus, mostly from North America, that adds colour and substance, and a degree of scent, to the flower garden at an otherwise difficult time, when it may have lost its summer flush and its autumn glories are only just awakening. In addition to upright border perennials that originate from moist, riverside places (such as *P. paniculata* and slightly smaller *P. maculata*), there are smaller, slumpier, little phlox that flower rather earlier in the season. Flowers are borne in fulsome, showy terminal clusters in colours ranging from white and pale lilac to magenta through all the pinks imaginable. Some flowers have centres in a contrasting colour, and there are even some recent introductions that are rather dizzy bicolours. Despite their traditional border associations, some of the more vivid coral-red, tall phloxes are suitable for inclusion in an exotic planting scheme.

Site and soil

Phlox thrive in sun or partial shade and well-prepared, fertile soil, into which plenty of organic matter has been incorporated. Grow tall border plants in a site that is not too arid in high summer, otherwise they may fall victim to powdery mildew. Smaller *P. divaricata* seems more tolerant of dry soil.

Plant all phlox in spring or autumn.

Buying guide

Phlox are easy plants to find at garden centres during spring. Border phlox of slightly smaller stature such as *P. maculata* 'Alpha' (lilac pink) and *P.m.* 'Omega' (white) are the most commonly offered for sale. A greater selection can be found for sale at specialist herbaceous plant nurseries.

Plant care

In spring, feed with a general fertilizer, then mulch around plants with compost or well-rotted manure. Protect new shoots from attack by slugs and snails.

Support the tallest border phlox in a way that does not cramp their elegant style. A simple, loosely encircling wire hoop or sticks and string are sufficient, as long as they are placed high enough around the tall stems, which become top-heavy when densely in flower – with potentially disastrous consequences after heavy rain.

PHLOX PRODUCE THEIR flowers in mid- and late summer, breathing new life into flower gardens after their peak. In this all-white scheme, phlox mingles happily with the flowers of cenolophium.

Frequently cut out any inconsequential shoots that are clearly not going to be robust enough to flower, to improve the look and vigour of the remainder, as well as to increase air circulation around the plant. This thinning may also keep powdery mildew at bay.

After it has finished flowering, give *P. divaricata* a soluble feed, to boost growth.

In spring, dig up phlox that start to produce shorter stems or smaller flowers (after three years or so) and replant in reinvigorated soil.

PHLOX AND THE "CHELSEA CHOP"

Phlox provide the best example of a plant that can have its size and flowering time manipulated by being cut back in early summer (see page 42). By experimenting you can find a method that suits you: either cut back all stems (by roughly half is usual), or just a few, or even just those on one side of the plant. Whatever you do, those shortened stems will branch, and subsequently produce slightly smaller flowerheads, two or three weeks later than would otherwise be the case.

Deadheading

Tweak off the first large heads of flowers on border phlox as they fade. They will then produce a smattering of later flowers.

On smaller front-of-border phlox, snip off spent flowers immediately after flowering has finished, by midsummer. This encourages the plant to make a new mini-thicket of shoots. These will not flower, but will make these semi-evergreen plants more dense and robust.

Overwintering

Border phlox are totally hardy and need no winter protection. Small phlox dislike winter wet and may, therefore, be short-lived.

Propagation

Divide border phloxes in spring or autumn (see page 44). Increase smaller phlox such as *P. divaricata* by softwood cuttings in summer (see page 46) or by the removal and potting up of straggly stems that have rooted themselves.

Recommended varieties

P. paniculata 'Monica Lynden-Bell'
Very delicate, pale pink flowers, with darker centres, are borne in mid- to late summer on this medium-height phlox. H: 75cm (30in); S: 40cm (16in).

P. paniculata 'David'
This vigorous phlox is possibly the most magnificent of the whites, and one that has a reputation for being resistant to powdery mildew. It flowers in mid- and late summer. H: 1.2m (4ft); S: 60cm (2ft).

P. divaricata 'Chattahoochee'
The colouring of this sprawling, dark-stemmed phlox is most attractive. The blue-mauve flowers become almost luminous at dusk, in early summer, and each has a darker, inky magenta eye. H: 30cm (12in); S: 45cm (18in).

P. paniculata 'Blue Paradise'
As long as you accept that "blue" in horticulture often means lilac/blue, then the dark-eyed flowers of 'Blue Paradise' will delight you during mid- and late summer. H: 100cm (39in); S: 40cm (16in).

Polemonium

The main flowering period of these delicate-looking, semi-evergreen perennials is usefully in late spring and early summer, when lilac-blue or white, sometimes pink, and occasionally yellow blooms are carried in loose clusters on tall, straight, branching stems. Many are from damp meadows in various parts of the northern hemisphere, and several species and hybrids are suitable for flower garden use. Polemoniums are grown not just for their attractive, five-petalled flowers but also for their almost geometrically arranged leaflets, resembling rungs on an old-fashioned step ladder, which gives the plant its common name of Jacob's ladder. Although hardy and perennial, polemonium plants are relatively short-lived.

Site and soil

Grow in fertile, well-drained but moist soil. Most polemoniums prefer a shady site. In drier soil the foliage will die back somewhat in summer, and in full sun it may scorch in some species.

Success with polemoniums is all about planting in a plot that suits that particular plant. In the right spot it is a relatively trouble-free plant. When planted in conditions that are not ideal, plants may become susceptible to powdery mildew. Some polemoniums like to share territory with, for example, hostas and hellebores.

Sow commercial seed in pots in a cold frame during spring or autumn.

Buying guide

Plants are normally on sale in spring, when the foliage is at its best and they are also in, or about to, flower. Plant them straight away.

Plant care

Tend plants carefully for their first season in the garden.

If the leaves do die back and become unsightly in hot summer weather, cut them away and apply a soluble feed to the soil around the roots, to encourage the growth of new leaves – and occasionally a further flush of flowers.

Deadheading

There is no advantage to deadheading sterile hybrids except to tidy up the plant after flowering. Species and named varieties that set seed should be deadheaded.

Overwintering

Polemoniums are hardy and need no winter protection.

Propagation

Divide polemonium in spring or autumn (see page 44). Seed collected or self-sown from non-sterile species and cultivars does not come true.

Recommended varieties

P. 'Lambrook Mauve' ♡
This sterile hybrid forms a robust clump of handsome leaves from which erect, branching flower stems emerge in late spring. The plentiful, open-faced, pale lilac-mauve flowers have yellow centres. H: 45cm (18in); S: 30cm (12in).

P. 'Northern Lights'
More compact than the above is 'Northern Lights', a sterile hybrid with pale blue, scented flowers that are produced from spring, on and off throughout the summer. H: 30-40cm (12-16in); S: 30cm (12in).

Polygonatum

A strong statement is made in shady parts of the garden by these elegant, rhizomatous woodland plants from the northern hemisphere. The most commonly grown hybrid, familiar to many gardeners as Solomon's seal, quickly spreads to create a small forest of green, arching, leafy stems with small, pendulous, green-tipped, white flowers carried daintily in summer. Stems and leaves remain attractive for the remainder of the season – the leaves turning vivid yellow in autumn.

Site and soil

These plants revel in moist woodland shade, and look particularly attractive where their flowers can be reflected in water. They also tolerate dry shade and will grow in fairly rooty woodland soil as long as it is well mulched in spring.

While in no way invasive, polygonatum does spread slowly. It is one of those plants that, after being planted in a specific place, to a large extent likes to decide for itself where it will grow comfortably and spreads out its rhizomes accordingly.

Recommended varieties

P. x hybridum ♀
Most gardeners are familiar with this elegant plant, producing sturdy stems and large, green leaves. White flowers are followed by bluish fruit. H&S: 1m (3ft).

P. odoratum var. pluriflorum 'Variegatum' ♀
With foliage that is edged in creamy white and young stems that are reddish, this plant makes a statement of a different kind. It has scented flowers, in small clusters, followed by black berries. H&S: 1m (3ft).

Buying guide

Plants are most frequently to be found for sale in nurseries in very early spring, when emerging stems – as thick as a little finger – will indicate the extent of the rhizomes in the pot. Plant them immediately.

Plant care

During their first growing season in a new site, take particular care of plants, ensuring they do not dry out.

In spring, apply a leafy organic mulch and protect new growth, which is moderately attractive to slugs. Also keep an eye out for the activities of Solomon seal sawfly. A preventative spray of all stems with a systemic insecticide as the leaves are emerging is effective.

Cut stems to the ground once they are no longer attractive, in late autumn.

Deadheading

Removal of the leafy flower stems is not appropriate, as they form much of the polegonatum's architectural presence in the garden.

Overwintering

Polegonatum rhizomes need no winter protection.

Propagation

Divide plants in spring, making sure that each piece of the rhizome has a visible growing point (see page 44).

Collect and sow seed when fresh in autumn, in a cold frame, after having removed the flesh. Plants raised from seed will take three years to flower from germination.

Potentilla

The herbaceous potentillas that originate from Asia and the Himalayas are colourful plants from the rose family and are thus related both to the long-flowering garden shrubs (*P. fruticosa*) with which gardeners may be familiar, and to strawberries. Their flowers somewhat resemble those of both. They are small, shallowly cup-shaped, usually five-petalled, and carried in loose sprays well above the generally palmate, somewhat hairy basal leaves. There are also varieties with double flowers. Flower colours are pale yellows, various shades of orange-red, through to some, such as *P. thurberi* 'Monarch's Velvet', that are a currently fashionable deep rich red. Most of these clump-forming potentillas produce a major flush of flowers in early and midsummer, and will go on flowering intermittently for the rest of the growing season.

Site and soil

Grow in moderately fertile soil and an open, sunny site, although potentillas are not fussy. Many of them make somewhat sprawling border plants.

Sow seed in pots in autumn, sprinkling it on the surface of sandy compost and covering it with grit.

Buying guide

Potentillas, particularly of the red varieties, are fairly easy to locate at garden centres, in spring or autumn. It would seem that yellow-flowered varieties, such as *P. recta*, are generally harder to track down and are more often found in the lists of specialist nurseries. Plant them in spring or autumn.

Plant care

Potentillas are trouble-free plants that need little attention apart from an annual mulch in spring and the application of a general fertilizer, also in spring.

Support the stems of clump-forming, semi-erect *P. recta* with a metal grid, as it carries slightly congested flowers, which can become top-heavy. Staking is usually unnecessary for those potentillas that have wide-spreading flowering stems – they simply lean attractively into neighbouring plants.

When plants die back completely in winter, cut away old stems and leaves.

SUN-LOVING POTENTILLAS carry masses of colourful flowers, which look like tiny, single roses, throughout summer.

Deadheading

Remove stems that have flowered right down to ground level, to induce the plants to produce a few fresh flowering shoots during the remainder of the season.

Overwintering

Potentillas are hardy and need no protection in winter.

Propagation

Increase potentillas by dividing the fibrous root system in early spring (see page 44).

Collect seed when ripe and sow it in autumn or spring. However, seed saved from cultivars will not come true.

BEST FOOT FORWARD

Potentillas mean many things to many people. Some cannot shake the image of jaded supermarket car park shrubberies, but these bushes can perform very well when cared for. Others will think only of the cottage-garden favourites, which bear brightly coloured blooms in spring and have more universal appeal. " 'Gibson's Scarlet'... no member of the race has flowers of so dazzling a scarlet... profuse... indispensible," wrote William Robinson, an enthusiastic Victorian advocate of natural gardening. While the colour and relaxed habit appealed to his sensibilities, many of the native potentillas seem to have other virtues. For example, *P. anserina* is often called traveller's ease or traveller's joy as its ground-hugging, silver leaves make inviting cushions on the roadside. Indeed, one 18th-century traveller also remarked: "Your carriers wear the leaves in their shoes, which keep them cool and prevent a too immoderate sweating of the feet, which causes a soreness in them."

Recommended varieties

P. 'Gibson's Scarlet' ♀
Neat, clump-forming 'Gibson's Scarlet' has large, brilliant scarlet flowers with darker centres carried above soft foliage for several weeks during early summer. H&S: 45cm (18in).

P. 'Gloire de Nancy'
When in bloom with its semidouble, deep red flowers, this old cultivar develops a sprawling habit. H&S: 45cm (18in).

P. recta var. sulphurea
The numerous, very pale creamy yellow flowers on this hairy perennial open a few at a time on erect stems over a long period from early to late summer. H: 60cm (24in); S: 45cm (18in).

P. 'Arc-en-ciel'
This is another variety with slightly untidy flower stems over clumps of green foliage. Flowers are red, yellowing with age. H&S: 30cm (12in).

Primula

Primulas are an enormous and varied plant family. The garden perennials dealt with here range in flowering height from a few centimetres to more than half a metre but all produce flower stems from a basal rosette of leaves. Some of the smaller primulas are recognizable as relations of the native European primrose and are shade tolerant, with open flowers produced on short stems, each with five fused petals. Auricula primulas, from the mountains of central and southern Europe, are also small in stature, have somewhat fleshy leaves, and bear distinctly marked flowers. Others, originating from damp sites in dappled shade in China and the Himalayas, are taller, the flowers of some (familiar as Candelabra primulas) being produced in whorls up stems that are often dusty-looking or (as in the Sikkimensis primulas) that have scented, hanging bells resembling giant cowslips.

Site and soil

Grow primrose types in dappled shade and moderately fertile, moisture-retentive soil that has been improved with leafmould or other organic matter.

Border auriculas do best in quite heavy soil, object to waterlogging or periods of drought, and prefer shelter from midday sun.

Tall Asian primulas prefer very moist, slightly acid soil enriched with well-rotted manure, in a site that has some midday shade.

Apart from double-flowered primrose varieties, most primulas grow easily from seed. This can be sown on the surface of seed compost in trays in an open cold frame as soon as it is ripe, or in spring.

Buying guide

Buy primulas as small plants in spring, when they are often sold in flower. Larger, moisture-loving primulas are also sold in flower in summer, when buyers can be sure of precise flower colours. Plant immediately.

Plant care

Look after young plants particularly well during their first season, while they become established. Prevent them from setting seed so that they put their energies into establishing good roots.

THIS PARTICULARLY PRETTY hybrid primrose – *P.* 'Guinevere' – produces a non-stop profusion of lilac-pink, yellow-centred flowers over bronze-tinged leaves from early to late spring.

If they are unsightly, remove old leaves on primrose-type primulas, when they die back during late summer. Plants will come back into leaf in autumn, when moisture levels in the soil rise.

Other primula types die back in early winter and remain dormant until the following spring.

PRIMULA PERFORMERS

Auriculas are the glamorous cousins of the native primrose. They are one of the few flowers to come in every colour of the rainbow, plus black and white. What generally keeps them in the realms of accepted good taste is their neat, uniform petals. The original *P. auricula* heralds from the mountains of central Europe, but the diversity comes from more than 400 years of breeding work by enthusiasts (once known as florists). There are now thousands of cultivars. Even in the 19th century there were hundreds of forms and, where no expense needed to be spared, they were arranged in spectacular auricular theatres. These tiered shelves were filled with pots so the plants look rather like a seated audience. A surviving example can be seen at Calke Abbey in Derbyshire, UK.

Deadheading

Deadheading will not encourage further blooms. Most primulas (apart from double varieties) produce masses of seed. Seed can be saved for sowing, but by simply leaving seedheads standing you will be encouraging the colony to spread naturally.

If seedheads of cowslip (*P. florindae*) and those of Candelabra primulas are not removed, they will remain attractive throughout the early part of the winter.

Overwintering

Primulas sold as garden plants are hardy and need no special winter protection.

Propagation

Sow seed as soon as it is ripe, or in spring.

Divide primrose types after flowering or in autumn (see page 44). Take basal cuttings (see page 45) or remove offsets, from mature plants, in autumn or spring.

Recommended varieties

P. vulgaris 'Lilacina Plena'
Also charmingly named 'Quaker's Bonnet', this form of primrose produces a profusion of double, lilac-pink flowers in spring. H: 10cm (4in); S: 15cm (6in).

P. bulleyana ♀
In late spring and early summer, whorls of coppery orange flowers are carried in tiers. This Candelabra primula has midgreen leaves. H&S: 60-75cm (24-30in).

P. florindae ♀
Above rosettes of red-ribbed, pale green leaves, rise tall stems of yellow or buff/orange flowers that smell strongly of dried ginger, during mid- and late summer. H: 1.2m (4ft); S: 1m (3ft).

P. auricula 'Cathy McLay'
A pretty auricula that flowers in April and May, each bloom having a distinct white 'eye'. H&S: 10-20cm (4-8in).

Pulmonaria *Lungwort*

Lungworts are an interesting group of plants that belong, together with forget-me-nots and comfrey, to the borage family and are mainly of European origin. They have two distinct periods of interest during the growing season. The first is in spring, when their slightly hairy stems carry eye-catching clusters of funnel-shaped flowers, in various shades of purple, blue, red, and white, above small and fairly insignificant leaves. Once the flowers have finished, the plants take on another life completely, producing a mass of wide and pointed, far more imposing leaves that form dense groundcovering clumps. Individual leaves are often spotted or substantially marked with white or silver, and they remain attractive for the rest of the growing season. The leaves are distinctly rough and can cause allergic reactions in some people.

Site and soil

Grow lungwort in full or light shade and leafy, fertile, moist but not waterlogged soil. It is, therefore, ideal flowering ground cover for a woodland garden.

Buying guide

Their shade-tolerance makes these popular plants and generally at least one variety can be found for sale in garden centres. Those with plain green foliage are generally sold in flower. Buy and plant them in spring.

Plant care

Protect new growth from attack by slugs and snails (see page 215).

When grown in very dry sites, lungwort is somewhat susceptible to powdery mildew. Tweak out the odd unsightly leaf individually; if the problem is acute, remove and dispose of all the blemished leaves and give the plant a deep drench using a soluble feed. This should ensure that a new batch of leaves is produced, most probably cleaner than before.

Once flowers have faded, remove them together with their stems (remember to wear gloves). When dealing with an established clump, grasp the stems and give them a sharp tug. Watering the plants afterwards and giving them a soluble feed will ensure that they produce plenty of large, attractive, new leaves.

PULMONARIAS ARE VALUED for their shade tolerance and early flowers – vivid blue in the case of *P.* 'Mawson's Blue'. The attractive foliage comes into its own once flowering is over.

In late autumn, clear away old foliage and apply a leafy organic mulch to the plants.

Deadheading

If flowers are not removed promptly, pulmonarias self-seed rampantly.

Overwintering

Lungwort is hardy and needs no winter protection.

Propagation

Divide plants after they have finished flowering, or in autumn (see page 44).

Self-sown seedlings may not come true, but you may find some interesting leaf and flower colour variations appearing as a result of letting plants seed about.

LIKE FOR LIKE

The name lungwort is not a pretty allusion, although it is one that would have offered hope to our ancient ancestors. It comes from the practice of "sympathetic magic", whereby it was thought that one thing can influence another if it bears a resemblance. In this case, the blotched leaves were seen to be similar to ulcerated and diseased lungs and could, therefore, help cure these ailments. As a result, Jerusalem sage (*P. officinalis*) must have been widely grown in Britain, as it has long since escaped apothecaries' gardens to grow wild in woods and hedgerows. Usually these are blue-flowered plants, but purple and white forms are occasionally seen. There are also rarer species. Unspotted lungwort, *P. obscura*, which as its name suggests has dark green leaves, is found in a few places in Suffolk, while the narrow-leaved lungwort, *P. longifolia*, grows wild in the New Forest and the Isle of Wight.

Recommended varieties

P. 'Blue Ensign'
This is a lungwort grown for the deep, true blue of its flowers. These are followed by clumps of plain, dark green leaves. H: 25-35cm (10-14in); S: 60cm (24in).

P. 'Trevi Fountain'
Cobalt-blue and deep pink flowers and silver-spotted leaves are characteristic of 'Trevi Fountain'. H: 30cm (12in); S: 60cm (24in).

P. 'Diana Clare'
If silvered foliage is what you are after, this is one of the most elegant varieties with its slender, pointed leaves. Light blue-purple flowers are produced from early to late spring. H&S: 30cm (12in).

P. saccharata 'Leopard'
The leaves on this more or less evergreen variety, which is also known as Bethlehem sage, are boldly spotted with silver, and the flowers are pink-red. H&S: 45cm (18in).

Ranunculus

To suggest that some gardeners deliberately plant buttercups and celandines (*R. ficaria*) in a border or woodland garden may seem a little odd, if not downright foolhardy in the case of celandines, as they are widely regarded as uncontrollable weeds. However, within this large and botanically complex genus, which grows extensively in the wild in temperate regions of the northern hemisphere, are several members that make quaint, attractive, and even quite glamorous, yellow- or cream-flowered garden perennials. The exception is Persian buttercup (*R. asiaticus*) – a tender, tuberous buttercup, which has flowers in all shades of red, orange, and yellow as well as white. The members of this vast and diverse buttercup family have different characteristics and have been categorized according to their cultivation requirements, which is helpful when deciding where to plant them.

Site and soil

Those species recommended here are useful in different parts of the garden.

All varieties of *Ranunculus aconitifolius*, *R. ficaria*, and *R. constantinopolitanus* need to be grown in moist but well-drained, humus-rich soil (group 1). *R. aconitifolius* and *R. ficaria* are shade-dwellers and thus suitable for a woodland garden, while *R. constantinopolitanus*, along with *R. bulbosus* (group 2), grow better in a sunnier bed or border.

Tender, tuberous *R. asiaticus* is cultivated as a colourful addition to an annual border or else can be planted in containers. It produces wonderful cut flowers. Start its tubers under glass. They need a sunny site and very well-drained soil when planted out.

CHILDHOOD CHOICES

The name *Ranunculus* comes from the Latin for frog, *rana*, because many species grow in damp places. So it is fitting that Beatrix Potter fills the illustrations for her tale about the friendly frog, Jeremy Fisher, with images of *Ranunculus*. There are buttercup leaves around the doors of his house, and the flowers appear near the water rats that disturb his lunch of butterfly sandwiches.

THESE BIG, BLOWSY buttercup-relations – tuberous, tender *R. asiaticus* – can be started under glass and planted out in the garden in summer. They are often grown simply for cutting.

Buying guide

None of these perennials is commonly found in garden centres, so will probably have to be bought from specialist nurseries. The exception is, perhaps, bronze-leaved *R. ficaria* 'Brazen Hussy', which is sold extensively as a single specimen – almost as a novelty plant – in small pots in spring, when at its most eye-catching. Plant it as soon as acquired.

Purchase small plants of *R. asiaticus* as plug plants in spring, or as tubers in autumn. Start them off in pots in a greenhouse in spring before planting them out in the garden.

Plant care

Given the right growing conditions, the perennials are trouble free, needing no more than a spring mulch of organic matter.

R. asiaticus is generally treated as an annual and replaced each year.

R. bulbosus naturally dies away in mid- to late summer, subsequently producing fresh foliage in autumn.

R. ficaria dies back completely by midsummer, vanishing without trace and only reappearing in very early spring the following year. Care should be taken not to dig up and accidentally disperse its bulbils when the plants are dormant.

Deadheading

Remove flowers and old flower stalks to improve the look of border buttercups; it will also slightly extend their flowering season.

R. asiaticus is an ideal cut flower, and cutting will effectively extend its flowering period.

Overwintering

Apart from *R. asiaticus*, these plants are hardy and need no special winter protection.

Propagation

Increase plants by division in spring or autumn (see page 44), or by removal (where appropriate, as in the case of *R. ficaria*) of basal bulbils. *R. constantinopolitanus* resents disturbance of any kind.

Recommended varieties

R. aconitifolius 'Flore Pleno' ♀
Shade-loving 'Flore Pleno' makes a clump of green, aconite-like foliage, with the tight, creamy white, double flowers carried in profusion above. H: 60cm (24in); S: 50cm (20in).

R. bulbosus 'F M Burton'
Another refinement of a common buttercup, this one has single, pale lemon flowers borne over hairy basal leaves. Plants are dormant between summer and autumn. H: 25cm (10in); S: 20cm (8in).

R. ficaria 'Brazen Hussy'
The whole of this plant – with its startling bronze leaves and its little, yellow flowers– is lustrous for a few weeks in spring. H: 5-10cm (2-4in); S: 20cm (8in).

R. constantinopolitanus 'Plenus'
This is the pretty, double form. It has clumps of softly hairy, dissected leaves in spring, and tight green-centred flowers in midsummer. H: 30-60cm (12-24in); S: 30cm (12in).

Rheum

These ornamental relations of edible rhubarb come from China and Tibet. They are much admired for their large and imposing basal leaves, which gradually unfold and power upwards on colourful stalks from their rhizomatous bases in spring. They also produce somewhat raggedy panicles of tiny, red flowers, which appear in midsummer on lofty stems. Rheums make handsome if somewhat space-greedy, specimen plants in grand and exotic planting schemes.

Site and soil

Rheums are lushest and most beautiful when grown in sun or partial shade and deep, rich, moist soil, although they will grow reasonably well in drier sites. As is the case with all red-leaved plants, rheums look extremely impressive where their fresh, new foliage can be seen backlit by sunshine.

Buying guide

Small rheums such as the hybrid R. 'Ace of Hearts' are easy to come by at garden centres. To find plants of larger varieties, you may need to visit an herbaceous or water-garden specialist nursery. Buy and plant rheums during spring or autumn.

Recommended varieties

R. palmatum 'Atrosanguineum' ♈
The whole plant is reddish in spring and the huge, deep green leaves remain red beneath. Deep pink-red flowers appear in summer. H&S: 2m (6½ft).

R. palmatum 'Red Herald'
'Red Herald' has darker red flowers and new growth that is even more purple-red than R. palmatum 'Atrosanguineum'. H&S: 2m (6½ft).

RHUBARB AND ROQUEFORT
As well as making fabulous foliage plants, R. x hybridum is the custard-friendly rhubarb. There are more than 130 cultivars held in the National Collection at RHS Garden Wisley, UK. And, in Yorkshire, UK, the forcing of rhubarb is a speciality that has been recognized with an EU designation. This puts the tender, pink stems at the same culinary heights and importance as Roquefort cheese and Parma ham.

Plant care

Rheums are tough plants with woody bases and are generally trouble free.

In spring, apply a moisture-retaining mulch.

Once the flowers have faded, cut the whole plant down to the ground, to encourage the production of new leaves. Also give a soluble feed. Then in autumn cut down any new foliage that may have grown.

Deadheading

Rheum does not need deadheading unless done so for aesthetic reasons.

Overwintering

Rheums are hardy and require no winter protection.

Propagation

Increase plants by division in early spring (see page 44).

Rodgersia

Moist woodlands in Myanmar, China, Korea, and Japan are the native habitat of these rhizomatous, clump-forming perennials with their huge and impressive foliage. Their heavily veined, crinkled leaves can be as much as 50cm (20in) across, with leaflets up to 25cm (10in) long. From midsummer onwards, plants produce dense panicles of tiny, petalless flowers in spikes up to 1m (3ft) tall. Flowers are long-lasting and in shades of dark ruddy pink and dull white.

Site and soil

Grow in partial shade and any moist, rich soil. When happy with their growing conditions, the rhizomes will spread mildly.

Although they are most often associated with a waterside planting, rodgersias are also suitable for the damper edges of a woodland garden. Their dramatic foliage would be impressive, too, in a more exotic, but of necessity slightly shaded, garden.

This is not a plant that can be squeezed into a tiny space, however, since the shade cast by the massive leaves, which get larger each year as the plant matures, could cause problems for plants growing nearby.

Buying guide

These plants are relatively easy to find in garden centres, particularly those that specialize in waterside planting. Buy and plant them in spring or autumn.

Plant care

Rodgersias are trouble-free, although slugs may damage young leaves (see page 215).

In spring, apply a moisture-retaining mulch with leafmould or composted bark, particularly if plants are not grown in soil that is permanently damp naturally. Brown-edged leaves indicate that the plant is too dry at the roots, so take remedial action.

When they become unsightly in late autumn, cut down dying leaves and old flower stems.

Deadheading

Deadheading is not beneficial or necessary, and the ruddy brown seedheads remain an attractive feature of the plant throughout early autumn, but remove any brown or scorched leaves for aesthetic reasons.

Overwintering

Although rodgersias are hardy, they should not be planted where frost can damage the new spring foliage.

Propagation

Propagate by division in spring (see page 44).

Recommended varieties

R. aesculifolia ♛
As the name suggests, the leaves very much resemble those of horse chestnut. Leafstalks and leaf veins are reddish brown, and the flowers are pink. H&S: 1m (3ft).

R. pinnata 'Superba' ♛
The bronze young leaves become dark green, glossy, heavily veined, and crinkled. The flowers are bright dark pink. H: 1-1.2m (3-4ft); S: 75cm (2½ft).

Rudbeckia

Perennial rudbeckias from North America are useful and attractive daisies, all of them yellow, some of them extremely tall, flowering more or less from early summer until the first frosts. Those that flower in mid- and late summer are particularly invaluable. Some plants are slightly undisciplined, spreading via rhizomes, while others are clump-forming. Smaller and stockier annual rudbeckia (*R. hirta*), which occasionally lasts a second season in a sheltered site, has the advantage that it can be slotted easily into a mainly perennial planting scheme without looking obviously, dizzily, annual. Many of these, too, are yellow, but there are also orange-red and bronze varieties – comfortable colours for late-season flowers. Rudbeckia flowers have a central disc raised into a substantial cone, which varies from yellow to black via purple. More than one variety may be called black-eyed Susan.

Site and soil

Grow in a sunny, open site and moderately rich, reasonably moist but well-drained soil that has been improved with organic matter.

Perennial rudbeckias look powerful when grown in large swathes, space permitting, and seem natural in a grassy planting scheme. When planted in a border, the tallest varieties will lean towards the light if they receive too little of it, and they are hard to support with any degree of subtlety.

Annual rudbeckias look particularly good if planted in large swathes, among grasses, and they are equally useful planted in twos and threes as gap fillers in a perennial border.

Sow seeds of perennial rudbeckias in containers in a cold frame in early spring. Annuals grown from seed should be started under glass in spring.

Buying guide

Plants of medium-sized rudbeckias (such as *R. fulgida* var. *sullivantii* 'Goldsturm') are easy to find at garden centres; others are less so, and it may be necessary to look further afield at specialist nurseries. Buy and plant rudbeckias in spring or autumn.

Most seed companies have various annual rudbeckias (hybrids of *R. hirta*) in their catalogues.

AT LEAST ONE clump of strong yellow daisies, such as these rudbeckias, should have a place in every garden. They positively bask in the last of the summer sunshine.

GOING FOR GOLD

Rather confusingly, golden *Rudbeckia* are commonly called coneflowers, just like *Echinaea*. However, the botanical name distinctly commemorates Olof Rudbeck (1630–1702). He was one of the most remarkable Swedes of all time – a botanist, anatomist, antiquarian, and founder of the Uppsala Botanic Garden. Fittingly, many rudbeckia are now equally distinguished in the garden. In recent years, cultivars such as 'Goldsturm' have become widely grown, and the range of orange- and brown-flowered annuals has increased to include reds and cream-tipped petals.

Plant care

In spring, give perennial rudbeckias a mulch together with a feed of general fertilizer. Tall plants may need the support of twiggy sticks if grown in exposed sites. In late spring, prune shorter, bushier plants down to about 45cm (18in) (the so-called "Chelsea chop", see page 42).

In autumn or winter, cut stems down to the ground.

Every couple of years, in spring, replace the central section of rhizomatous spreaders with some offcuts from their outermost growth.

If cut down and tidied up in spring, annuals may flower a second year.

Deadheading

Removal of faded flowers will improve the look of the plants and, particularly in the case of *R. hirta*, will promote more flowering.

Overwintering

Perennials are fully hardy. *R. hirta* may survive mild winters if given the protection of a dry mulch.

Propagation

Divide perennial rudbeckias in spring or autumn (see page 44), or sow their seed in early spring. Saved seed from annuals does not come true, and self-sown seeds will germinate too late to flower in the current season.

Recommended varieties

R. fulgida var. sullivantii 'Goldsturm' ♈
Probably one of the best and most popular of the rudbuckias, it is robust and very free-flowering with golden-yellow, black-centred flowers. H: 75cm (30in); S: 30cm (12in).

R. maxima
Stems up to 2–3m (6½–10ft) high are produced on this big border beast, which bears enormous flowers with slightly drooping petals. H: 2–3m (6½–10ft); S: 1.2m (4ft) or more.

R. hirta 'Indian Summer' ♈
This is a short-lived perennial grown as an annual, with the possibility that it will go on for another year. H: 60cm (24in); S: 30cm (12in).

R. 'Herbstsonne' ♈
Late-flowering 'Herbstsonne' carries sulphur-yellow flowers, each with a green cone, between late summer and midautumn. H: 1.5–2.5m (5–8ft); S: 60–75cm (2–2½ft).

Salvia *Sage*

The *Salvia* genus is a large and diverse group, from Europe, northern Africa, North and South America, and Asia, that includes shrubs (some hardy, some tender), subshrubs (woody-based perennials), herbaceous perennials, and a few annuals. Not unnaturally, European and North American sages tend to be more hardy than those from hotter climates. Sages belong to a family that includes deadnettles; they have very recognizably similar flowers, with distinct upper and lower lips, and the stems are square rather than rounded. Flowers of many perennial salvias are in the blue/mauve/ purple range, but there some vibrant reds, too. Foliage is often highly aromatic, and not always pleasantly so, as anyone will know who has accidentally brushed past the tall and ethereally beautiful but treacherously malodorous *S. sclarea* var. *turkestanica*.

Site and soil

Most sages need to be grown in full sun and well-drained soil that is not too rich.

Buying guide

Buy sages when good plants become available. Common culinary sage in its various forms is easily found in garden centres, either as very small plants (probably growing in slightly unsuitable, loam-free compost) or in 1 litre pots. Visiting a specialist herb grower can be an eye-opener, however, and will provide an introduction to many other more unusual species and varieties.

Herbaceous perennial sages are numerous, too, and several nurseries specialize in unusual varieties, some of them rather tender.

Plant care

Vigorously growing sages bought during spring will undoubtedly have spent time with the protection of a polytunnel and should, therefore, be carefully hardened off before planting.

Plant all sages in spring and tend them extra carefully for their first year. Thereafter a topdressing of garden compost or rotted manure, applied in spring, is all the plants may need.

In early spring, prune shrubby sages grown for their leaf colour, to keep them in bounds and encourage

AN OLD, COTTAGE-GARDEN favourite, *Salvia nemorosa* 'Ostfriesland' (East Friesland) bears masses of rich purple flowers on compact plants over a long period in midsummer.

them to produce pristine new foliage – but this will result in few flowers.

Once their flowers have faded, lightly trim back those sages grown principally for their flowers and give them a soluble feed.

SAGES AND LEAF HOPPERS

Many sages and their relations (nepeta, for example, which has similarly aromatic leaves, and phlomis), become mysteriously shabby, particularly during hot summer, with pale, mottled leaves. The damage is the work of tiny, sap-sucking leaf hoppers that live and breed on the backs of the leaves. They are noticeable only if you tap the plant, whereupon they fly up *en masse*. Once identified, spraying plants with a systemic insecticide sorts out the problem very quickly. Or you can trim the plants back, which helps physically to remove some of the insects, and/or use a contact insecticide that is suitable for food crops.

Deadheading

Deadhead or lightly shear sages, to promote a second flush of flowers.

Overwintering

As long as they are not planted in soil that is winter-wet, or in very heavy clay, sages are quite hardy – apart from those that originate in hotter climates. Take insurance cuttings of any sages that are borderline tender (see below).

Propagation

Take softwood cuttings from non-flowering shoots in the growing season (see page 46). Divide herbaceous clumps during spring (see page 44).

Recommended varieties

S. officinalis 'Purpurascens' ♀
One of the most ornamental of the culinary sages, 'Purpurascens' is a subshrub with dustily purple leaves and deep blue-violet flowers. H: 45–60cm (18–24in); S: 100cm (39in).

S. x jamensis 'Raspberry Royale' ♀
Autumn sage is a shrubby hybrid with slightly sticky leaves and spikes of small, bright raspberry-pink flowers in summer and autumn. H&S: 60cm (2ft).

S. candelabrum ♀
Blue-purple, typical sage flowers are carried on long outward leaning stems, so this subshrub needs space to look its best. It has stems that are reddish at the base and wrinkled leaves. H&S: 75cm (30in).

S. x sylvestris 'Blauhügel' ♀
This is a clump-forming, blue-flowered perennial sage, 45cm (18in) high, with dense, branching stems. It blooms in early summer and again later if sheared after flowering. H&S: 45cm (18in).

Sanguisorba

Being subtle-coloured, stylish, and of a suitable scale (apart from perhaps the tallest species), sanguisorbas are useful for a small garden or border, or even for a wilder, grassy garden. Big, bruising, show-off border plants these are definitely not, and nor are they vista-blockers – their slim stems and flowers adding admirable lightness to any planting scheme. The culinary herb salad burnet is a dwarf member of the sanguisorba tribe, which originates in the northern hemisphere, where several species grow in a variety of damp places – moist meadows and riversides. Leaves are divided into numerous small leaflets that have toothed edges and are almost feathery-looking. In some species, the foliage turns an attractive, bright yellow in autumn. The flowers – wine-red, pink, or white – are bottlebrush in style and upright or softly drooping, depending on the species.

Site and soil

Grow in moist soil and sun or part shade. Sanguisorbas dislike very dry soil and hot sun.

They definitely need to be planted in groups rather than singly. Small, new plants that throw up only two or three flower stems can get a little lost in the general border hurly-burly.

Whether they look good and earn their keep or not depends largely on whether sanguisorbas stand straight and tall. It would seem that the more substantial the clump, the easier it is to support the stems.

Sow sanguisorba seed in containers in a cold frame in spring or autumn. Germination may be erratic.

Buying guide

Not commonly found in garden centres (apart from the culinary herb), sanguisorbas are more readily sourced from specialist herbaceous nurseries. Buy and plant them during spring or autumn.

Plant care

These are easy to grow, trouble-free plants if given the correct, moist, cool growing conditions.

In spring, spread a moisture-retaining mulch of compost around sanguisorba plants, and then give them a feed of general fertilizer. Also put in place a veritable forest of twiggy sticks, to support plants as they grow taller.

ONE OF THE tallest and stateliest of this airy-flowered, moisture-loving tribe is *Sanguisorba canadensis*. It bears flowers like upright, white candles on 2m (6½ft) high stems.

WIDER APPRECIATION

Say the word "sanguisorba" and, until recently, few gardeners would have much to comment. The genus was known through a widely grown herb – salad burnet – which adds a nutty and cucumbery sharpness to garnishes. Curiously, the herbalist Gerard thought salad burnet would "make the hart merry and glad, as also being put in wine, to which it yeeldeth a certaine grace in drinking". Today, though, there is a growing interest in the other species and cultivars. One nurseryman noted: "Burnets are among rising stars of the horticultural stage. Needless to say, they are exemplary when used in association with grasses." Leading the way is *S.* 'Cangshan Cranberry', which produces dusky red flowers on self-supporting stems between early and late autumn. Another fuzzy pink to look out for is *S.* 'Blackthorn', which can reach 2m (6½ft) high. Although *RHS Plant Finder* listed, both are not widely available yet, but they are beacons for the great potential of sanguisorba for the future.

Deadheading

Those species that age gracefully (with good colour) can be left standing until autumn, when they are cut back to ground level.

Deadhead other species, to smarten up the plants. It may also promote some extra flowering and will prevent excessive self-seeding, which can be a problem.

Overwintering

Sanguisorbas are hardy and need no special winter protection against frost.

Propagation

Divide plants in spring or autumn (see page 44). Collect and save seed (see page 46), then sow it in autumn or spring. Where several species are grown together, saved seed is likely to throw up some odd hybrids. If required, transplant self-sown seedlings in spring.

Recommended varieties

S. officinalis 'Arnhem'
Above a clump of long green leaves, the early to midsummer flowers form a mass of dark maroon, ovoid buttons that age to rust-brown and are held on wiry stems. H: to 2m (6½ft); S: 75cm (2½ft).

S. hakusanensis
This Japanese species has large, grey-green, divided leaves and stems carrying large, drooping, vivid pink, fluffy flowers in mid- to late-summer. H: 40–90cm (16–36in); S: 40cm (16in).

S. 'Tanna'
Somewhat like a miniature *S. officinalis*, 'Tanna' has dark, button-like flowers appearing over mounds of neat, blue-green foliage. It is relatively drought tolerant. H: 30–50cm (12–20in); S: 30cm (12in).

S. albiflora
Grey-green foliage and upright, showy, slightly fluffy, white flowerheads typify this short form. H&S: 60cm (24in).

Saxifraga

The plants in this huge genus, many of which are shade tolerant, come from mountainous regions of Europe, Asia, and North America. Some are evergreen with tough, almost leathery rosettes of leaves, while other evergreens form tight hummocks, with foliage that could best be described as mossy-looking. There are also deciduous saxifrages, with almost fleshy, shiny, lobed leaves, which are often beautifully coloured, and very obviously related to the heucheras. Flowers of saxifrages come in various shades of pink, red, and white, are five-petalled, and often star-shaped. In low-growing species, the summer flowers appear to clothe the matted foliage and are borne singly, on short stems, whereas they are held above the shiny foliage in soft clusters in taller species, such as shade-loving *S. fortunei*, which is one of the last woodland plants to flower, in early autumn.

Site and soil

Grow mossy-leaved saxifrages in light shade and moist yet well-drained, neutral to alkaline soil. When sited in soil that is too dry, mossy saxifrages will die back unattractively. They make good plants for the edge of a shady path, and several varieties with different coloured flowers growing together look eye-catching. They will also spread about in a moisture-retaining gravelly area.

Rosetted *S. fortunei* grows best in a dappled woodland setting in leafy soil that can be slighty acid. This moisture-loving species will be much smaller, leafing up and flowering later, if it is too dry.

S. x urbium is the least demanding of all saxifrages, capable of growing well in complete shade and even in poor soil. *S.* Southside Seedling Group plants look effective planted on their own in a trough or pot filled with John Innes No 3 potting compost mixed with a little organic matter.

THE HUMMOCKY GROWTH and mossy foliage of many saxifrages are perfect in gravel and on the edge of stony paths. The little, massed, starry flowers are the icing on the cake.

Species can be cultivated from commercial seed sown in autumn in pots in an open cold frame.

Buying guide

Most garden centres sell a small selection of mossy and rosette-forming saxifrages, many of which are not specifically named. They are usually in tiny pots accompanied by various other small alpines. The best plants are always available in spring. *S.* Southside Seedling Group plants are often sold while in flower during late spring or early summer. All saxifrages should be planted as soon as they are acquired.

Plant care

Saxifrages are generally trouble-free plants, and the rosette-forming species are surprisingly tough.

In spring, mulch around plants with organic matter. The exception is *S. x urbium*, which seems to need nothing whatsoever in the way of nurturing.

Protect against vine weevil grubs (see page 216), which may be a problem particularly for saxifrages that are grown in containers.

Deadheading

The removal of whiskery, old flower stems on *S. x urbium* and on *S.* Southside Seedling Group plants definitely improves the looks of each, although it does not result in the production of further flowers.

Snipping off the old flowerheads of mossy saxifrages is one of those jobs that gardeners with not enough to do might undertake.

Overwintering

Saxifrages are hardy but constant winter wet can take its toll, and some mossy saxifrages will die back somewhat. *S. fortunei* dies right back in winter and may not start to grow again until midsummer.

Propagation

Divide mossy-leaved saxifrages in spring (see page 44).

Detach individual rosettes of foliage, with a little section of stem attached, in spring. Press them gently into the surface of sandy compost in a pot, where they should root within a few weeks.

Recommended varieties

S. 'Firebrand'
This mossy-leaved saxifrage has particularly fine, glowing red flowers over compact growth.
H: 1-3cm (½-1in);
S: 15-20cm (6-8in).

S. Southside Seedling Group ♀
The leaf rosettes of this saxifrage are attractive in their own right. Arching stems bear red-blotched, white flowers in early spring. H: 30cm (12in); S: 20cm (8in).

S. x urbium 'Miss Chambers'
A rather more refined version of London pride, this saxifrage has notched leaves and red-eyed flowers. H: 30cm (12in); S: indefinite.

S. 'Cumulus' ♀
Large, white flowers appear in summer over a tight mound of mossy foliage. H: to 5cm (2in); S: 25cm (10in).

Scabiosa

Pincushion-flowered plants seem to hold a special place in many gardeners' hearts. These charming plants from dry, sunny parts of the Mediterranean region grow well among other cottage-garden plants and are exceptionally useful for the cut-flower gardener. A succession of flowers, generally blue, pink, creamy white, or maroon, are produced for weeks on end from early summer. The fine flower stems stand well above the often long, slightly hairy leaves at ground level.

Site and soil

Grow in full sun and slightly alkaline soil that is well drained. Lighten up heavy soil with plenty of organic matter, before planting in spring or autumn.

Buying guide

Perennial scabious plants are generally easy to find in garden centres and specialist nurseries in spring or autumn. Eye-catching, blue- and black-flowered perennials have become extremely popular and fashionable. They, too, are easy to find in garden centres, sometimes rather prematurely in flower and very possibly in pots of slightly unsuitable, loam-less compost in early spring. Plants bought like this should be carefully hardened off before being planted out later in spring.

Sow seed in spring, in containers in a cold frame.

Plant care

These plants are generally trouble-free but can lose their vigour after two or three years. Dig them up and either divide them (see page 44) or simply replant them in

THE WAVING PINCUSHION heads of scabious can look softly effective when massed together in a grassy garden.

reinvigorated soil. *S. atropurpurea* is extremely short-lived so does not need such treatment.

In spring, put in short twiggy sticks to stop front-of-border plants from sprawling unattractively. Grow taller plants through a metal grid, which will give their lower stems just a little bit of backbone.

In winter, cut stems down to ground level. Plants retain a few basal leaves at this time of year. In spring, as new leaves appear, remove the old foliage, to tidy up plants.

Deadheading

Cutting flowers for use in the house encourages a succession of floral interest all summer. Deadhead any blooms that you do not want, even though this means some fairly time-consuming snipping. It is, however, a task that is definitely worth the effort for all scabious.

Overwintering

Scabious are hardy unless grown in winter-wet soil or heavy clay that has not been sufficiently opened up with organic matter at planting time.

Propagation

Increase plants by division in spring or by taking basal cuttings in spring (see page 45). Saved seed can be sown in pots in a cold frame in spring.

IT'S ALL IN THE NAME

Rarely available as a cut flower today, *S. caucasica* was widely grown in Britain between the world wars. It has long stems and a long-flowering period, making it an ideal cut flower. The strong blues were always the most popular, but competition to supply those blooms was a cut throat business. As a result one Solihull salesman suggested to prominent Bristol breeder, James House, that it would be easier for him to sell large quantities if a scabious was named after him. The salesman's name was Clive Greaves, and the plant chosen has gone on to outperform all other blue cultivars in reliability and productivity. Ironically, the rather puritanical James House would probably not have named it 'Clive Greaves' if he knew more of the man – he had a weakness for women and wine.

Recommended varieties

S. caucasica 'Clive Greaves' ♛
Plentiful flowers are produced in mid- and late summer on this large-flowered, lavender-blue scabious. It has long, greyish basal leaves. H&S: 45-60cm (18-24in).

S. atropurpurea 'Chile Black'
For "black", of course, read maroon. On this outstanding, short-lived perennial are white "pins" that adorn each perfect "pincushion". H: 60cm (24in); S: 30cm (12in).

S. 'Butterfly Blue'
This is a little, prolific-flowering, lilac-blue scabious, 30cm (12in) high, for the front of the border. If deadheaded, it flowers non-stop from early summer onwards. H&S: 40cm (16in).

S. columbaria subsp. **ochroleuca**
An invaluable feature of this cream, small-flowered scabious is its ability to distract the eye from neighbouring flowers that may be past their best by midsummer. H&S: 1m (3ft).

Sedum *Iceplant*

Quite how spectacularly successful, sun-loving *Sedum* gained the common name iceplant is anybody's guess. However, most plants in this genus, of which there are 500 or so species, come from temperate or cool regions north of the equator, and some of the distinctly ground-hugging ones grow mostly in tight spots – in crevices, on poor mountain soils, and even on roofs. Meanwhile, the clump-forming species are an imposing lot: stems and leaves are fleshy, frequently stout and upright, and in grey-green or (in many recently introduced varieties and hybrids) dusty pink or purple. Tight, flat heads consisting of numerous small, star-shaped flowers, in white, creamy pink, or various shades of red, open in late summer and early autumn, and many of them change colour attractively as they age. The flowers are extremely attractive to bees and butterflies.

Site and soil

Grow in an open, sunny site, not crowded by other leafy border plants, in moist but well-drained, moderately fertile soil. Clump-forming iceplants grown in rich soil tend to become floppy.

Iceplants make an interesting, almost architectural statement in the garden both when in flower and growing upwards and outwards in spring and summer, and again in autumn until late winter when their handsome flowerheads are dry, browning, and old. These plants look good in a gravel garden or among grasses and make an imposing feature at the front or on a corner of a border.

Buying guide

These are popular plants, and in spring it is easy to find them in most garden centres, particularly those with colourful stems and leaves.

Iceplants are often sold looking delicious in bud, yet the flower colours of some of the newer introductions may be somewhat at odds with the soft, mellow, leaf/bud colours.

Before purchasing, gently turn the chosen plants out of their pots to check for the presence of vine weevil grubs, which will show as a distinct lack of young, white roots on the edge of the rootball. Reject any that are not pest-free. Plant iceplants in spring or autumn.

IN MID- AND LATE summer, the buds of sun-loving sedums such as *S.* 'Herbstfreude' ('Autumn Joy') are handsome in their own right. The moment the colourful flowers open, the bees move in.

BEWARE OF THE ENEMY

Vine weevil grubs adore the roots of iceplants, and snails may damage their lower leaves, particularly if they become hemmed in by other plants. There is also a moth that lays its eggs among the shoot tips in early summer, and their caterpillars quickly spin gauzy webs and destroy flower buds; if not checked in time – by cutting off the shoot tips and spraying the plant as soon as the webs are seen – the whole plant will drop its leaves.

Plant care

Although tough, iceplants need protecting from slugs and snail damage (see page 215), and also attack from vine weevils (see page 216).

In spring, divide clumps that have become too wide and cumbersome or, if they are vigorous and floppy, lift them and replant without reinvigorating the soil. (The action of disturbing their roots seems to retard growth usefully.)

Iceplants respond brilliantly to the "Chelsea chop" (see page 42), and if cut down by half in early summer will produce more (but smaller and, therefore, less heavy) flowers on shorter stems.

When the seedheads become unsightly, cut the stems right down using secateurs. Do not leave this task until spring, as it will become difficult to avoid damaging the emerging new growth.

Deadheading

Remove flowering heads only if damaged, as the brown seedheads look attractive throughout winter.

Overwintering

Iceplants are hardy in a cool-temperate climate. In winter, however, do not inadvertently cover the crown of the plant with an organic mulch, which might encourage it to rot.

Propagation

Divide in spring (see page 44) or take stem cuttings in spring or early summer (see page 45). Stems root easily – even in a glass of water. Iceplants may also self-seed, but seedlings will not necessarily come true.

Recommended varieties

S. telephium (Atropurpureum Group) 'Purple Emperor' ♀
This upright hybrid has red stems and deep purple leaves. Large flowerheads open to pink-purple flowers that darken with age. H&S: 50cm (20in).

S. spectabile 'Brilliant' ♀
Pale green stalks and leaves are topped by star-shaped, bright pink flowers in late summer on this clump-forming perennial. H&S: 30-45cm (12-18in).

S. telephium (Atropurpureum Group) ♀
Purple leaves, red stems, and flowers that open soft pink are produced by this iceplant. It has a slightly open growth habit. H&S: 70cm (28in).

S. 'Vera Jameson' ♀
The tiny flowers on this iceplant are particularly eye-catching, each being darker pink in the centre, while the stems are purple and the leaves are pinkish. H: 20cm (8in); S: 40cm (16in).

Stachys

Stachys is a diverse genus of plants from temperate regions of the northern and southern hemispheres, with numerous common names that may be familiar: betony, woundwort, lambs' ears, and hedge nettle. Indeed, stachys is related to deadnettles, and many of them have leaves that give off a distinctive, somewhat foetid smell when crushed. It is the ground-hugging, rhizomatous perennial *S. byzantina* and its various forms with which most gardeners are familiar. It makes an excellent weed-smothering ground cover at the front of a border, especially when flanking a sunny path. However, there are some clump-forming, more upright perennial stachys that are useful in a flower border as well. All stachys leaves are often softly hairy, and the flowers, borne on often densely tiered spikes, are small, tubular, and pink or purple.

Site and soil

Grow in full sun and somewhat poor, sharply draining soil those species with hairy leaves as well as those with grey- and felty-leaves such as *S. byzantina*. In all these plants, nutrient-rich soil produces overtall, heavy flower spikes.

Other species tolerate less than full sun, and moist or even waterlogged situations.

Those gardeners who just like the ground-hugging, silver leaves of *S. byzantina* take the trouble to remove the flowers since they become somewhat heavy and untidy after heavy rain. Yet there is an alternative variety, *S.b.* 'Silver Carpet', that they could use and which scarcely flowers at all.

Buying guide

Grey-leaved, ground-hugging *S. byzantina* is commonly sourced from garden centres and can be bought all the year round. It seems to establish more reliably, however, if bought and planted in spring. Indeed, plants acquired on a dreary autum/winter day will be highly unattractive and bedraggled and remain so until the following growing season is well under way.

Other species and varieties are harder to track down, although their historic "medicinal" status means that they may be found in specialist herb nurseries. Plant these also during spring or autumn.

UPRIGHT PERENNIALS SUCH as *S. officinalis*, with dense spikes of purplish flowers and weed-smothering foliage, are less well known than the ground-hugging varieties with silvery lambs' ears leaves.

REFLECTING PAST NEEDS

The term *officinalis* is a medieval Latin one meaning "of use in the apothecary". It indicates that the many plants described thus originally had a medicinal use. In addition to stachys, lavender and sage are just two further examples of plants with an *officinalis* species.

Plant care

Protect plants well from slugs and snails (see page 215), which are particularly partial to the new growth of stachys; otherwise plants may take some time to get into their stride in spring.

In spring, as growth starts, remove unproductive older rhizomes from *S. byzantina* and tidy away any remaining foliage made unattractive from winter cold.

Deadheading

Removal of old flower spikes tidies up plants considerably in late summer, but it will not extend the flowering season.

Overwintering

Plants are hardy and need no frost protection. However, if *S. byzantina* is grown in a less than ideal site (that is, with imperfect drainage coupled with no winter sun), it may perish.

Propagation

Increase stachys by division in spring (see page 44).

ADAPT AND SURVIVE

The British may complain about the weather, but wet summer days are essential to keep borders blooming. In parts of the world where rain is scarce, plants have adapted to cope with the hot, dry conditions. *Stachys byzantina*, from the Middle East, shows several of these cunning ploys. The silver leaves reflect light, and so heat, away from the plant. The dense coating of hairs that gives the plant its common name, lambs' ears, help trap water evaporating from leaf pores (stomata), conserving moisture. Finally, the thick rhizomes store water just like a cactus, but on a smaller scale. The resulting plant thrives in sunny, dry borders, even in the UK.

Recommended varieties

S. officinalis 'Hummelo'
This front-of-border variety has dense rosettes of slightly hairy, evergreen leaves with toothed edges. In early summer to early autumn, it produces spikes of deep purplish pink flowers. H: 20-40cm (8-16in); S: 40cm (16in).

S. byzantina
From a rhizomatous mat develop loose rosettes of felty, green foliage above which are carried thick, equally felty spikes of tiny, insignificant, pink flowers from mid- to late summer. H: 30-38cm (12-15in); S: 60cm (24in).

S. macrantha 'Robusta' ♔
The broadly oval, green leaves are wrinkled and hairy. Dense whorls of purple-pink flowers are produced between late spring and late summer. H&S: 60cm (24in).

S. byzantina 'Big Ears'
As the name suggest 'Big Ears' is a more imposing form of *S. byzantina*. It has huge, felty "ears", each up to 25cm (10in) long, and purple flowers. H: 45cm (18in); S: 60cm (24in).

Tagetes *Marigold*

The sharp colours and aromatic, even pungent foliage of annual marigolds, natives of South and Central America and Africa, are not to everyone's taste. However, there is no denying that these easy-to-grow annuals are useful for adding long-lasting splashes of orange and russet-red to a hot, sunny planting scheme from late spring to autumn. Marigold hybrids fall into several groups. African marigolds (derived from *T. erecta*) all have densely double, single-coloured, pompon flowers in yellows and oranges. French marigolds (derived from *T. patula*) carry smaller, double flowers that are coloured and marked yellow, red-brown, and orange. Afro-French marigolds have some of the characteristics of each, bearing numerous, smaller, semidouble, yellow/orange flowers, often marked red-brown. Delicate-flowered Signet marigolds are grown in greenhouses as a whitefly deterrent.

Site and soil

Grow in full sun and moderately fertile soil.

Sow seeds in a seed tray or pot filled with loam-based seed and cutting compost, in early spring. Cover them with glass until they germinate. Harden off seedlings before planting them out once there is little risk of frost. You can also sow marigolds *in situ* in late spring but they will flower later than those raised under glass.

THERE IS NO DENYING you get a lot for your money with annual marigolds. From a packet of seed (and with a little effort) you receive brilliant flowers that simply go on and on and on...

Buying guide

All the major seed companies sell a wide selection of seeds, most as mixtures, some as single varieties. New varieties carrying interesting, different colour variations are produced by seed companies almost every year, it would seem.

Marigold seedlings, sometimes already prematurely in flower, can be bought in midspring from garden centres, mail order companies, and online. If appropriate, pot them on so they can develop more until it is time to plant them out in the garden. Gradually harden them off first, however.

Plant care

Pinch off the first flower to make each plant bush out and become sturdier.

During the growing season, give container-grown marigolds a weekly feed with a soluble, high-potash fertilizer (such as tomato food), to encourage the continuous production of flowers.

Towards the end of summer, pompon-flowered marigolds may fall victim to downy mildew (botrytis) after periods of wet weather. Snip off and destroy all affected flowers at once (see page 214).

Once marigolds have become unsightly, pull them up and put them on the compost heap.

Deadheading

Remove marigold blooms constantly to ensure that they keep flowering through to autumn.

Overwintering

Marigolds will have died back completely before winter.

Propagation

Seeds from hybrids will not come true, so there is no point in saving seed to sow the following year, unless a seriously dizzy mixture is what you want.

Recommended varieties

T. patula 'Lemon Gem'
This small Signet marigold makes a mound of fine foliage that is almost hidden, from late spring to early autumn, by masses of small, lemon-yellow flowers. H: 23cm (9in); S: to 30cm (12in).

T. patula 'Favourite Red'
The single, mahogany-red flowers, each with a yellow centre, are borne over a long period on this French marigold of some elegance. H&S: to 30cm (12in).

T. 'Zenith Orange'
The deep yellow, almost carnation-like flowers of this imposing Afro-French marigold are more wet-weather resistant than most of this type. H&S: 30cm (12in).

T. patula 'Mr Majestic'
Mahogony-coloured stripes on yellow petals make this French marigold particularly eye-catching. H&S: 30cm (12in).

Thalictrum

These tall and handsome border perennials - also known as meadow rue - are buttercup relations. They grow naturally in moist meadows and slightly shady places in many parts of the world. The genus includes a number of extremely tall and - given their height - surprisingly erect plants. All thalictrums have very divided and somewhat unusual foliage, often bluish in colour; in some species, it resembles that of maidenhair fern (*Adiantum*) while in others it is more like that of aquilegias. The flowers, too, are refined, being individually tiny but with prominent, colourful stamens. The blooms, which are in lilac, soft mauve, pink, white, or pale yellow, are held aloft in delicate and spriggy panicles or those that are soft and almost fluffy-looking. Thalictrums are, therefore, a useful group of plants with an understated, almost diaphanous elegance.

Site and soil

Grow in a partially shaded site and moist soil that has been enriched with plenty of organic matter.

Most thalictrums are back-of-the-border plants, although they also look at home in a wilder woodland site and will grow well there as long as the soil is not too dry.

Buying guide

Buy and plant thalictrums in spring or autumn. *T. delavayi* seems to be the most commonly found thalictrum, in particular the form 'Hewitt's Double'. Others are harder to source - particularly the larger species, some of which (such as *T.* 'Elin') grow to a height of as much as 3.5m (11ft) in one year.

Plant care

In spring, feed plants with a general fertilizer and apply a mulch of garden compost or other organic matter.

Protect new growth late in spring from attack by slugs and snails (see page 215).

Stake tall species securely if grown in very rich soil.

At the end of autumn, cut plants down to the ground.

Every three years in spring, divide *T. delavayi* 'Hewitt's Double' and replant in reinvigorated soil (see page 44). Other thalictrums can be left undisturbed for longer.

CLOUDS OF DELICATE foliage are produced by *Thalictrum aquilegiifolium* 'Purpurea'. After midsummer, this foliage is topped by delicate, soft-focus flowers.

GETTING IN A KNOT

The airy blooms of *T. delavayi* are irresistible in a vase. However, if they are specifically grown as a cut flower, they are best kept well apart from each other at 90cm (3ft) spacings. As plantsman Graham Stuart Thomas explained, if planted any closer: "The flowers get entangled and make one say Cardamine! and Damnacanthus!; they are impossible to separate, but of course help hold each other in place in the garden." Thalictrums go well with *Aster* x *frikartii* 'Mönch', *Rudbeckia fulgida* var. *sullivantii* 'Goldsturm', and long-flowering, mauve *Phlox maculata* 'Alpha'; and, thankfully, these companions don't require staking – unlike the thalictrums.

Deadheading

In midspring, shorten thalictrums – the so-called "Chelsea chop" (see page 42). When so treated, taller species and varieties can be persuaded to flower later and at two-thirds the height. Otherwise, deadhead plants for aesthetic reasons, so that lower, smaller flowers appear more prominent.

Overwintering

Thalictrums are hardy but go completely dormant – and therefore invisible – for a long period over winter. Care should be taken, until you know your border geography well, to mark where winter-dormant plants are sited so that you are not tempted to plant anything in the space their roots occupy.

Propagation

Increase thalictrum by division in spring.

Recommended varieties

T. delavayi ♀
Divided leaves and flowers that are lilac and yellow, occasionally white, from midsummer to early autumn, adorn this very pretty and popular species. H: 1.5-2m (5-6½ft); S: 60cm (2ft).

T. aquilegiifolium 'Thundercloud' ♀
The pale bluish green foliage is eye-catching well before the purple flowers are produced between late spring and midsummer. H: 1.2m (4ft); S: 50cm (1½ft).

T. rochebrunianum
This is one of the tallest species. It has very divided, dull green leaves. Robust, purplish stems are topped by a haze of lilac and pale yellow flowers. H: 2m (6½ft); S: 50cm (1½ft).

T. lucidum
Creamy sulphur-yellow flowers on a branched head are carried between early and late summer, along with narrow, shiny green leaves. H: 1-1.2m (3-4ft); S: 50cm (1½ft).

Trillium

And now for something completely different. Trilliums, also known as wake robin and wood lily, are a genus of rather other-worldly-looking plants that come mainly from North America (especially the Appalachian mountains), but also from the Himalayas and Japan. In spring, single stalks emerge and each produce three leaves, sometimes mottled, in the centre of which gradually appear pointed buds, each with three petals. (It is clearly the coincidence of threes that give the genus its name.) The buds of those from North America (sessile trilliums) are stalkless and tend to remain closed and pointed, while most Asian species (pedicellate trilliums) carry flowers on short stalks and have petals that open wider. Flowers are white, pink, red-brown, or yellow. And the allure? Spreading clumps of these curious flowers are a really lovely sight in a cool, shady position in light woodland.

Site and soil

Trilliums are fussy about growing conditions, and even when they are happy it takes years to establish a substantial colony from their slowly spreading rhizomatous base.

Most will succeed only if they are planted in the shade under the canopy of deciduous trees in leafy, slightly acid to neutral soil that remains moist at least while they are in their visible growing stage. *T. cuneatum* grows well in soil that is more alkaline.

AMERICAN BEAUTY

Trilliums are just as much part of an American woodland in spring as bluebells are in Britain. As a result, *T. grandiflorum* became the state wild flower in Ohio, USA, in 1982. And over the border in Canada, there are two official uses: the species was named as the provincial emblem of Ontario in 1937; and a stylized flower also appears on the official flag of the province's French-speaking people.

Buying guide

Trilliums have become rather modish in recent years, and they are sold in spring at smarter garden centres singly in

SOMETHING DISTINCTLY SPECIAL to embellish the woodland floor in spring is *Trillium sessile* 'Rubrum'. Find the right spot for it and the colony will gradually expand year by year.

pots, as seedlings or offsets that are just coming into flower for the first time. (They cannot be sold bare-rooted as the rhizomes deteriorate rapidly once they dry out.) In order to be sold when in flower (no one would buy them otherwise), trilliums have to be nurtured for up to five years. The plants are, therefore, expensive.

Plant new purchases straight away in soil that has had masses of leafmould dug into it in advance.

Plant care

Before they start to grow in spring, trilliums appreciate a feed with a general fertilizer as well as the application of a light topdressing of well-rotted leafmould spread over their root area.

Monitor plants carefully during the short weeks before they start to die back, and mark their positions clearly. Trilliums flower one year on the energy built up the previous year after flowering, so the longer they stay in leaf before dying down, the better they will flower the following year.

Deadheading

The plants - leaves and flowers - die down naturally, so deadheading is not applicable here.

Overwintering

Trilliums are completely dormant during winter and need no protection. New growth, however, may be damaged by late frosts.

Propagation

Divide plants immediately after the flowers have faded. Propagation by division, however, is not for the faint hearted. Therefore, if you have a flowering clump that is starting to spread its rhizomes slowly about, it would be safer to leave things alone and let nature take its course.

To split up a trillium clump, dig up the entire plant and cut off 2.5cm (1in) of rhizome, severing its terminal bud. Dust the cut surfaces with fungicide when they are dry. Plant the cut section immediately; it will eventually make shoots from the dormant buds. The severed section with its terminal bud can also be planted, and it may make a second plant that will flower the following year.

Growing trilliums from seed is such a lengthy process that it is, therefore, somewhat impractical.

Recommended varieties

T. grandiflorum ♀
One of the showiest, white pedicellate trilliums is this beautiful plant. Above dark green, pointed leaves, its stout stems bear large, white, open flowers that fade to pink. They appear in spring and early summer. H&S: 30cm (12in).

T. cuneatum
Clump-forming T. cuneatum has quite rounded leaves that are somewhat mottled, and carries pointed, sessile, dark maroon brown flowers in spring. H: 40cm (16in); S: to 30cm (12in).

T. chloropetalum var. giganteum ♀
The leaves are large and mottled on this giant trillium, and the fragrant, sessile, spring flowers range in colour from white to deep garnet-red. H: 50cm (20in); S: 20cm (8in).

T. luteum ♀
This is a robust, sessile trillium that is tolerant of alkaline soils. It has slim-petalled, lemon-scented, yellow flowers, in spring, and its mottled leaves are almost rounded. H: 10-40cm (4-16in); S: to 30cm (12in).

Tropaeolum *Nasturtium*

A bright and jolly ragbag of leafy, orange-, yellow-, or red-flowered nasturtiums scrambling all over the place is, I am sure, one of the most uplifting, albeit somewhat unsophisticated, sights in a late summer garden. But there are 80 or so different species of these climbing and scrambling plants, mostly originating in cool mountainous regions of Central and South America, some of them herbaceous perennials. All climbing nasturtiums scramble around in the same way, by bending their long leafstalks to form crooked elbows with which they grasp onto trellises and other plants for support. They all have spurred flowers, some more tubular than others. There are also dwarf plants with interesting leaves and flowers of more subtle hues, some only slightly trailing and others that don't budge at all.

SCRAMBLING ANNUAL NASTURTIUMS like these (*T. majus*) create a riot of colour wherever they go. The perennials are more subtle and harder to please, but efforts are well rewarded.

Site and soil

Grow the annual *T. majus* as well as its hybrids and cultivars in poor soil, for maximum flowering potential. Non-trailing annuals are suitable for the front of a sunny border, semi-trailers do well in containers, while trailing annuals look good climbing over trellises, and through shrubs and hedges.

Plant the perennial climber *T. speciosum* in moist, humus-rich, neutral to acid soil, positioning it so the delicate rhizomatous roots are in cool, leafy shade. Plant it where its extremely fine stems can scramble upwards easily (it does well growing up yew).

Grow *T. tuberosum* in full sun and deeply cultivated, moist but well-drained soil that has masses of organic matter added to it. This generally tender species can prove to be hardy if grown against a year-round warm and sunny house wall. It generally flowers very late during summer.

Sow seed of annual nasturtiums either *in situ* in late spring or in pots of compost under glass in midspring; plant out when the weather warms up. Plants from seed sown *in situ* will flower later and for longer.

Buying guide

Seeds of most annual nasturtiums are easy to find at garden centres, although the interestingly coloured variations tend to sell out early in the growing season, so they may need to be ordered direct from the supplier.

Plants of *T. speciosum* are not often available, but when they are on sale they are usually in the early stages of leaf growth in early summer and somewhat vulnerable.

Plants of *T. tuberosum* are hard to source, and it may be necessary to track them down at a specialist nursery, by mail order, or online.

Plant care

Annuals need little special care, except protection from blackfly and the caterpillars of the large white butterfly if these are a problem (see page 216). Pull up plants and compost them when they die back in autumn.

In its first year, nurture *T. speciosum* extra carefully, making sure it does not dry out at the roots. After the first year, the rhizomes will have spread out underground and little shoots may appear at some distance from the originals. Apply a leafmould mulch each spring.

Keep *T. tuberosum* well watered in dry spells.

Deadheading

It is important to deadhead annual nasturtiums, which will otherwise go to seed and stop flowering. The exception is *T. majus* 'Hermine Grashoff' (see right). Towards the end of the season, seed can be collected and saved (see page 46); plants will almost inevitably have dropped seed themselves as well.

Deadheading perennials does not extend their flowering season, which seems to fade away as temperatures fall.

Overwintering

T. speciosum is hardy, but will die back completely until very late spring the following year.

T. tuberosum is tender, and unless grown in a warm and completely sheltered site will need to be lifted in autumn, stored in frost-free conditions, and replanted in spring.

Propagation

In spring, increase annuals by seed that has been saved from the previous season. Some cultivars of annual *T. majus* (such as 'Hermine Grashoff') do not set seed and must be propagated from basal or soft cuttings in spring or early summer (see page 45).

Perennials are best propagated by division (see page 44). In early spring, divide rhizomes of *T. speciosum*. In autumn when dormant, separate tubers of *T. tuberosum*.

Recommended varieties

T. majus 'Empress of India'
The purple-green leaves of this dwarf, bushy cultivar form a perfect backdrop for the rich bright scarlet flowers in summer and autumn. H: 30cm (12in); S: 30cm (12in).

T. speciosum ♀
Vivid red flowers create a fine splash of colour as this sought-after, tiny-leaved nasturtium scrambles through evergreen shrubs in late summer. H: to 3m (10ft); S: indefinite.

T. majus 'Hermine Grashoff' ♀
This strong-growing climber produces masses of bright red, double flowers and must be propagated by stem-tip cuttings. H: 3m (10ft) or more; S: indefinite.

T. tuberosum var. lineamaculatum 'Ken Aslet' ♀
Exotic-looking 'Ken Aslet' has grey-green leaves and long-spurred, red/orange, tubular flowers borne on purple stems. H: 3–6m (10–20ft); S: indefinite.

Verbascum

Verbascums, of which there are some 300 species, come chiefly from Europe and Turkey, where they grow on poor, dry soil. In recent years, they have become enormously popular cottage-garden plants because of their vertical structure and colourful flowers, and numerous new hybrids and cultivars have been introduced. Most verbascums are biennial, a few being at best short-lived perennials. However, such is their ability to seed themselves around that once you slot one or two into your garden you tend to have them for ever. Leaves of many verbascums are soft, grey, and woolly, while others are darker green with toothed edges. All form attractive wide rosettes in their first year of growth. In year two, the flower stems are produced, erect, some of them lofty, some branched, bearing five-petalled flowers often with colourful "eyes" in shades of yellow, white, mauve, or pinkish buff.

Site and soil

Grow in full sun and soil that is well drained and moderately fertile. Although naturally happiest growing in open ground (leaf rosettes and their spires look particularly dramatic in a gravel garden, for example), verbascums also thrive in the more crowded environment of a garden border, either popping up as random-looking singletons or planted in groups.

Buying guide

Because they are now so fashionable, plants of the numerous new, somewhat smaller garden varieties of verbascums are easy to find at garden centres. Such plants are likely to be short-lived perennials.

Plants of the older, tall, and white-woolly-leaved biennial species are less often available at garden centres, so first-year seedlings may have to be begged from friends – unless you can source them from specialist nurseries.

Seed suppliers now list numerous colourful verbascum hybrids in their catalogues. Sow seed in pots or trays of loam-based seed and cutting compost in a cold frame either in late summer or in early spring.

Plant care

Verbascums seldom need staking.

Pick off by hand caterpillars of the striped mullein moth, or use a systemic insecticide in early summer.

WHETHER GROWN IN a mixed crowd, as here, or as stately singletons, the vertical stems of verbascums are invaluable in any planting scheme.

If undetected, the caterpillars may shred verbascum leaves in a matter of days.

Pull up exhausted biennials, but be careful where you discard them as their seeds may infest a compost heap.

In autumn, cut perennials down to the ground. They will re-emerge in late spring.

Deadheading

In midsummer, cut to the ground healthy plants of more robust, dark green-leaved hybrids and cultivars – of *V. chaixii*, for example – to encourage a welcome second crop of spires in early autumn.

For other verbascum, deadheading is really a matter of aesthetics. Individual flowers appear up the stems in what seems like an almost random manner, so they flower over a long period of time and maintain an attractive if somewhat increasingly husky brown-looking presence for weeks – while, of course, they are ripening and casting about a lot of seed.

Overwintering

Plants should generally survive winter unprotected.

Propagation

Species can be grown from seed, in autumn, but in most cases saved seed will produce unpredictable hybrids. Self-sown seedlings can be moved around in their first autumn; if they are transplanted in spring before they flower their spires are likely to be shorter.

In spring, it is possible but not easy to propagate verbascum from root cuttings or by the careful removal of side rosettes of perennial plants.

MAGICAL MULLEIN

Mullein (*V. thapsus*) is a towering perennial that has attracted similarly tall stories over the centuries. In antiquity, it was a magical herb given to Ulysses to protect him from Circe, the powerful enchantress who turned Ulysses' men into pigs. This tale probably has deep links with the idea that the flower stalks of mullein can be used as torches to keep witches at bay; but, paradoxically, the witches were also said to use the herb in their potions.

Recommended varieties

V. chaixii 'Album' ♀
One of the best and most versatile verbascums is 'Album'. It has dark grey-green leaves and white flowers each with a maroon eye. Self-seedlings come true. H: 1m (3ft); S: 50cm (1½ft).

V. 'Norfolk Dawn'
The flowers on this vigorous and large-flowered verbascum are a subtle biscuity-buff colour. H: 80cm (32in); S: 50cm (1½ft).

V. 'Jackie'
Slightly tender and distinctly sun-loving 'Jackie' is a smaller plant altogether. It produces dark green leaves and pretty, peachy pink flowers on short spikes. H: 60cm (2ft); S: 30cm (1ft).

V. 'Cotswold Beauty' ♀
This extremely handsome hybrid is deservedly popular. Pale coppery flowers, with purple eyes, open from darker bronze buds in summer. H: 1.2m (4ft); S: 45cm (18in).

Verbena

Gardeners may be familiar with the colourful but slightly gangly, spreading bedding verbenas, usually grown as annuals and particularly useful as container plants. However, they may know less about their bolt-upright relations, some of which will add height and a certain architectural quality to a sunny border. Verbenas are natives of both North and South America and not reliably hardy. They thrive in a sunny, sheltered garden and most will self-seed – sometimes to excess. On the upright border perennials, the individually tiny flowers are borne on shoot tips and open from dusky dark buds, either in clusters or small spires, a few flowers opening at a time over a long period. The flowers, which are much loved by butterflies, are in subtle shades of deep lilac-purple, pink, mauve, and white, whereas bedding verbenas produce bold red, purple, white, or sharp pink blooms.

Site and soil

Grow all verbenas in full sun and soil that is very well drained. As well as sun, sharp drainage is the main requirement of perennial verbenas, which tolerate fairly poor soil.

Low-growing, spreading bedding verbenas do particularly well in containers filled with John Innes No 2 compost.

Bring on plug plants under glass until they are ready to be planted out in early summer.

Buying guide

Low-growing verbenas are easy to find among the bedding plants at garden centres in late spring. *V. bonariensis* is also readily available; many gardeners for whom it has become a weed express surprise that the plant is offered for sale at all. Its shorter, brighter-

WITH ITS VIGOROUS growth and flowers of a particularly lovely violet-blue, *V.* 'La France' is one of the very best of the hybrid verbenas, at its happiest spilling out of a summer container.

flowered relation *V. rigida*, often erroneously sold as an annual, is often grouped among the bedding plants.

Plant care

On all winter-surviving verbenas, cut back old growth to just above the lowest green shoots, in midspring.

Also in midspring, pinch out the shoot tips on young plants, to encourage them to branch.

Apply a monthly, balanced soluble feed when in flower. Despite this, bedding verbenas may flower less profusely in prolonged periods of cool, cloudy weather.

Verbenas do not need staking.

Protect bedding verbenas against powdery mildew (see page 215) and leaf hoppers in hot summers (see page 216). Taller verbenas are less prone to these problems.

Deadheading

Before late summer, shorten flower stems on border perennials by one-third to one-half to stimulate the production of sideshoots that will flower before autumn. This also makes the plants more branching and stocky.

Removing old flowerheads on bedding verbenas is a fiddly exercise carried out chiefly for aesthetic reasons, as such verbenas do not set seed. Nevertheless, it is probably a task worth doing.

Overwintering

When bedding verbenas have stopped flowering, by early autumn, either treat them as annuals and pull them up or trim back the plants and keep them relatively dry in a frost-free cold frame or greenhouse for winter.

V. rigida may survive the winter outside if protected by mulch, while *V. hastata* may be killed by long-term winter wet. *V. bonariensis* is more reliably hardy, and is one of the last of the summer flowers to give up in autumn, at which point blue tits enjoy picking off the seeds. Cut *V. bonariensis* down to within 30cm (12in) of the ground; it will survive short periods of frost and snow.

Propagation

In spring, sow seed or take softwood cuttings (see page 46). The border perennials all self-seed. If appropriate, move self-sown seedlings to their new site in spring; this should not retard their growth.

Recommended varieties

V. rigida ♀
This tuberous verbena looks like a shorter version of *V. bonariensis*, or an upright version of an annual. It carries rich purple flowers over a long period in summer. H: 60cm (2ft1in); S: 30cm (1ft).

V. hastata
The young growth and upright habit look very like *V. bonariensis*, but this verbena has more widely branching stems bearing candelabra-like, mauve-purple flower spikes. H: 1.5m (5ft); S: 25cm (10in).

V. bonariensis ♀
Being tall, rigid, and slender, this plant looks best planted *en masse* so that its stems form a see-though, green forest topped by a haze of maroon-purple flowers. H: 2m (6½ft); S: 60cm (2ft).

V. 'Sissinghurst' ♀
One of the best and most robust of the bedding verbenas is 'Sissinghurst', which carries masses of sugar-pink flowers throughout the summer months. H: 20cm (8in); S: 45cm (18in).

Veronica

One look at the flowers of some of the plants illustrated here will tell you that they are all close relations of that much disliked but pretty, blue-eyed lawn weed, lesser speedwell. The veronicas - the common name of all of them is speedwell - are all natives of temperate parts of the northern hemisphere, mainly Europe. With one or two exceptions, all have flowers that are white or pale blue, true blue, or blue-purple. Although they share certain characteristics - leaf arrangement and the shape of individual flowers- they seem to be a diverse lot when you look at their general growth habit with an unbotanically trained eye. The prolific flowers of some of the border veronicas are carried in fine, upright spires, while others are more like those of the lawn weed: they sprawl over the edges of a path and any flower spires appear to clothe the entire plant loosely, untidily, but very prettily.

Site and soil

Grow border veronicas in full sun or partial shade and moderately fertile, moist but well-drained soil.

Sow seed (generally supplied commercially as mixed colours) in containers in a cold frame in autumn.

FRIEND AND FOE

Alpine plants are usually cherished and cosseted by gardeners, who create cold frames, airy glasshouses, and rock gardens to provide the perfect conditions. Unfortunately, though, one introduction had no trouble feeling at home. The sender speedwell (*V. filiformis*) was considered to be a pretty ornamental when it was introduced to the UK from the Caucasus (the area north of Turkey and south of Russia) in the 1830s. It offers a mass of striking, blue flowers in late spring and early summer and creates an extensive mat. The problem came when it escaped the rockery and headed for the lawn. It was far happier here, quickly leading to its reclassification from alpine to weed, especially as speedwells are resistant to the majority of lawn weedkillers available to amateur gardeners. However, with the rise in interest in creating meadows, this plant is once again finding favour as a partner for buttercups in a flowery mead.

EASY-TO-GROW veronicas provide a flower garden with some of its best blues. Shown here are the elegant racemes of *V. exaltata*, which flowers for a long period in midsummer.

Buying guide

Many veronicas are at their most alluring in late spring and early summer, popping up for sale in garden centres and at the first plant fairs of the year. Plants bought and planted in flower need extra care and attention, including cutting back immediately they have performed, in order to allow the plant to develop a strong root system. It will also ensure an even better show the following year.

Plant care

During their first season, remove fading blooms from young plants immediately, so they concentrate on root production, and ensure plants are not swamped by later-performing perennials in the border.

Protect plants from powdery mildew, to which they are particularly susceptible in late summer if they become dry at the roots (see page 215).

Every few years in autumn or spring, divide well-established clumps and replant in reinvigorated soil (see page 44).

Support taller species with twiggy sticks, as stems can flop badly after rain.

In autumn, cut plants down to ground level.

Deadheading

Once they start to fade, shear off the first flush of flowers on early flowering veronicas and give them a soluble feed. They will then produce fresh leaves and a smaller autumn flush.

Late flowerers will not reflower if treated this way.

Overwintering

Veronicas are hardy and need no winter protection.

Propagation

Sow seed in autumn or divide border veronicas in autumn or spring.

Recommended varieties

V. austriaca subsp. teucrium 'Crater Lake Blue' ♀
The spike-like racemes of this compact veronica are the most outstanding, true blue. It flowers in summer over a long period. H: 25cm (10in); S: 25cm (10in).

V. umbrosa 'Georgia Blue'
This is a lovely, sprawling but bushy veronica with white-eyed, deep blue flowers and purplish leaves. Plant it at the front of a border. H: 10cm (4in); S: 60cm (24in) or more.

V. gentianoides ♀
Matt-forming V. gentianoides has dark green leaves and produces short, upright spires of pale blue (or darker blue or white) flowers in early summer. H: 25–45cm (10–18in); S: 45cm (18in).

V. longifolia 'Blue John'
Flowering in mid- to late summer, this is an upright border perennial with long, pointed, midgreen leaves and tall, fine spires of tiny blue flowers. H: to 1m (3ft); S: 30cm (12in).

Veronicastrum

There are only three species in this genus, which is closely related to *Veronica*. Only one of them - *V. virginicum* - is in general garden cultivation; it comes from the woods, meadows, and prairies of North America. Veronicastrums make extremely elegant, back-of-border plants, which, unlike most of the veronicas, flower in the second half of the growing season, from midsummer to early autumn. As such, they are extremely useful, especially as a restful foil for the often loud-coloured, late summer daisies. Their growth is more refined, erect, and architectural than the large, late veronicas, too. Veronicastrums have pointed, midgreen leaves arranged in neat whorls around each dark stem. Super-slim, tall, and generally upright spires of tiny flowers - in pinks, mauves, or whites - are borne on the top of each stem, as well as on lower side branches.

Site and soil

Veronicastrums thrive in moist but well-drained soil and produce the most upright flowering stems, and more of them, if grown in full sun. They are most impressive when grown in substantial clumps, their flowers forming a soft-focus haze of colour.

Buying guide

It may be necessary to source veronicastrums from specialist nurseries as they are not commonly found for sale at garden centres. Buy and plant them during spring or autumn.

Veronicastrum seed is not commonly found commercially.

Plant care

Veronicastrums are easy to grow, but can be plagued by fungal diseases (see page 215) if growing conditions are not to their liking.

In spring, feed plants with a general fertilizer, to improve performance, then apply a mulch around each plant.

Shorten flower stems in late spring to make the plant shorter and more sturdy - the so-called "Chelsea chop" (see page 42).

Stake plants to prevent them flopping when in flower, if they are grown in part shade.

THIS WHITE-FLOWERED form of *Veronicastrum virginicum* is at its best in a grand setting, where its textured foliage and refined flower spikes can be viewed *en masse* from a distance.

Old flowerheads look attractive through winter, and can be left standing until they become unsightly. The seed can be collected and saved, if required (see page 46).

Every three years or so, in autumn, divide well-established, expanding clumps and replant them (see page 44).

Deadheading

Remove the central spire of each shoot as it fades to prolong flowering somewhat and to improve the look of the plant.

Overwintering

Veronicastrums are hardy plants and need no special frost protection.

Propagation

Plants left standing in winter may self-seed.

In autumn, sow saved seed in a cold frame, or increase mature clumps by division, also in autumn.

DEEP ROOTS

Stately *V. virginicum* comes with a string of common names from its native USA. The descriptive black root is most common. However, Culver's root, Culver's physic, and physic root are frequently used and seem to refer to Dr Culver, the 18th-century American physician who used the black roots for their laxative and emetic properties. This follows the Native Indians' practices for *V. virginicum*. The Seneca Indians used it as a herb to induce vomiting in ceremonial purifications, and the Chippewa Indians adopted the root as a blood cleanser. Of course, this is now a plant that should be taken only under medical supervision, but it makes a fine garden plant. It is a striking, upright perennial so works well with plants of contrasting habits. Try growing cultivars such as *V.v.* 'Pointed Finger' with the plumes of *Calamagrostis brachytricha*, the rosy blooms of *Persicaria amplexicaulis* 'Blotau', and inky *Salvia nemorosa* 'Caradonna'.

Recommended varieties

V. virginicum 'Apollo'
'Apollo' has an upright habit and produces lilac-blue flower spikes from midsummer to early autumn. H: 0.9–1.8m (3–6ft); S: 50cm (20in).

V. virginicum 'Fascination'
Some of the lilac-blue or rich pink flower spikes grow fused together (fasciated – hence the quirky varietal name), giving the plant a curious twisted look. H: 0.9–1.8m (3–6ft); S: 50cm (20in).

V. virginicum 'Lavendelturm'
Stems on this variety are very branched and carry lavender-blue spikes. H: 0.9–1.8m (3–6ft); S: 50cm (20in).

V. virginicum 'Pointed Finger'
The central flower spike is exceptionally long on this extremely elegant plant, hence its name. The flowers are pale lilac-blue. H: 0.9–1.8m (3–6ft); S: 50cm (20in).

Viola

This is a huge genus. There are some 500 species from scattered temperate sites all over the world, so botanists have divided them into several distinct groups. Of these, the most familiar and popular garden plants are the perennial violas (created through complicated hybridization), some of which are almost evergreen, and their larger-flowered, biennial relations – the pansies. The perennial violas with which we are concerned here are compact and tufted, with a multi-stemmed root system. Their flowers are small and often scented, borne for several weeks throughout summer. (Biennial pansies, which flower on and off throughout winter and spring, have similar-shaped but larger faces; they grow from the ground on a single stem, and carry flowers on bent-over branches.) Two members of the viola family can become garden weeds: dog violet (*V. riviniana*) and sweet violet (*V. odorata*).

Site and soil

Grow in sun or partial shade and fertile, neutral to slightly alkaline soil that has been enriched with organic matter.

Violas are good front-of-border plants that can, if appropriate, be allowed to sprawl upwards and flower in among other plants. *V. cornuta* thrives on the outer margins of a woodland garden.

Seed of most violas is hard to find commercially since many violas set seed poorly.

Buying guide

Numerous violas are now commonly to be found in garden centres, generally already in flower in spring and early summer. Plant them up straight away and deadhead immediately, to encourage the formation of a good root system.

Plant care

In spring, as growth starts, feed, mulch, and tidy up any overwintered plants.

Deadheading

Deadheading and cutting back are extremely important to maintain a continuous supply of flowers on all violas. *V. cornuta*, in particular, gets extremely straggly: cut it back quite hard in midsummer, if not before, even though this means sacrificing quite a lot of flowers. Then give

AFTER A MIDSUMMER haircut to tidy it up, lovely, little, shade-tolerant *V. cornuta* will start flowering all over again and may go on doing so until autumn.

these perennials a soluble feed, to boost performance and discourage disease. Plants will respond instantly by developing new shoots that will flower within a couple of weeks of such surgery.

Overwintering

Violas are hardy as long as they are not growing where the soil becomes sunless and waterlogged in winter.

Propagation

Because they are short-lived, propagate from your viola plants regularly.

Divide *V. cornuta* in spring or autumn (see page 44).

Take softwood cuttings of lush viola growth in summer (see page 46).

Seed can be saved from those that set seed readily (such as *V. sororia*). Sow it in trays filled with seed and cutting compost in an open cold frame as soon as it is ripe. Plants will not come true, however.

SWEET SMELL OF SUCCESS

Sweet violas, or violets, were once grown in profusion as a cut flower. They were said to be Queen Victoria's favourite bloom, and were famously grown in the south-west of England and transported to Covent Garden market in London, UK. Charles Dickens wrote in *All Year Round*: "We have a large number of street vendors of flowers and they cry 'Penny a bunch, violets!'" By the middle of the 19th century, however, the French began to take over this lucrative market, much to the detriment of one grower, George Lee. Worried by the situation, Lee was walking home from church and stopped to pray for providence to intervene. And, as the story goes, he opened his eyes and a beautiful violet lay at his feet (in truth, Lee actually bred it at his nursery in Clevedon, near Bristol). It was this violet that he named after his queen, 'Victoria Regina', and sent a bunch to her each birthday. As a result, he and the variety went on to become a huge success.

Recommended varieties

V. cornuta ♀
This is a spreading, sprawling perennial with rhizomatous roots and lightly scented, mauve flowers There are beautiful white and cream cultivars. H: 7–15cm (2½–6in); S: 20–40cm (8–16in).

V. sororia 'Freckles'
During spring and summer, prettily speckled flowers adorn this spreading, rhizomatous viola, which self-seeds readily. H: 10cm (4in); S: 20cm (8in).

V. corsica
Narrow-leaved *V. corsica* has yellow-throated, purple flowers in summer and is suitable for container growing. H: 20cm (8in); S: 30cm (12in).

V. 'Etain'
Not only are the petals beautifully shaded but the large flowers of 'Etain' are also scented. It needs a warm position in order to do well. H: 15cm (6in); S: 30cm (12in).

Zantedeschia

Zantedeschia - a plant with an exotic-sounding name - comes from moist soil, swamps, and lake margins in southern and East Africa. It is often called calla lily or arum lily, although it does not, in fact, belong to the lily family at all. Zantedeschia is grown for its unusual, white or coloured spathes, produced in spring or summer. From a tuberous root, it produces leaves that are often heart shaped, sometimes more strappy, but always decorative in their own right and borne on long stems. Most zantedeschias grown in gardens are hybrids, and in cold regions most of them should be regarded as marginally tender. While the white callas have unfortunately become somewhat associated with funerals, there are now some less sombre, distinctly colourful hybrids that can take their place in an exotic garden scheme, and are more tolerant of drier conditions. Zantedeschia make good cut flowers.

Site and soil

Grow in full sun or light shade and moist soil to which a lot of organic matter has been added. If zantedeschia are grown in too shady a position, plants may produce leaves but no flowers. Plant deeply, with 10cm (4in) of soil over the crowns.

Colourful and less hardy zantedeschia can be grown in containers. These should be roomy, and filled with a mixture comprising 80 per cent rich, loam-based potting compost (John Innes No 3) and 20 per cent leafmould or garden compost.

Buying guide

Zanthdeschias are most often sold potted and in flower in garden centres, sometimes in their indoor plant areas, and even in smart florists' shops. It should be noted that plants with white- or green-splashed spathes (forms of *Z. aethiopica*) are much hardier than those with colourful spathes, which should be regarded as container plants.

Hardier zantedeschias can be planted outside, having first been carefully acclimatized to life outdoors. They may not flower for their first year after they have been planted out in the ground.

Plant care

In spring, give these greedy plants a feed of garden compost or well-rotted manure.

THE SOMBRE FLOWERS of moisture-loving zantedeschia look almost unreal. They are excellent for cutting, if you can bear to spoil the waxen tableau with your secateurs.

Also in spring as growth starts, tidy up evergreen and semievergreen plants.

Protect plants from aphid infestation, and keep a wary eye out for fungal leaf spots (see page 215).

Deadheading
Remove old flowers after they have faded, at which point the plants become handsome foliage plants for the remainder of the season.

Overwintering
In mild areas during frosty weather, protect the crowns of more hardy zantedeschias with a deep organic mulch.

Move container-grown zantedeschia into a cool greenhouse or conservatory during winter.

Propagation
In spring, before growth starts, divide tuberous roots (see page 44).

AN ITALIAN ROMANCE
Z. aethiopica lends enchantment to one of the "world's most romantic gardens". It's a title often applied to Ninfa, just south of Rome in Italy. The garden around the ruined Roman town is so entwined with roses that it creates an image that would do credit to Edward Burne-Jones' *Sleeping Beauty* series. Yet this is also a water garden, as crystal clear streams filled with dancing waterweed criss-cross the land. All along these waterways and ditches are self-seeded *Z. aethiopica*, unfurling their pure white blooms. In midspring, they form a picture-perfect partnership with blue tassel-blooms of wisteria and flamboyant, pink tree peonies. And it only seems right that zantedeschia should grow so well at Ninfa, as this plant is actually named in tribute to an Italian botanist and physican. Giovanni Zantedeschi (1773–1846) studied in Verona and Padua, and went on to publish 10 works on the flora of the nearby province of Brescia.

Recommended varieties

Z. aethiopica 'Crowborough' ♆
Often called the Crowborough lily, this is one of the hardiest varieties and has long, pure white spathes. H&S: 90cm (3ft).

Z. 'Black Star'
"Black" (that is, very deep maroon) flowers, dark-edged, mottled leaves, and dark stems typify this marginally tender perennial. H: 60cm (2ft); S: 30cm (12in).

Z. aethiopica 'Green Goddess' ♆
The yellow-centred spathes are irregularly streaked white and green, and the dull green leaves may be evergreen in mild areas. H&S: 90cm (3ft).

Z. 'Picasso'
This semi-evergreen, marginally tender hybrid produces white-spotted, glossy, green leaves and satiny spathes that are purple within, white at the edges. H: 90cm (3ft); S: 50cm (20in).

Year planner

Early spring

While early spring is often a harsh time in cool-temperate gardens, by late spring there is generally a lot going on. And by getting the garden up to scratch in early spring, you will save a lot of work later on. This is also a good time to visit those public gardens that are open early in the season. By observing their bones you can learn a lot about how to space, support, and otherwise maintain plants and gardens. This is high season in many woodland gardens – many woodlanders producing their best show before the leaf canopy closes overhead.

Frost protection Check on slightly tender plants such as cannas and dahlias left *in situ* and protected with a dry mulch (straw or bracken, for example) that has been pegged down under a layer of fleece. Put a couple of slug pellets in under the mulch as a precaution against loss of young growth.

Greenhouse plants In unheated greenhouses beware of cold nights, and on sunny days, in an attempt to keep botrytis (downy mildew) at bay, open the door for an hour or so, for ventilation. Autumn-germinated sweet pea seedlings may have made a surprising amount of new growth and may need to have their shoot tips pinched out, to encourage bushy growth and a good root system.

Slugs Soil-dwelling slugs will be active in any mild weather, and this is definitely the time to assess the defence systems before border plants start to put out their first tender shoots. Rudbeckias, hostas, and delphiniums are notoriously vulnerable.

Feeding By now the weather and soil may be warm enough to start serious border work. When all your plants are cleared up, cleaned up, and in the right place, spread balanced fertilizer around each bed and border at the rate recommended on the packaging (generally a fistful per square metre/square yard). Work it into the top few centimetres of soil with a long-handled, small-headed fork.

Mulches If you have a residual weed problem, spread a thick blanket of organic mulch such as garden compost or leafmould over the soil. To encourage certain plants to self-seed, concentrate the mulch thickly around individual plants. Also mulch plants that are particularly susceptible to mildew – knautia, phlox, and some asters, for example – to retain moisture around their roots, or move them to a site that is less crowded, sunny, and dry if the problem proves insurmountable.

Move bulbs Shoots of spring bulbs should be pushing their way up through the ground by now, so, if you have some naturalizing in grass, be careful where you tread, and don't mow. Move any bulbs that had been overlooked and show up in the wrong place. If replanted with as much soil attached to their roots as possible, they should still grow and flower well.

Snowdrops Thin these out or plant new snowdrops when in the green – that is, just after flowering but before their leaves fade.

Twiggy supports Cut hazel sticks from hedges (before they leaf up) to use later as simple twiggy supports for small, floppy perennials.

Meadow maintenance Mow summer-flowering meadow gardens to keep the grass in check.

Late spring

This is a time of enormous change as the first spring flowers come and go, and gradually the borders become a mass of greenery and growing expectations. There is a lot to do.

Seeds Now you can get on with a lot of seed sowing under glass or outside in the soil (warm up the soil with a cloche), always following guidelines on packets.

Cuttings Take softwood or basal cuttings from perennials such as penstemons (see pages 46 and 45), and ensure that they do not dry out during the coming weeks.

Hardening off Plants grown under the protection of glass and also all those bought in strips or trays from garden centres will need to be hardened off (out by day, in by night) for a week or so before they can cope with the harsher conditions of life in the garden.

Container-grown planting You can get away with planting out the vigorous potted perennials that are now flooding the nurseries and garden centres, but be aware that they will not have had time to get their roots into the compost around them. They will, therefore, need special nurturing for the entire growing season, if they are to thrive.

Plant supports Get stakes and other supports into place in your borders before they are needed, so that plants grow up through them and are hidden. This is a time-consuming job needing a lot of thought, since different plants may need different types and heights of support (see page 41). But it is a task that gets easier year by year as your familiarity with plants grows, and it makes an enormous difference to the general success of all flower gardens.

Lilies Replace the original stick (provided when the plant was bought) with a stout stake in each pot of lilies and tie the stems to it carefully as they grow.

Spring bulbs Remove the seedheads and flower stalks of daffodils. Let all spring bulbs die down naturally since their leaves are needed to make the flower buds for the next year. If your bulbs are scattered around the garden and their leaves annoy you, consider grouping them together in one place, which will make them more tolerable and manageable; do this transplanting now before you forget where they were. Tulips should also be deadheaded. Their leaves die down quite quickly, after which the bulbs can be lifted and stored until late autumn or they can be left *in situ* (with markers so you don't accidentally put a spade through them).

Tender plants These (cannas and dahlias, for example) can literally come out of wraps if they were left *in situ*. If they were overwintered in a dry, frost-free garage or shed, plant them out now, in the ground. At the same time, insert any support stakes, rather than run the risk of stabbing the tubers later.

Slugs and snails Check vulnerable plants and barriers almost daily. Go on nocturnal snail-hunting expeditions, armed with a torch, and put out beer traps to catch these pests (see page 215).

Other major pests Watch out for and destroy lily beetles, which will be emerging from hibernation in the ground and are often to be seen first on fritillaries. Apply a preventative systemic insecticide to lilies to deter this destructive pest and others such as seldom-seen capsid bugs (the activities of which can decimate some herbaceous geraniums and other perennials).

The "Chelsea chop" Cut back by half any perennials that you want to reduce in size or whose flowering you want to delay by a few weeks (see page 42). If you have never done this and are hesitant to do so, try it with a tough *Phlox paniculata*, on which the technique is absolutely foolproof.

Early summer

This is the time when many perennials and biennials get into their stride, when flower gardens are full of flowers that are just happening or just about to happen. By taking a daily walk around your garden, inspecting the flowers and plants, you will generally notice problems and spot small jobs that need doing. Yet this is one of the best times in the garden, and so it should be enjoyed in a sedentary position as often as possible.

Visual reminder Take photographs of your flowers as an *aide-mémoire* for when you may adjust your garden planting scheme in the future. If you are so inclined, make a few notes as well. Also, visit other gardens and take pictures (with the owners' permission) of flowers and flower combinations you like. Ask questions and always have a notebook with you.

Deadheading Do this job daily if you can, in order to extend the flowering season of each plant by as much as possible and prevent it from putting energy into seed production. Using slim-bladed scissors, remove not just spent flowerheads but also lengths of stem as well, down to a point where a new tiny flower bud can be seen (see page 42). If you want to save seed, leave some seedheads to ripen.

Cutting back As flowers eventually fade, cut plants right back - leaves and all - if they are untidy. Some perennials will flower again (particularly with the help of a watered-in feed, if the weather is hot and dry).

Watering Do this mainly for new and vulnerable plants. Try to water early in the morning or, even better, do it in the evening (see page 40). Do not water plants when the sun is on them.

Pest protection Slugs, snails, and many other pests are less active in hot weather, but caterpillars of various sorts may attack individual plants (nasturtiums, for example) and start to strip the foliage. Generally to be found on the backs of leaves, if you spot them early you can pick them off by hand before the infestation becomes life-threatening.

Fungal diseases Mildew (indicated by powdery-grey leaf surfaces and slow growth) can take hold on some plants, particularly those packed closely together and growing in very dry soil (see page 215).

Remove the diseased (generally lower) leaves from hollyhocks that show symptoms of rust (orange spots on leaves).

Emergency supports Prop up any plants that have flopped after a sudden rainstorm, using twiggy sticks or purpose-made, bendy, metal, Y-shaped stakes.

Late summer

Flower gardens with a high population of annuals will be coming into their own now, as will those with later-flowering perennials (asters and heleniums, for example) and the slightly tender perennial dahlias and cannas. As summer starts to wind down it is time to take stock of your perennial planting: you may be very conscientious about selecting plants that flower in early and high summer, but less good at leaving space for later summer performers.

Summer meadow areas Cut down fading flowers and leave them lying for a few weeks to drop their seed. Then gather up the dry remains.

Deadheading Keep up the deadheading of annuals to prolong the summer for as long as possible.

Collecting seed Keep an eye on seedheads you have left to ripen, in order to collect seed. You could even put a small plastic bag over each head to ensure that the seeds do not escape while your back is turned. Put seed to be saved in a cool, dry place (see page 46).

Forward planning By now, most flower gardens are getting to the end of their season, so this is a good time to start making plans for the following year. Indeed, if you are wanting to make extensive changes to your flower borders, get on with the major work while the soil is warm, motivation is high, the days are still quite long, the size and stature of your existing plants is still obvious, and serious rains are inevitably about to arrive.

Autumn

Before the soil cools down and the days shorten even further is a great time to be working productively in a flower garden.

Cutting back Start to cut down perennials that are damaged by autumnal weather and have become unsightly, but don't feel the need to cut everything down all at once. For the moment, save anything that looks good or is providing enjoyment and food for birds. Given half a chance, for example, blue tits behave like trapeze artists on the tall, seed-carrying stems of *Verbena bonariensis*.

Annuals Pull up and compost annuals and biennials. Plant sweet peas in modules or pots in an unheated greenhouse. Leave them to grow very slowly during winter.

Composting Cut the woodiest plant stems into short lengths before composting them. Be aware that the seed of prolific plants, such as verbascum, fennel, and red orach, may well not be killed off in a domestic composting system and may thus go on to infest your garden, so treat such plants with caution.

Dividing plants Propagate plants by division (see page 44) and replant the new divisions so they have time to become established before the soil cools down. Indicate where you have put them with labels or markers in the soil – most perennials effectively vanish during the winter months and by the following spring you may not remember the new layout of your planting scheme.

Tender plants Move container-grown, slightly tender plants into a place that is at least dry, and preferably frost-free. Any plants that cannot actually be put under cover should be protected with dry bracken or straw held in place with horticultural fleece.

Planting bulbs Spring-flowering bulbs such as alliums, daffodils, and fritillaries should be planted as soon after they are acquired as possible. Tulips and camassias can wait until late autumn.

Soil improvement Whenever you plant and transplant in autumn, always add as much well-rotted organic matter as you can muster – this is the key to maintaining the health of your soil and it should become as automatic as putting on a seat belt before you start your car.

Tuberous perennials Lift tender tuberous plants once the temperatures have seriously dropped away, and dahlias have had their foliage nipped by the first light frosts; store them in dry compost somewhere frost-free. Alternatively, cut them down and leave in the ground, covering them with bracken or straw pegged down under fleece. They may well survive in the ground in some cool-temperate areas without this covering, but growth will be very slow, and probably not very sturdy, the following spring.

Oriental hellebores Remove the old, evergreen leaves of Oriental hybrid hellebores and mulch their crowns with leafmould.

Winter

How much work you do in your garden in winter depends entirely on the weather and your general inclination to be outside.

Tender plants If you have not already moved slightly tender plants in containers under protective cover for the winter, do so without delay.

Composting Collect all the dead leaves around the garden and cage them up to rot. (It will take 18 months or more before they can be used to mulch woodland plants and added in as a general soil conditioner.) Give the contents of your compost bins a good stir.

General tidy up Remove wooden plant stakes and clean them up for the following year. Metal ones can be left *in situ* unless you regard them as unsightly. Also clean your hand tools, and wash and stack up old plant pots. Sort out your saved seed. Look through your photographs and notes, and make plans for the coming year.

Planting lilies Bulbs become available in mid- or late winter. Plant them as soon as they arrive. They are easier to protect from lily beetles and snails if grown in a heavy pot of soil-based compost. For convenience, insert a slim, short marker stick (such as a wooden kebab stick) beside each lily bulb; these can later be replaced with taller support canes.

Problem solver

It would be wonderful to think that if you took on board and acted on the wealth of useful information about plants and gardening in books (and on the internet), everything would turn out just as beautiful as the illustrations in *Grow Your Own Flowers*. But gardening - exterior decoration - isn't like that. You don't tour nurseries and garden centres clutching colour swatches, confidently matching this to that and expecting the result to be seamless perfection and colour harmony, nor can you plump up your plants when they look a bit flat - as if they were a row of sofa cushions. In the unpredictable world of the garden, bad things sometimes happen.

NEW PLANTS THAT FAIL

Failure of plants to establish well could be caused by imperfect planting techniques. For example, there may be air pockets around the roots if the plant was not firmed into the ground well. Or plants may have been insufficiently watered at planting time, which would cause them to have difficulty in establishing new roots in the soil, however meticulously the site was prepared. If you identify these problems quickly enough, you can rescue the situation by replanting and watering thoroughly (see "Preparing and planting", page 30).

If a wilting plant still fails to perk up, dig up the plant and examine its roots. Look for obvious problems - rot or other damage, or something as mundane and depressing as an infestation of vine weevil grubs (see page 216). Wash soil off the roots, cut stems down to reduce the stress on them, and hospitalize the patient in a pot of John Innes No 2 somewhere out of strong sunlight for a week or two, after which it can be carefully planted again.

The problems of many longer-term ailing plants can be attributed to fundamentally daft planting decisions - if, for example, you are growing lavender in deep shade or rodgersia on a sunny bank. In such places, these plants will never thrive.

PLANTS THAT DON'T FLOWER WELL

This could be down to lack of light or else overfeeding a plant by giving it an unnecessary amount of nitrogen-rich fertilizer. But remember, if the soil has been properly prepared there really is no need for additional fertilizer in the first year. And some very floriferous plants - many of which come from hot, dry places - really do perform a bit better in soil that is not very fertile. Annuals, however, can always be given a soluble, high-potash feed every two weeks or so to boost their floral performance.

DISEASES AND PESTS

Here are some of the more common ills that can befall your plants and pests that can disfigure or even kill them.

Fungal diseases

Apart from being disfiguring, fungal diseases seriously retard a plant's growth. Symptoms most often occur some time after midsummer.

Treat fungal diseases with a copper-based fungicide. Systemic fungicides offer greater protection and are more effective if used preventatively or at the first signs of trouble. Although new growth on plants that have been sprayed with systemic fungicide may be cleaner, a plant once diseased will always be susceptible as long as its growing conditions don't improve. Therefore, mulch the plant, to increase moisture retention in the soil, or move the affected plant to a moister or more open site. Also practise good general hygiene: keep tools clean and in good condition; promptly remove and burn or otherwise dispose of diseased material (never compost it); keep pots and seed trays scrupulously clean, using a plant-friendly disinfectant; and clean plant stakes and canes in autumn before storing them.

Downy mildew (botrytis) This is caused by damp air and damp soil. Garden plants that rot at the base generally do so because they are growing in too moist a site. Annuals and tender perennials may rot at the bases of stems, and also in any rain-sodden flowerheads, if they are overwatered and sunless. Plants develop areas with distinct grey fur on them, and leaves may yellow before blackening and dying. Annuals may be killed by a severe infection. Cut off any affected parts on perennials and biennials (but do not compost), then spray the whole plant with a fungicide.

Downy mildew in a greenhouse is capable of wiping out whole trays of seedlings within hours (this is referred to as "damping off"). To prevent infection, drench seed compost with a fungicide formulated for the purpose, and ensure there is good ventilation around seedlings. Remove affected parts on a mature plant and then spray it with a fungicide, to help to control the spread of infection. Clear and wash down the greenhouse annually.

Fungal leaf spots These affect herbaceous plants such as pansies and primulas. Typically, leaves will develop black or brown spots with yellow margins. Remove spotty leaves, including any on the ground, which may harbour spores. Leaf spots are difficult to treat, but a spray with a systemic fungicide may help to stop the spread of the disease.

Powdery mildew White-dusty leaves, initially on the upper surfaces, are evidence of this fungal disease. Powdery mildew takes hold generally in the second half of summer. It develops in plants that are dry at the roots and is particularly troublesome where plants are overcrowded so that air circulates badly around their massed stems and foliage. Some plants are more likely to suffer than others.

Rust Orange-spotted leaves that yellow and die are a sign of rust. Some plants are more susceptible than others: on ageing hollyhocks, rust is almost unavoidable, for example. Tweak off rusty leaves where they can be reached (they will eventually drop anyway, and if they do they should be picked up to prevent spores from lingering). A systemic fungicide applied early in the season helps to protect plants from rust.

Viruses
Many viruses show as a mottling and puckering of the leaves over an entire plant, and this is accompanied by a general failure to thrive. Since they are so difficult to diagnose, most gardeners tend to treat symptoms with everything they can think of and only finally give up and say "it must be a virus" when no other cures work. As viruses are incurable, dig up and burn infected plants. A similar replacement should not be planted in the same spot.

Pests that damage shoots, buds, and leaves
Slugs and snails There are numerous ways of tackling this most pressing and depressing of gardening problems. They include the following.
• Water the soil with a solution containing microscopic nematodes that eat slugs from within.
• Protect plants with wide, thick barriers of coarse grit, sheep-wool pellets, even coffee grounds, which slugs and snails are loathe to cross.
• Erect more permanent physical barriers using copper, which work by giving slugs and snails mild electric shocks.
• Bait slugs and snails with bran or drown them in beer traps.
• Scatter slug pellets of various types, some of them acceptable to organic gardeners.
• Hunt the garden on a warm, moist evening (armed with a small container of salty water in which to drop the slugs and snails). This method can be staggeringly fruitful.
• In dry weather, search crusty clusters on walls and in garden debris for gangs of dormant snails, and promptly dispose of them.

Sap suckers and leaf nibblers
It is easy to get overanxious about garden creepy crawlies, but in general adopting a live-and-let-live attitude is helpful. Certainly no one nowadays should habitually tour the garden with their finger on the trigger of a spray bottle of malodorous killer-gunk.

However, there are some pests that seriously disfigure and even kill plants. While there are plenty of contact insecticides (some plant- or soap-based and so suitable for organic gardeners) that you can use as soon as you spot pests present on plants, leaf pests are most efficiently controlled preventatively with carefully timed and specifically targeted use of systemic insecticides. To work out when to use preventative sprays it really helps if you learn about the life cycle of the individual pests with which you may have a problem. This knowledge may enable you to interrupt that cycle at some stage and thereby forestall or lessen their impact.

The effects of systemic sprays (and also, for containers, systemic soil drenches and plant pins) can last for several weeks, while the effects of contact sprays will continue only for days. Use garden chemicals as little as possible and then do so only late in the evening, when bees and beneficial insects are not active. As much as possible, work with nature in encouraging natural predators, be they birds, ladybirds and other beetles, hedgehogs, hoverflies, or frogs. A small pond will provide a focus in your garden for many of these creatures, and, while garden hygiene is all-important, always leave some areas wild for these helpful garden friends.

Aphids With your fingers, brush away small localized infestations of greenfly and blackfly, which nestle on the stems of various open-flowered daisies, for example, as well as on shoot tips, in spring and early summer.

Capsid bugs These small and fast-moving, colourless or greenish bugs inject a shoot-deforming poison into buds as they suck the sap. Snip off damaged shoot tips: the next ones produced may flower. Use a preventative spray on vulnerable plants (such as hardy geraniums) in late spring, and repeat a few weeks later.

Caterpillars Those of the large (or cabbage) white butterfly are troublesome on nasturtiums and plants that belong to the cabbage family, while those of

lesser-known moths can cause problems – one of the worst being the mullein moth (see page 198). Apply a preventative systemic spray in early summer.

Earwigs These dark brown, slender, fast-moving beetles, with pincers on their back ends, delight in eating petals, particularly of double flowers. They are nocturnal feeders so you may be able to catch and destroy a few by shaking flowers at night. You can also bait them by providing alternative hiding places: for example, a small, upturned flower pot stuffed with paper or straw on top of a cane.

Leaf hoppers Resembling minuscule grasshoppers, these live on the backs of leaves. Use a systemic insecticide and/or a contact one, especially in summer. See also page 179.

Spider mites Scarcely detectable with the human eye, spider mites breed and spread rapidly in hot, dry summers. They cause browning and curling inward of leaves (where they can sometimes be seen on the fine webs they spin). Cut down and dispose of damaged foliage. Clusters of females (bright orange) hibernate under plant ties and in crevices, so garden hygiene is important.

Vine weevils Vine weevil grubs (white, C-shaped, brown-headed grubs, 0.5cm/¼in long) feast on soft, new roots, particularly those of plants growing in containers. Be vigilant when buying plants. Use carefully timed biological or systemic soil drench, and add a grit mulch, 2cm (¾in) deep, over the potting compost. Symptoms of infestation by the black, snouty-nosed, flightless beetles include neatly notched, lower leaf edges on evergreen shrubs and leathery-leaved, evergreen herbaceous plants. To catch adults in the act of feeding at night, place newspaper under plants, which you then tap gently.

Whitefly These minute, white-winged, moth-like insects are mainly a greenhouse pest and are superficially similar to leaf hoppers (see above). Catch them with sticky traps or introduce a parasitic wasp. The smell of tagetes plants is reputed to put off whitefly.

Flower listings

Glossary of terms

annual A plant that completes its growing cycle in one year.

basal [leaves] Leaves that grow from the base of a stem.

beard [iris] A tuft, or zone of hairs, for example on the falls of bearded irises.

biennial A plant that completes its life cycle in two years.

bract A modified leaf at the base of a flowerhead.

bulb An underground organ, consisting of a short, disc-like stem bearing fleshy scale leaves and one or more buds, often enclosed in protective scales.

bulbil A small, immature bulb often formed at the base of a mature bulb.

cold frame An outdoor, unheated, glazed growing frame used for propagating hardy plants.

copper adhesive tape A type of tape applied around the circumference of a plant container, to deter slugs and snails.

corm A solid, bulb-like stem bearing buds but without fleshy scale leaves.

corymb A broad, flat-topped or domed, racemose flowerhead.

crown The basal portion of a herbaceous plant where the roots and aerial parts or overwintering buds meet.

cultivar (contraction of "cultivated variety") A plant raised or selected in cultivation for a particular character or combination of characters and that retains these distinct characteristics when propagated by appropriate means.

cyathium [plural, cyathia] The inflorescence of the genus *Euphorbia*.

deciduous [of trees and shrubs] Shedding leaves annually at the end of the growing season.

disbud To remove surplus buds so better-quality flowers are borne.

dormancy The suspension of growth (in winter or high summer).

double digging Incorporating organic matter into soil via systematic trench digging.

drill A narrow, straight furrow in soil into which seed is sown.

ericaceous compost Lime-free potting compost that is suitable for acid-loving plants.

evergreen [of trees, shrubs, and perennials] Retaining leaves all year.

F₁ hybrid The vigorous, uniform, first-generation offspring derived from crossing with distinct, pure bred lines.

fall [iris] The semi-pendent part of an iris flower.

fleece A frost-protective membrane that can be placed over plants.

genus [plural genera] The category of plant classification, between family and species, consisting of one or more similar species.

hardy Tolerant of low temperature.

herbaceous [plant, border] Refers to a plant that dies back and becomes dormant.

hybrid/hybridize Naturally or artificially produced offspring of genetically unlike parents.

loam Highly fertile, well-drained, moisture-retentive, humus-rich soil containing equal parts of clay, sand, and silt.

lobe A segment on a leaf that is usually but not necessarily rounded.

monocarpic Refers to plants that flower and fruit once and then die.

mulch A layer of material applied on the soil to improve its moisture retention and (as in organic mulches) fertility.

node The point on a stem from which leaf buds, leaves, and shoots develop.

NPK content The primary constituents of a plant food comprising its nitrogen (N), phosphorus (P), and potassium (K).

offset A short lateral shoot that produces roots and shoots at the tip and is used for propagation, as in sempervivums.

panicle A much-branched inflorescence with separate flower-bearing branches – a branched raceme would be a good example. See also raceme.

pedicellate With stalks that bear single flowers.

perennial A non-woody plant that lives for more than two years.

perlite Light granules of volcanic minerals that are added to potting compost to improve aeration.

pinch out The removal of the growing tip, with finger and thumb or sharp secateurs, in order to promote more vigorous growth from shoots lower down the stem.

planting out The transfer of plants to their final growing site.

plug plant A small developing plant whose growth has been forced well in advance of its normal planting-out date. It is just large enough to handle by its seed leaves.

potting on The transfer of small seedlings individually into small pots to grow on before being planted out.

raceme A flowerhead with the blooms appearing along an unbranched central stem. See also panicle.

rhizome A horizontal, root-like stem growing at or below ground level.

riddle A sieve for refining garden soil.

runner A trailing stem that roots from the apex or nodes giving rise to plantlets.

semievergreen [of trees and shrubs] Retaining most or some leaves all year.

semiripe [cuttings] Cuttings taken from partially ripened but still pliable new shoots in mid- to late summer.

sessile [of flowers or leaves] Having no stalk.

shrub A perennial, woody, many-stemmed plant, generally smaller than a tree.

silver sand Fine, clean sand (such as sandpit sand) that, unlike builders' sand, contains nothing that would harm plants.

softwood [cuttings] Cuttings taken from young, non-flowering shoots that have not yet started to harden, from spring to early summer.

spur An extension of a petal or sepal, often containing nectar.

stamen The male part of a flower, that is, filament, connective, and anther.

standard [iris] The erect, inner part of an iris flower.

stratification The practice of chilling seeds, which in the case of the seed of some plants is necessary before germination can take place.

subshrub A woody-based plant with soft stems.

systemic [of chemicals] Refers to chemicals that are absorbed by the plant through its leaves, stems, and/or roots so that they become unpalatable to leaf-eating, root-eating, or sap-sucking insects and their offspring.

taproot The main, downward, strongly growing root of a plant.

tender Refers to plants that may be killed by temperatures lower than 5°C (41°F).

tilth Finely cultivated, raked, and riddled soil suitable for seed sowing.

tree A plant with a crown of branches coming from a single, woody stem.

tuber A swollen root or underground stem from which roots and shoots grow.

umbel A flat or round-topped inflorescence in which the flower stalks arise from the same point.

variegated Refers to the irregular arrangement of pigment.

variety The category of plant classification below species; the naturally occurring variant of a species.

vermiculite A mica-like mineral that is added to potting compost to improve aeration and moisture retention.

Index

Acknowledgements

Author's acknowledgements

I am extremely grateful to a lot of good people: firstly, I would like to thank the posse of RHS and publishing people - notably Rae and Helen, Leanne and Joanna - for all their hard work and for managing - just - to keep my nose to the grindstone when I would far rather have been outside among my flowers. Thanks also to Leigh for his fantastic feature boxes. And then there is my family: I will be forever grateful to my late parents, gardeners and botanists both, who first sent me off down the endless garden path, and to my son Henry, who was technically invaluable and, as always, a tower of strength. I am also indebted to my gardening friends for putting up with me rabbiting on about the book, and particularly those at Merriments Garden and Nursery in East Sussex, a favourite stamping ground of mine. I am, of course, thankful to fellow gardeners and writers - too numerous to mention - whose work I used to back up my own knowledge, learnt by hands-on experience. Lastly, I would like to pay tribute to my great friend, plantsman extraordinaire Richard Zatloukal, who died suddenly shortly before I was commissioned to write this book. His tome, Zat's Perennials, is a great source of inspiration and each time I dip into it his glorious wit just makes me smile.

Picture credits

Alamy Angela Jordan 155 br; Anna Yu 191 ar; Christopher Burrows 58 bl, 151 bl, 167 bl, 173 bl, 179 bl; Cuboimages srl 191 al; FloraImages 102 br; Holmes Garden Photos 129 br, 142 c, 164 b; ImageState/Gary Smith 20-21; Jim Allan 140 c; John Glover 83 br, 127 bl, 159 ar; Martin Hughes-Jones 82 bl; MBP-one 97 bl.

Derry Watkins Special Plants 113 bc, 65 bl.

Edelweiss Perennials 173 ar.

FloraPix.nl Todd Boland 207 bl.

Fotolia Diana Leadbetter 184; adisa 36; an24 88; Bev Evans 172; diligent 182; Fyle 190; LianeM 65 a; Matti 121 a; Nuncia 22 l; Scott Slattery 86; Tatiana 84; tazzymoto 14, 22 c.

GAP Photos Carole Drake 161 ar; Clive Nichols 181 al; Dianna Jazwinski 117 bc; FhF Greenmedia 38; Friedrich Strauss 44 l, 44 c; Geoff du Feu 117 b; J S Sira 41 r, 127 al; John Glover 7 l & r; Jonathan Buckley 30 all; Jonathan Buckley/design Christopher Lloyd 15 r; Juliette Wade/design Roger and Fay Oates 44 r; Maddie Thornhill 179 al; Matt Anker 97 br; Neil Holmes 118 c; Pernilla Bergdahl 8 l; Rice/Buckland 35.

Garden Collection Derek Harris/Sissinghurst Castle Garden 12; Jonathan Buckley/demonstrated by Alan Titchmarsh 32 bl, bc & br.

Garden World Images 55 br, Andrea Jones 101 b, 209 ac; Anthony Baggett 136 ac; C Linnett 169 al; Chris Harris 140 a; Christopher Fairweather 80 ac; D Gould 99 ar; Dave Bevan 64 b, 69, 102 a; Deni Bown 144 br, 149 c, 167 ar; Flowerphotos/Dave Zubraski 154, /Jonathan Buckley 121 c; Gilles Delacroix 51 a & bc, 55 al, 58 al, 59 a, 66 bl, 72 a, 77 a, 148 br, 151 a, 165 a, 171 ar, 191 br, 203 al & ar; Glenn Harper 85 ac, 95 al, 102 bl; Jacqui Dracup 181 bl; Jenny Lilly 108, 111 ac, 152; John Gunn 129 bl; John Martin 111 b, 141 c, 181 ar, 194, 209 b; John Swithinbank 46 all, 103 a, 209 bc; Jonathan Need 9, 91 b, 203 bl; Juliette Spears 189 a; L Mack 70 ac; Lee Thomas 51 b, 58 ar, 99 bl, 112, 113 ac, 138 bc, 171 al, 175 a, 193 ar, 198; Leonie Lambert 95 bl; Liz Cole 141 b, 148 bl; Liz Every 163 a, 195 ac; Liz Kirton 68 a; MAP/Frédéric Didillon 161 al, /Nathalie Pasquel 91 bc, 121 b; Martin Hughes-Jones 85 bc, 93 bc, 107 bl, 109 a & b, 110, 113 b, 115 ar, 127 al, 141 a, 159 br, 180, 193 bl, 204; N+R Colborn 8 r, 70 bc; Nicholas Appleby 52; Philip Smith 62 bl, 157 bl; Rita Coates 59 b, 80 b, 89 ac, 174 a, 181 br, 195 bc; Rodger Tamblyn 138 b; Rowan Isaac 170; Sine Chesterman 72 bc, 196; Steffen Hauser 203 br; Terry Jennings 175 bl, 189 bc; Tony Cooper 70 b, 95 br; Trevor Sims 57, 77 c, 78 bl, 95 ar, 101 bc, 118 b, 129 al & ar, 132 a, 149 a, 150 a, 157 br, 158, 192, 193 br, 197 al & bl, 199 al, 205 ac.

Marianne Majerus Garden Images Marianne Majerus 85 b.

Missouri Botanical Garden PlantFinder Alan Stentz 138 ac.

Octopus Publishing Group 2 ar, bl & br, 75, 82 a, 96, 98, 100, 114, 116, 118 a, 122, 130, 137, 143, 160, 164 a, 166, 168, 178, 186, 200, 202, 206, 208, 128, 156, Andrew Lawson 87 a & bc; David Sarton/design David Domoney 50, /design John Wood 15 l, /design Tom Stuart-Smith 15 c; Jane Sebire 26; Jo Whitworth 37; Marcus Harpur 2 al; Mark Bolton 142 a, /design Tom Stuart-Smith 13, /design Xa Tollemache with Jon Kellett 60; Sarah Heneghan 6, 17 all, 31, 43, 47 all, 54, 62 a, 63, 70 a, 71, 74 a & br, 80 a, 81 bl & br, 82 br, 90, 91 ac, 92, 93 a & ac, 94, 103 br, 104, 105 b, 106, 107 ar, 111 a, 119, 124, 125 bc, 126, 135, 139 b, 140 b, 145, 147, 157 ar, 162, 163 ac, 167 br, 175 br, 176, 179 ar, 188, 189 ac, 197 ar, 201 al, 205 a.

Photolibrary Group design Bridgemere Gardens 48-9; age fotostock/Brian Durell 201 ar; Cuboimages/Paroli Galperti 65 br, 146 bc; Garden Photo World/Georgianna Lane 72 ac; Garden Picture Library/A S Milton 127 br, /Alan Bedding 39, /Alec Snaresbrook 78 a, /Anne Green-Armytage 83 bl, /Carole Drake 183 bc, /Chris Burrows 89 bc, /Chris L Jones 189 b, /Clive Boursnell 28, /Clive Nichols 29, 142 b, /David Burton 16, /Eric van Lokven 27, /Gary K Smith 33 l & r, 34, /Howard Rice 58 br, 89 b, 155 bl, 173 br, /Lynne Brotchie 10-11, /Mark Bolton 133, /Michael Davis 149 b, /Richard Felber 25, /Stephen Hamilton 41 c, 45 all, /Stephen Robson 18, /Suzie Gibbons 42, /Maria Mosolova 85 a, GardenPix Ltd 66 & 83a; imagebroker/FB-Rose 139 a.

P-Pod.Co.Uk Ltd 161 br.

RHS Herbarium 41 l, 51 ac, 61 ac, 64 a, 74 bl, 101 ac, 111 bc, 115 bl & br, 120 ac, b & bc, 131 bl, 136 a, 138 a, 146 a & b, 151 br, 155 al, 159 bl, 163 bc, 177 bl, 183 a & ac, 199 ar, 209 a; Ali Cundy 53 ar, 97 al & ar, 131 al, ar & br, 134 b, 150 bl & br, 174 bl & br, 191 bl; Barry Phillips 53 bl, 55 ar, 76 a, b & bc, 91 a, 117 a, 134 a & ac; Carol Sheppard 59 c, 64 bc, 73 c, 76 ac, 77 b, 79, 81 a, 87 ac, 93 b, 105 ac, 115 al, 123 b & bc, 125 ac & b, 132 c, 144 al & bl, 148 al & ar, 153 ar & br, 155 ar, 161 bl, 169 ac & ar, 205 bc; Caroline Beck 99 br; Cecile Moisan 62 br, 99 al, 144 ar, 159 al, 173 al & bl; Christopher Whitehouse 109 bc, 195 a; Gilles Delacroix 185 bl & br; Graham Titchmarsh 53 al & br, 61 a & b, 64 ac, 68 ac, b & bc, 72 b, 73 b, 80 bc, 89 a, 101 a, 103 bl, 105 a, 132 b, 134 bc, 136 b & bc, 157 al, 164 c, 165 b & c, 169 bl, 171 bl & br, 177 ar & br, 183 b, 185 al, 193 al, 195 b, 197 br, 207 al & ar; Jacquie Gray 78 br, 201 br; John Trenholm 32 al, ac & ar, Leigh Hunt 61 bc, 120 a, 123 ac, 177 al; Philip Smith 125 a; Philippa Gibson 56 bl & br, 87 b, 109 ac, 113 al, 139 c, 153 bl, 179 bl, 185 ar, 199 bl, 207 br; Susan Grayer 199 br; Tim Sandall 107 br, 169 br, 205 b; Wendy Wesley 117 ac, 187 all; Wilf Halliday 66 br, 107 al, 153 al, 167 al; Zebrina Rendall 22 r, 55 bl, 105 bc, 123 a, 146 ac, 163 b.